Advanced Studies in Diginomics and Digitalization

Series Editors

Lars Hornuf ⓘ, Faculty of Business and Economics, Technische Universität Dresden, Dresden, Germany

Herbert Kotzab ⓘ, Coggin College of Business, University of North Florida, Jacksonville, USA

Markus Pelger, Management Science and Engineering, Stanford University, Stanford, CA, USA

The book series 'Advanced Studies in Diginomics and Digitalization' features the latest research in economic topics related to the digitization of labor, financial, and product markets. Books published in this series are primarily monographs and edited volumes that present new research results, both theoretical and empirical, on ethical, socio-political, psychological, economic and politically relevant questions about new digital markets. All books are published in print and digital formats and disseminated globally.

Lars Hornuf • Sonja Mangold • Yayun Yang

Data Privacy
and Crowdsourcing

A Comparison of Selected Problems in China,
Germany and the United States

 Springer

Lars Hornuf
Faculty of Business and Economics
Technische Universität Dresden
Dresden, Germany

Sonja Mangold
Faculty of Business Studies and Economics
University of Bremen
Bremen, Germany

Yayun Yang
Faculty of Economic Law
Southwest University of Political
Science and Law
Chongqing, China

This work was supported by University of Bremen

ISSN 2731-0477   ISSN 2731-0485   (electronic)
Advanced Studies in Diginomics and Digitalization
ISBN 978-3-031-32063-7   ISBN 978-3-031-32064-4   (eBook)
https://doi.org/10.1007/978-3-031-32064-4

This Springer imprint is published by the registered company Springer Nature Switzerland AG
The registered company address is: Gewerbestrasse 11, 6330 Cham, Switzerland

Foreword

This book, "Data Privacy and Crowdsourcing. A Comparison of Selected Problems in China, Germany and the United States" deals with a highly topical and hardly dealt with subject area. Crowdsourcing, understood as a principle for organizing work, can manifest in very different forms. Be it crowdfunding or crowd work, paid or unpaid, cooperative or competitive, internal or external or mixed, there are many different forms of crowdsourcing in our increasingly platformized world. This subject area triggers numerous legal questions, arising, for example, from the dissolution of the classic "business site" as a place of work, questions about intellectual property in and around the content created on such platforms, and so on. This book addresses the relevant issue of data protection, going above and beyond Europe and additionally looking at the two largest other markets for crowdsourcing: China and the United States.

The analyses of the legal aspects have been well done and edited in a platform-independent way. Even though more information on the respective platforms, especially in China and the United States, would be very exciting, the insights remain fundamentally very relevant and are presented in a target-oriented manner. It is particularly worth mentioning that this work provides Western readers with an insight into Chinese data protection law—a subject area that is otherwise treated as a black box in the Western world. In addition, a highly exciting topic is raised toward the end: the presumption of a Brussel's effect, i.e., that potentially higher data protection standards could spread from the European Union to other systems. This outlook deserves further elaboration. I wish the work the great dissemination it deserves and readers a useful reading.

St. Gallen, Switzerland   Jan Marco Leimeister

Funder Information

This book received financial support from the Data Science Center at the University of Bremen and the Hans Böckler Foundation.

Contents

1 Introduction 1
   References 3

2 Players in the Crowdsourcing Industry 5
   2.1 Segments of the Crowd Industry 5
   2.2 The Chinese, German, and U.S. Markets 9
   2.3 General Market Trends 14
   References 15

3 Data Protection Law in Germany, the United States, and China 19
   3.1 Data Privacy and Crowdsourcing in Germany: Legal Instruments,
       Aspects of Contract Law, Consumer Protection,
       and Competition Law 19
       3.1.1 Legal Sources for Data Processing 19
       3.1.2 Data Security: At the Interface Between Data Protection
            and IT Security Law 22
       3.1.3 Protection of Personal and Sensitive Data 23
       3.1.4 Particularities of Data Protection: Company Information,
            Consumer and Employee Data 23
       3.1.5 Basic Principles of Data Processing 24
       3.1.6 Pseudonymization and Anonymization as Data Protection
            Measures 26
       3.1.7 Consent as the Central Legitimation of Data Processing . . 27
       3.1.8 Algorithm-Based Decision-Making: Risks of
            Discrimination, Solution Approaches 28
       3.1.9 Rights of Data Subjects 29
       3.1.10 The Data Protection Impact Assessment: Self-Evaluation
            in the Case of High-Risk Data Processing 30
       3.1.11 Internal and External Data Protection Controls 31
       3.1.12 Sanctions 31

3.2   Data Privacy in Digital Business in the United States: Fragmented
       Rules, State Pioneers and the Prominent Role of the Federal Trade
       Commission   32
       3.2.1   Patchwork of Privacy Regulation   32
       3.2.2   Data Security: Numerous Legal Sources   34
       3.2.3   Protection of Personal and Sensitive Information:
                No Single Definition   35
       3.2.4   Protection of Consumer and Employee Data   37
       3.2.5   Main Principles of Data Processing: Sector-Specific and
                State-Specific Approaches   38
       3.2.6   Anonymization and Pseudonymization   39
       3.2.7   Consent for Data Processing: Limited Legal
                Requirements   40
       3.2.8   Regulation of Algorithmic Decision-Making: Steps and
                Gaps   40
       3.2.9   Individual Rights: Scattered Rules   41
       3.2.10   Requirements for Data Protection Risk Assessments   42
       3.2.11   Internal and External Enforcement   43
       3.2.12   Sanctions   43
3.3   Data Privacy and Crowdsourcing in China   44
       3.3.1   Various Sources of Law for Data Processing: A Brief
                Overview   44
       3.3.2   Data Security   49
       3.3.3   Protection of Personal Identifiable Information and
                Sensitive Data   50
       3.3.4   Particularities of Data Protection: Company, Consumer,
                and Employee Data   51
       3.3.5   Basic Principles of Data Processing   53
       3.3.6   Anonymization and de-Identification as Data
                Protection Instruments   55
       3.3.7   Consent as the Standard for Legitimation of Data
                Processing   56
       3.3.8   Automated Decision-Making   57
       3.3.9   Rights of Data Subjects   58
       3.3.10   Data Protection Impact Assessment   60
       3.3.11   Internal and External Data Protection Supervision   61
       3.3.12   Sanctions   64
3.4   Similarities and Differences in Regulatory Approaches   65
       3.4.1   Particularities of Norm-Setting in the Field of Data
                Privacy   65
       3.4.2   Data Security Standards   67
       3.4.3   Protection of Personal and Sensitive Data   67
       3.4.4   Collection of Company Information and Consumer
                and Employee Data in the GDPR Broadly   68

3.4.5   General Principles of Data Processing, Privacy by
         Design and by Default   68
3.4.6   Anonymization and Pseudonymization   69
3.4.7   Consent for Legitimizing Data Processing   69
3.4.8   Regulation of Algorithmic Decision-Making   70
3.4.9   Individual Rights   70
3.4.10   Data Protection Impact Assessment   70
3.4.11   Enforcement Mechanisms   71
3.5   Interim Result and the Aspect of Regulatory Competition   71
References   72

4   Privacy Statements in China, Germany, and the United States   81
4.1   Processing of Data   81
4.2   Processing of Data by Third Parties   102
References   130

5   Summary and Conclusion   131
5.1   Increasing Regulation and Regulatory Competition   131
5.2   Processing of User Data   131
        5.2.1   Privacy Statements as Main Source of Information   131
        5.2.2   Processing of Crowdworkers' Data   132
        5.2.3   Collection of Sensitive Data   132
5.3   Processing of Data by Third Parties   133
        5.3.1   Data Sharing   133
        5.3.2   Use of Social Plugins and Web Analytics   133
        5.3.3   Use of Cookies   134
        5.3.4   Data Protection Efforts by Platforms and Outlook   134
References   135

Appendices   137
A. Chinese Crowdsourcing Platforms   137
        A.1 Platforms with a Privacy Statement   137
        A.2 Platforms Without a Privacy Statement   139
        A.3 Platforms with No Website   140
B. German Crowdsourcing Platforms   141
        B.1. Platforms with Privacy Statements   141
C. US Crowdsourcing Platforms   142
        C.1. Platforms with Privacy Statements   142
        C.2. Platforms Without a Privacy Statement   148
        C.3. Platforms with No Website   149

About the Authors

Lars Hornuf completed his PhD at the Faculty of Economics of the Ludwig Maximilian University (LMU) in Munich in 2011 and subsequently received his habilitation in the field of business administration in 2019 at the University of Regensburg. Previously, he was a junior researcher at the Ifo Institute for Economic Research and a research associate at the Institute of International Law at the LMU. He has been a visiting scholar at UC Berkeley, Stanford Law School, Duke University, Georgetown University, the CESifo, and the House of Finance at Goethe University Frankfurt. In 2014, he became assistant professor of law and economics in the Department of Economics of Trier University. From 2016 to 2021, he was an affiliated research fellow at the Max Planck Institute for Innovation and Competition. In 2017, Lars Hornuf became a full professor of business administration, specializing in the areas of financial services and financial technology at the University of Bremen, and recently a fellow of the CESifo research network. Since spring 2023, he has been a full professor of business administration specializing in financial services at Technische Universität Dresden. He has worked on numerous projects related to crowdsourcing and data privacy and raised external funding from the Deutsche Forschungsgemeinschaft and the German Ministry of Finance, among others. Since spring 2022, he has been a principal investigator of the research project "Platform Work and Data Privacy in a National and International Perspective," which is supported by the Hans Böckler Foundation. His research interests also include fintech, law and finance, and behavioral science. Media including *The Economist* and *Foreign Policy* have reported on his research findings.

Sonja Mangold is an assessor in law. Following her two state examinations in law, she worked as a research associate at the Collaborative Research Center 597 (*Sonderforschungsbereich* "Transformations of the State") in Bremen (Germany) from 2012 to 2015. She completed her PhD in the field of transnational labor law and EU anti-discrimination law in 2018. Her doctoral thesis received the Hugo Sinzheimer Award in 2019 from the Hugo Sinzheimer Institute for Labor and Social Security Law (Frankfurt a.M.) and the BMT Award 2019 from the Faculty of

Law at the University of Bremen. Sonja Mangold is currently working as a post-doctoral researcher at the Faculty of Business Studies and Economics at the University of Bremen. Since spring 2022, she has been a principal investigator of the research project "Platform Work and Data Privacy in a National and International Perspective," which is supported by the Hans Böckler Foundation. Her current research interests include consumer data protection laws from a comparative law perspective, regulation of new digital business models, alternative and cooperative forms of regulation, and law and economics theories.

Yayun Yang completed her PhD at the Faculty of Law of the University of Bremen in June 2021. Previously, she received a master's degree in economic law from the China University of Political Science (CUPL) and the master of European and international law (LL.M.), which was awarded by the University of Hamburg in 2016 under the double master program at the China-EU School of Law of the CUPL. In 2022, Yayun Yang became a lecturer at the Faculty of Economic Law of the Southwest University of Political Science and Law in Chongqing, China. Her research interests include labor law, gender equality law, and data protection law.

List of Figures

Fig. 2.1 Work process for microtasks. Dotted lines show possible divergences from the standard work process and might be platform-specific 6

Fig. 2.2 Work process in online freelancing. Dotted lines show possible divergences from the standard work process and might be platform-specific 7

Fig. 2.3 Estimations of the German crowdworking market 12

Fig. 4.1 Frequency of providing a privacy statement. Distinction by country. Number of privacy statements $N = 485$ 83

Fig. 4.2 Frequency of crowdsourcing segments. Distinction by country. Number of evaluated privacy statements $N = 416$ 84

Fig. 4.3 Frequency of separate and integrated privacy statements. Distinction by country. Number of evaluated privacy statements $N = 416$ 84

Fig. 4.4 Frequency of separate and integrated privacy statements. Distinction by crowdsourcing segment. Number of evaluated privacy statements $N = 416$ 85

Fig. 4.5 Law applicable to data processing if a law was explicitly mentioned. Distinction by crowdsourcing segment. Number of evaluated privacy statements $N = 416$ 86

Fig. 4.6 Frequency of privacy statements indicating that personal or personally identifiable information is being processed. Distinction by country. Number of evaluated privacy statements $N = 416$ ... 88

Fig. 4.7 Frequency of privacy statements that differentiate between data collected from crowdworkers and from other groups (clients, visitors to the website). Distinction by country. Number of evaluated privacy statements $N = 416$ 89

Fig. 4.8 Frequency of privacy statements that differentiate between the data collected from crowdworkers and from other groups (clients, visitors to the website). Distinction by crowdsourcing segment. Number of evaluated privacy statements $N = 416$ 90

Fig. 4.9   Frequency of privacy statements reporting which personal data are
            processed. Distinction by country. Number of evaluated privacy
            statements $N = 416$ 90
Fig. 4.10   Types of personal data processed according to the privacy
            statement. Distinction by country. Number of evaluated privacy
            statements $N = 416$ 91
Fig. 4.11   Types of personal data not processed according to the privacy
            statement. All U.S. platforms. Number of evaluated privacy
            statements $N = 268$ 92
Fig. 4.12   Types of personal data processed according to the privacy
            statement. Distinction by crowdsourcing segment. Number of
            evaluated privacy statements $N = 416$ 93
Fig. 4.13   Special categories of personal data processed according to the
            privacy statement. Distinction by country. Number of evaluated
            privacy statements $N = 416$ 94
Fig. 4.14   Special categories of personal data not processed according to the
            privacy statement. All U.S. platforms. Number of evaluated
            privacy statements $N = 416$ 95
Fig. 4.15   Type of company-related data processed according to the privacy
            statement. Distinction by country. Number of evaluated privacy
            statements $N = 416$ 96
Fig. 4.16   In which contexts are the IP addresses of the users processed?
            Distinction by country. Number of evaluated privacy statements
            $N = 416$ 98
Fig. 4.17   Is a reason given for processing personal data? Distinction by
            country. Number of evaluated privacy statements $N = 416$ 99
Fig. 4.18   Is a reason given for processing personal data? Distinction by
            crowdsourcing segment. Number of evaluated privacy statements
            $N = 416$ 99
Fig. 4.19   Which reason is given for processing personal data? Distinction
            by crowdsourcing segment. Number of evaluated privacy
            statements $N = 416$ 100
Fig. 4.20   Which reason is given for processing personal data? Distinction
            by country. Number of evaluated privacy statements $N = 416$ ...   101
Fig. 4.21   Is it specified how long data are stored or when data are deleted?
            Distinction by country. Number of evaluated privacy statements
            $N = 416$ 101
Fig. 4.22   Is it specified how long data are stored or when data are deleted?
            Distinction by crowdsourcing segment. Number of evaluated
            privacy statements $N = 416$ 102
Fig. 4.23   Are data processed anonymously or pseudonymously? Distinction
            by country. Number of evaluated privacy statements $N = 416$ ...   103
Fig. 4.24   Are data processed anonymously or pseudonymously? Distinction
            by crowdsourcing segment. Number of evaluated privacy
            statements $N = 416$ 104

Fig. 4.25   Are personal data published? Distinction by country. Number of
            evaluated privacy statements $N = 416$ 104
Fig. 4.26   Are personal data published? Distinction by crowdsourcing
            segment. Number of evaluated privacy statements $N = 416$ 105
Fig. 4.27   For what reason are personal data published? Distinction by
            country. Number of evaluated privacy statements $N = 416$ 106
Fig. 4.28   For what reason are personal data published? Distinction by
            crowdsourcing segment. Number of evaluated privacy
            statements $N = 416$ 106
Fig. 4.29   Are personal data shared with third parties with consent?
            Distinction by country. Number of evaluated privacy statements
            $N = 416$ 107
Fig. 4.30   Are personal data shared with third parties with consent?
            Distinction by crowdsourcing segment. Number of evaluated
            privacy statements $N = 416$ 107
Fig. 4.31   Are personal data of crowdworkers shared with crowdsourcing
            companies or other clients? Distinction by country. Number of
            evaluated privacy statements $N = 416$ 108
Fig. 4.32   Are personal data of crowdworkers shared with crowdsourcing
            companies or other clients? Distinction by crowdsourcing
            segment. Number of evaluated privacy statements $N = 416$ 108
Fig. 4.33   Is there an exhaustive statement on what personal data are shared
            with third parties? Distinction by country. Number of evaluated
            privacy statements $N = 416$ 109
Fig. 4.34   Is there an exhaustive statement on what personal data are shared
            with third parties? Distinction by crowdsourcing segment.
            Number of evaluated privacy statements $N = 416$ 109
Fig. 4.35   What personal data are shared with third parties? Distinction by
            country. Number of evaluated privacy statements $N = 416$ 110
Fig. 4.36   What personal data are shared with third parties? Distinction by
            crowdsourcing segment. Number of evaluated privacy statements
            $N = 416$ 112
Fig. 4.37   For what purpose are personal data shared with third parties?
            Distinction by country. Number of evaluated privacy statements
            $N = 416$ 113
Fig. 4.38   For what purpose are personal data shared with third parties?
            Distinction by crowdsourcing segment. Number of evaluated
            privacy statements $N = 416$ 114
Fig. 4.39   Is it indicated to which third parties data are shared? Distinction by
            country. Number of evaluated privacy statements $N = 416$ 115
Fig. 4.40   Is it indicated to which third parties data are shared? Distinction by
            crowdsourcing segment. Number of evaluated privacy statements
            $N = 416$ 116

Fig. 4.41   Is it stated that personal data will only be passed on to third parties
            in exceptional cases? Distinction by country. Number of evaluated
            privacy statements $N = 416$ 116
Fig. 4.42   Is it stated that personal data will only be passed on to third parties
            in exceptional cases? Distinction by crowdsourcing segment.
            Number of evaluated privacy statements $N = 416$ 117
Fig. 4.43   Are personal data collected from third parties? Distinction by
            country. Number of evaluated privacy statements $N = 416$ 117
Fig. 4.44   Are personal data collected from third parties? Distinction by
            crowdsourcing segment. Number of evaluated privacy statements
            $N = 416$ 118
Fig. 4.45   Does the company's website use social plug-ins or are third-party
            services integrated? Distinction by country. Number of evaluated
            privacy statements $N = 416$ 118
Fig. 4.46   Does the company's website use social plug-ins or are third-party
            services integrated? Distinction by crowdsourcing segment.
            Number of evaluated privacy statements $N = 416$ 119
Fig. 4.47   Does the company's website use social plug-ins or are third-party
            services integrated? Distinction by country. Number of evaluated
            privacy statements $N = 416$ 120
Fig. 4.48   Are behavioral, usage, or movement data processed or are
            tracking services used? Distinction by country. Number of
            evaluated privacy statements $N = 416$ 121
Fig. 4.49   Are behavioral, usage, or movement data processed or are
            tracking services used? Distinction by crowdsourcing segment.
            Number of evaluated privacy statements $N = 416$ 121
Fig. 4.50   Number of analytics services used by companies. Distinction by
            country. Number of evaluated privacy statements $N = 416$ 122
Fig. 4.51   Frequency of analytics services used by companies. Distinction by
            country. Number of evaluated privacy statements $N = 416$ 123
Fig. 4.52   Number of advertising services used by companies. Distinction by
            country. Number of evaluated privacy statements $N = 416$ 124
Fig. 4.53   Frequency of advertising services used by companies. Distinction
            by country. Number of evaluated privacy statements $N = 416$ ...   125
Fig. 4.54   Does the company provide information on the use of cookies?
            Distinction by country. Number of evaluated privacy statements
            $N = 416$ 126
Fig. 4.55   Does the company provide information on the use of cookies?
            Distinction by crowdsourcing segment. Number of evaluated
            privacy statements $N = 416$ 126
Fig. 4.56   Frequency with which the privacy statements provide an
            exhaustive or non-exhaustive list of what data are transmitted
            through server log files. Distinction by country. Number of
            evaluated privacy statements $N = 416$ 127

Fig. 4.57   Frequency with which the privacy statements provide an
            exhaustive or non-exhaustive list of what data are transmitted
            through server log files. Distinction by crowdsourcing segment.
            Number of evaluated privacy statements $N = 416$ 127
Fig. 4.58   Frequency of data processed by log files. Distinction by
            crowdsourcing segment. Number of evaluated privacy statements
            $N = 416$ 128
Fig. 4.59   Frequency of data processed by log files. Distinction by
            crowdsourcing segment. Number of evaluated privacy
            statements $N = 416$ 129

Chapter 1
Introduction

The objectives of this book are threefold. First, we provide a concise overview of the crowdsourcing markets in China, Germany, and the United States and highlight recent market trends. Second, we examine the data protection laws in these three jurisdictions and show the extent to which crowdworkers and other platform users (website vistors, clients) are protected. Third, we analyze and compare data privacy practices on crowdsourcing platforms and highlight how they relate to legal rules. Finally, we provide a conclusion and, based on our functional and empirical legal investigations, show where there is a need for improvement in the legal rules and data protection practices.

Data has been dubbed the "new oil" (Economist, 2017) driving the business models of the digital economy, but there are considerable privacy risks for those operating in the digital space. People whose livelihoods depend on crowdworking can be particularly affected, since the use of their data can be essential for them, namely when data processing no longer opens up any employment opportunities for them or their wages are reduced to a minimum (Kittur et al., 2013). Given the paucity of research on the extent of crowdworking markets, we provide a brief overview of the phenomenon in Chap. 2. For this purpose, a systematic analysis of academic literature and industry reports is carried out. Chapters 3 and 4 constitute the core of this book. The analysis of data protection laws in Chap. 3 is based on a rigorous legal analysis. Like others before us in different areas of law (Kraakman et al., 2017), we have chosen a functional approach to examining the legal rules. In our study on privacy practices in Chap. 4, we follow Dorfleitner and Hornuf (2019) and empirically examine the privacy statements of crowdsourcing platforms. We extend their study by comparing privacy statements across three different countries and by comparing the crowdsourcing industry to another industry in which sensitive data is processed: the financial technology industry. In line with the classification of Boudreau and Lakhani (2013), we also examine differences between crowd complementor, crowd labor market, collaborative community, and crowd contest platforms. The analysis of privacy statements enables us to examine, among other

L. Hornuf et al., *Data Privacy and Crowdsourcing*, Advanced Studies in Diginomics and Digitalization, https://doi.org/10.1007/978-3-031-32064-4_1

things, which data platforms process, why they process this data, and to whom they transmit it. Based on the empirical analysis, conclusions can be drawn regarding ways in which transparent platforms deal with data processing and inform users through privacy statements. Assuming that platforms are transparent in their privacy statements, conclusions can also be drawn about how fairly crowdworkers are treated in the respective jurisdictions.

We have chosen China, Germany and the U.S. for our comparison because these countries are home to some of the largest crowdsourcing platforms. They are also among the four largest economies in the world, alongside Japan. All three countries have made significant legislative advances in the area of data protection. Although we generally follow the alphabetical order throughout this book, putting China first and the U.S. last, we deviate from this order in Chap. 3, *Data Protection Law in Germany, the United States and China*. The reason for this is that our legal analysis follows the chronological development according to which the EU General Data Protection Regulation (GDPR), which is applicable in Germany, has represented a decisive step in terms of data protection and became binding on May 25, 2018. The state of California followed suit and enacted a consumer protection law similar to the GDPR, which went into effect on August 14, 2020. The Chinese Personal Information Protection Law (PIPL), a unified and comprehensive data protection instrument, became effective on November 1, 2021. Since some of the individual laws have very similar content, a chronological presentation makes sense in Chap. 3, particularly because the question of legal adaptations is best answered in this way.

In sum, we find that as of now, there are no specific regulations for protecting data on crowdsourcing platforms in China, Germany, or the U.S. However, in all three countries, there has been an increase in the number of laws and regulations being developed to address the handling of data on these platforms in recent years. In studying how crowdsourcing platforms handle data protection and analyzing information from 416 privacy statements, we find that German platforms tend to rely mostly on the GDPR for their data processing, while U.S. platforms refer to a variety of international, European, and state-level legal sources on data protection. Chinese crowdsourcing platforms, which are often not accessible to foreign users, do not generally reference the GDPR in their privacy statements. Some U.S. platforms were particularly clear about which data they do not process, as indicated in their privacy statements. When we compared the privacy practices of crowdsourcing platforms with those of the German financial technology sector, we observed that pseudonymization and anonymization are used much more frequently on crowdsourcing platforms in Germany. Most privacy statements did not provide a thorough explanation of which personal data are shared with third parties, despite mentioning that data is shared with such parties. We believe that these findings have important implications for the crowdsourcing industry, and the policymakers and scholars concerned with data privacy and crowdsourcing.

References

Boudreau, K. J., & Lakhani, K. R. (2013). Using the crowd as an innovation partner. *Harvard Business Review, 91*(4), 60–69, 140.

Dorfleitner, G., & Hornuf, L. (2019). *FinTech and data privacy in Germany: An empirical analysis with policy recommendations*. Springer.

Economist. (2017, May 6). The world's most valuable resource is no longer oil, but data. *The Economist*. Accessed January 10, 2023, from https://www.economist.com/leaders/2017/05/06/the-worlds-most-valuable-resource-is-no-longer-oil-but-data

Kittur, A., et al. (2013). The future of crowd work. In *CSCW 2013 – Proceedings of the 2013 ACM conference on computer supported cooperative work*, pp. 1301–1317. Accessed January 10, 2022, from https://doi.org/10.1145/2441776.2441923

Kraakman, R., et al. (2017). *The anatomy of corporate law: A comparative and functional approach*. Oxford University Press.

Chapter 2
Players in the Crowdsourcing Industry

2.1 Segments of the Crowd Industry

The term *crowdsourcing* was coined by Howe (2006) as a portmanteau of the words "crowd" and "outsourcing" (Leimeister & Zogaj, 2013). Howe defines crowdsourcing as an outsourcing of activities traditionally performed by dedicated actors—usually internal staff—to an unspecified and preferably large group of people via an open call (Howe, 2010). The World Bank coined the term "online outsourcing" for the same phenomenon and, like Howe, defined it as a contractual relationship between foreign workers and clients for the provision of services or the execution of tasks via internet-based marketplaces or platforms (World Bank, 2015). The "crowd" to which the activity is outsourced does not necessarily have to be outside the company. Internal crowdsourcing, in which the workforce acts as a crowd, is also widespread, such as at IBM and Daimler (Öhrler & Spies, 2015; Schäfer, 2015). However, broader changes in industrial relations have resulted in external crowdsourcing. Cappa et al. (2019) show, for example, that the announcement of a crowdsourcing campaign positively affects the expectations of a firm's future profits as measured by its stock market performance.

With external crowdsourcing, a company (the *crowdsourcer*) posts tasks or task packages on an internet platform and calls on the *crowdworkers* to complete the tasks. The requirements are described so specifically that they can be completed by any properly trained internet user without further consultation with the client. The activities outsourced in this way are diverse. The World Bank distinguishes between *microwork* and *online freelancing* in crowdsourcing (World Bank, 2015). Microwork breaks projects down into microtasks that can be completed in seconds or minutes. On the part of the crowdworkers, only basic mathematical and/or reading skills are required to complete these tasks. For example, tasks are about labeling images, editing text, or categorizing data and products. As Fig. 2.1 shows, the work process for microtasks is highly standardized and meant to minimize direct communication between employees and customers.

© The Author(s) 2023
L. Hornuf et al., *Data Privacy and Crowdsourcing*, Advanced Studies in Diginomics and Digitalization, https://doi.org/10.1007/978-3-031-32064-4_2

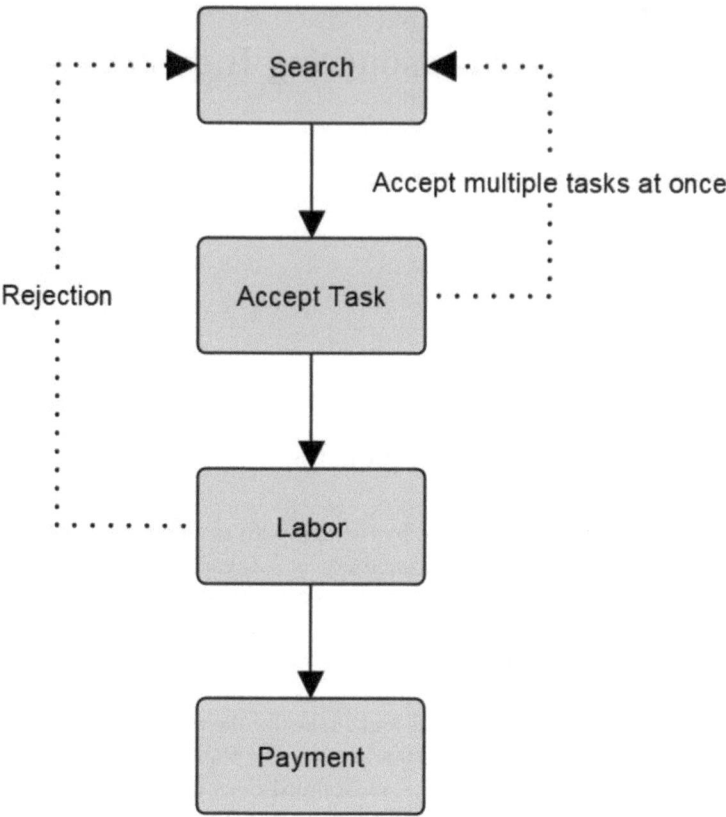

Fig. 2.1 Work process for microtasks. Dotted lines show possible divergences from the standard work process and might be platform-specific (Source: Hornuf & Vrankar, 2022)

Online freelancing is the outsourcing of professional services to crowdworkers, who usually must have relevant technical or professional qualifications. The tasks are often larger projects that are completed over a longer period of time—several days, weeks or even months. Examples of these tasks are the creation of designs or program codes, or the solving of mathematical or scientific problems (Däubler & Klebe, 2015; Leimeister & Zogaj, 2013; Risak, 2015). Figure 2.2 shows the work process for online freelancing, which is slightly less standardized and encourages communication between crowdworkers and crowdsourcers.

For many crowdworkers, microtasks could represent a gap-filling activity that is carried out between other activities and which pays a relatively low wage (Teevan, 2016; Newlands & Lutz, 2021). Some scholars have therefore criticized the working conditions in crowdworking and have described them as precarious (Kittur et al., 2013; Schriner & Oerther, 2014; Hara et al., 2018; Whiting et al., 2019). In investigating 105 mean hourly wages in crowdwork that were reported in 22 different studies, Hornuf and Vrankar (2022) have found evidence that working on microtasks

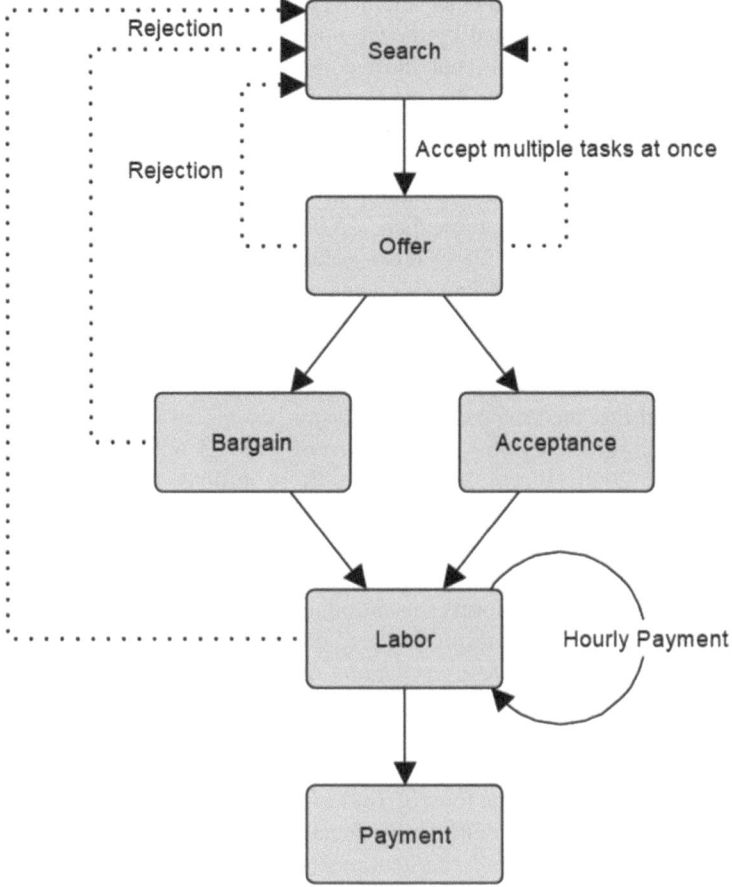

Fig. 2.2 Work process in online freelancing. Dotted lines show possible divergences from the standard work process and might be platform-specific (Source: Hornuf & Vrankar, 2022)

results in wages ranging from $3.78 to $5.55 per hour on average. Online freelancers earn $4.87 to $20.88 per hour on average, which is up to three times more than microtask workers. However, when factoring in unpaid work, such as searching for tasks and communicating with requesters, wages of online freelancers tend to be much more similar to the wages of microwork.

Another distinction scholars often make is whether platforms restrict activities to a specific region or whether they can in principle be carried out from anywhere in the world (Rani et al., 2021). This definition relates somewhat to the distinction between microwork and online freelancing. While microwork can often be performed from anywhere in the world, online freelancers are often locked into a specific region, for example when it comes to delivering food or groceries. Activities that are limited to specific regions are also often referred to as "gig work" (Heiling & Kuba, 2017).

Crowdsourcers typically use an internet platform to advertise their tasks. The platform is sometimes operated by the crowdsourcers themselves, such as at IBM (Klebe & Neugebauer, 2014), but most commercial providers such as Amazon Mechanical Turk, Clickworker, Freelancer, Innosabi, TopC or Twago operate platforms that can be used by anyone. The business of these platforms has grown rapidly in recent years. According to information in the literature, Freelancer alone has over 14.5 million users working on 7.2 million projects (Däubler & Klebe, 2015). The German platform Twago lists more than 225,000 registered experts with more than 80,000 advertised projects with an order volume of over 400 million EUR on its website (Twago, 2023). Well known clients who advertise tasks via the platform include AOL, BMW, Deutsche Telekom, Facebook, Google, Honda, Intel, Manhattan Cosmetics, Microsoft, NSA, Panasonic, Postbank and Walt Disney (Klebe & Neugebauer, 2014; Däubler & Klebe, 2015; van Delden, 2014). For 2013, the World Bank estimated that the crowdsourcing industry had global sales of 2 billion U.S. dollars, and considered a global sales volume of 15 to 25 billion U.S. dollars to be conceivable in 2020 (World Bank, 2015). It is difficult to say whether these estimates actually bore out, as there are hardly any current and reliable figures for this market. However, if one looks at the development of individual market players, these aggregate figures do not seem exaggerated.

Another taxonomy of platforms was introduced by Boudreau and Lakhani (2013) and relates to the specific work processes to complete the tasks and their remuneration. Their first category are *crowd labor markets* and often relate to external crowdsourcing. The activities are most similar to what the World Bank defines as *microwork*. Well known examples of such platforms are oDesk, Clickworker and Amazon Mechanical Turk. This particular category of crowdwork is considered by some scholars to be an extreme form of Taylorism (Kittur et al., 2013; Aloisi, 2015), defined as dividing a large, intellectually demanding task into many small tasks, all of which can be completed with minimal mental effort.

The second category Boudreau and Lakhani (2013) define are *crowd contests*, which are competitions in which participants submit their work. Again, the interaction with crowdsourcers is kept to a minimum. Typical tasks include designing a logo or a web page or solving a company's problem. Well known examples of platforms include 99designs, DesignCrowd, GoPillar, Hatchwise, HYVE, and Topcoder. The remuneration of crowdworkers depends on the crowdsourcer, which ranks the work that has been submitted. In some cases, a worker may not receive payment, despite completing the work.

Crowd complementors offer products, software, or services within an ecosystem built and maintained by a company and thus generate value for the company, as well as for users in that specific ecosystem. They often receive a fixed fee for their contribution that has been *ex ante* defined by the platform and is charged by the company providing the ecosystem or platform. Typical tasks in this third category of crowdsourcing include developing an app, recording a video, or uploading a song or photo. Well known examples of platforms are the Google Play Store, iTunes, Soundcloud, and YouTube.

The fourth and final category of crowdsourcing is *collaborative community* platforms, which often involve innovation contests among regular employees of a company or users of a product who receive no additional compensation for their activities on the platform. Collaborative communities are typically dedicated to a greater purpose. Activities are often unpaid and performed as a hobby, which instead of money pays off in terms of experience or recognition in the respective community. Typical tasks include developing open-source software, translating, and helping other users on the same platform. Well known examples of platforms are Apache, Translate, and Wikipedia.

2.2 The Chinese, German, and U.S. Markets

In China, crowdsourcing is commonly known as the Witkey model. The term Witkey is short for "key of wisdom" and was coined in 2005 by Liu Feng, a researcher at the Chinese Academy of Social Sciences (CASS) (Liu, 2008). In the same year, Liu created the Witkey internet platform, which aims to leverage CASS's expert resources and scientific achievements to address the technological problems faced by companies (Liu, 2008). In building the platform's website, Liu established an area on the internet where problems can be solved through online platforms and the solvers are paid similarly to freelancers. Liu defined the Witkey model as a "new Internet model in which human knowledge, wisdom, experience and skills are converted into real income through the Internet" (Liu, 2008).

Crowdworkers are also often referred to as *witkey* in China. They are "people who convert their wisdom, knowledge, ability and experience into real income by solving problems in the field of science, technology, work, life and learning on the Internet, and thus make their knowledge, wisdom, experience and skills economically valuable" (Liu, 2008). The term "crowdsourcing" as it is used in the Chinese context not only refers to the Witkey model, but also to the tasks on the platforms that can be completed offline. A typical example of offline crowdsourcing is food delivery platforms such as Meituan. In principle any Chinese citizen can register on the platform and become a delivery driver. Because the crowdsourcing platforms defined in this book exclude those that only deal with offline tasks, only the Witkey platforms in China are considered in the legal and empirical analysis, and hence fall under the definition of crowdsourcing used in the present book.

In October 2019, we found 145 Chinese crowdsourcing platforms that fall under this definition. Most of these platforms remain active, while around 28% of the initially active services had ceased to be available by May 2022. Originally, Chinese crowdsourcing platforms were mainly crowd contest platforms (Huang & Wang, 2015). Today, all four types of crowdsourcing platforms that have been classified by Boudreau and Lakhani (2013) exist. Even before the terms crowdsourcing or *witkey* arose, crowdsourcing platforms existed in China. For example, K68 was founded in 2003 as allegedly the first Chinese crowdsourcing platform (CCTV, 2006). Since the establishment of the K68 platform, diverse tasks and projects that can be done through the internet have been published there.[1] In 2022, the platform is still active with around 2.8 million users, and around 28,000 companies have used it so far as a crowdsourcing platform to find crowdworkers to carry out relevant tasks.[2] Many different types of tasks are currently published on the K68 platform, such as graphic design, architectural or decorative design, translation, new product testing, and naming (for example, a company, a product or a baby). The platform falls under both categories: crowd labor market and crowd contest platform.

Since 2005, Chinese crowdsourcing platforms have experienced rapid development. According to the 2010 *China Witkey Industrial White Paper* (iResearch, 2010), the total registered users of Chinese crowdsourcing platforms already exceeded 20 million in 2010, when the cumulative transaction volume exceeded 300 million CNY, or 39 million EUR.[3] Among crowdsourcing platforms, the Zhubajie platform, which was founded in 2005, ranks first in terms of the number of registered users and cumulative transaction volume. In 2013, the number of registered users of this crowdsourcing platform reached over ten million.[4] It was reported that the platform's annual transaction volume reached 7.5 billion CNY in 2015, amounting to over 80% market share (PEdaily.cn, 2016).[5] There are now around 28 million registered users of the Zhubajie crowdsourcing platform.[6]

According to the 2010 *China Witkey Industrial White Paper* (iResearch, 2010), a survey conducted in 2010 among 355 crowdworkers shows that 17% of the respondents did not earn anything on the crowdsourcing platforms; 31.5% earned less than 100 CNY a month on the platforms[7]; more than 50% earned more than 100 CNY a month; and only 3% earned more than 2000 CNY.[8] By 2017 there were around 30 million Chinese crowdworkers serving approximately 190,000 companies and individuals worldwide, generating a total business turnover of 5 billion CNY, or approximately 700 million USD (Huo et al., 2017). While more recent data is difficult to obtain, given the rapid development of Chinese crowdsourcing platforms and the strong growth of registered users over the past decade, we can expect that the income of crowdworkers in China's crowdsourcing market has increased significantly.

---

[1] See the website of the K68 platform company (https://www.k68.cn/).

[2] The data were provided by the president of the K68 platform company Mr. Yan Qixing through a telephone interview on March 12, 2022.

[3] Based on an average exchange rate in 2021 of 7.6369 CNY per 1 EUR, 300 million CNY is approximately 39 million EUR.

[4] The data is available at the website of the *Zhubajie* platform (https://www.zbj.com).

[5] The data were disclosed on the 2016 "Internet+" China Service Fair organized by the Internet Society of China. For more details see PEdaily.cn (2016).

[6] The data is available at the website of the *Zhubajie* platform (https://www.zbj.com)

[7] Based on an average exchange rate in 2021 of 7.6369 CNY per 1 EUR, 100 CNY is approximately 13 EUR.

[8] Based on an average exchange rate in 2021 of 7.6369 CNY per 1 EUR, 2000 CNY is approximately 261 EUR.

For Germany, Serfling (2018) defines crowdworkers as natural persons who earn at least part of their income by performing paid work via internet platforms or smartphone apps, carried out online or offline. In his definition, he explicitly excludes work that takes place within a company, that is, work that could be described as internal crowdsourcing. In terms of employment status, crowdworkers can be self-employed, full-time or part-time employees for another company, but also non-employed people such as students or pensioners. In Germany, too, a large number of activities can be subsumed under the term crowdwork. These include microtasks with short processing times, which are carried out via such platforms as Clickworker, Streetspotr and Testbirds. But there is also crowdsourcing in the form of competitions for design jobs, which can, for example, be carried out on the jovoto platform, as well as innovative and complex problem-solving tasks aimed at highly qualified professionals, such as on the twago platform (Nierling et al., 2020).

The most ambitious project providing comparative data for crowdworking activities in the European Union is the COLLEEM survey, an international research project of the European Commission's Joint Research Council. The first pilot wave of the survey was completed in 2017 and gathered a total of 32,389 responses from 14 member states. The survey found that 10.4% of the adult population in Germany have been involved in crowdworking activities (Pesole et al., 2018). In 2018, the German Federal Ministry of Labor commissioned another study, which was conducted by Serfling (2018) and estimates that 4.8% of the German electorate engages in crowdworking activities. A year later, Serfling (2019) estimated that 4.0% of the German population are active and 2.3% past crowdworkers. In other publications, estimates of the extent of crowdwork range from 0.27% of German-speaking adults (Bonin & Rinne, 2017) to 12% of the total German adult population (Huws et al., 2016). Pongratz and Bormann (2017) estimated a projected number of up to 300,000 active German crowdworkers in 2017 (see Fig. 2.3 for an overview).

More recently, Mrass et al. (2020) took a different approach and surveyed 21 crowdworking platforms with headquarters or at least a physical presence in Germany. They found that the average number of registered crowdworkers on these platforms is 93,909 people. The crowdworking platforms themselves estimated that in 2017 there were 1,162,059 crowdworkers in Germany, which was probably an overestimate given that inactive users were most likely also taken into account by the responding platforms. Mrass et al. (2020) also provide information about the size of the platforms. The average crowdworking platforms employed 23 people. Sales increased sharply from 2015 to 2016, with an average growth of 90%. The surveyed crowdworking platforms themselves estimated the total revenues of the German crowdworking platforms in 2016 at 45 million EUR. The total revenue generated by crowdworking platforms with a physical location in Germany amounted to 203 million EUR.

Empirical evidence in Germany shows that crowdworkers are unlikely to be part of the labor force and that Germans often pursue crowdsourcing as a secondary activity (Vandaele, 2018). However, crowdsourcing is increasing in the traditional working population (Nierling et al., 2020). According to Krzywdzinski and Gerber (2020), two-thirds of crowdworkers worked a maximum of 10 hours per week on a

Study	Huws, Spencer, & Joyce (2016)	Bonin & Rinne (2017)	Pesole et al. (2018) COLLEEM survey	Serfling (2018)	Serfling (2019)
Percentage of crowdworkers	12%	2.9% (0.85% corrected)	10.4% adjusted estimate 11.8% initial estimate	4.8%	2.6%
Definition of the population	Resident population (16–70 years)	German speaking resident population (adults, older than 18 years)	Resident population (adults, 16–74 years)	German electorate (adults, older than 18 years)	Resident population in Germany (older than 15 years)
Survey dates	April 1–4, 2016	April 12–June 20, 2017	Second half of June, 2017	June 2017–April 15, 2018	July 2017–October 15, 2018
Data collection method	Online survey carried out by Ipsos-MORI as part of its regular iOmnibus online survey	Computer assisted telephone interviews	Online survey aimed at being representative of all internet users between 16 and 74 years old in the selected countries	Online survey using an open-access web-panel of internet users	Online survey using an open-access web-panel of internet users
Sampling method	Non-probability sampling	Random sampling	Non-probability sampling	Non-probability sampling	Non-probability sampling
Sample size	2,180	10,017	2,292	376,750	495,000

Fig. 2.3 Estimations of the German crowdworking market. Source: Nierling et al. (2020) and own additions

platform, suggesting that crowdwork was, if at all, a secondary activity for them. According to the *The Online Labour Index,* an endeavor carried out by the Oxford Internet Institute (Stephany et al., 2021), which provides global statistics on the gig economy, the majority (37.1%) of global online freelance labor demand was located in the U.S., but only 5.7% of the global online freelance labor supply. In Germany, global online freelance labor demand was 2.3% of demand and 0.6% of supply (Online Labour Index, 2020). In the United States, 35% of those surveyed worked more than 20 hours per week on the platforms, which means that platform work was more likely the main source of income for crowdworkers. Around 40% of respondents in the U.S. performed platform work as a part-time job of 10 hours or less per week. According to Krzywdzinski and Gerber (2020), only 16% of crowdworkers in Germany reported that their platform income accounted for more than 50% of their total income. In the United States, the figure was just under 33%. This difference between Germany and the United States applied to crowdworkers on both microtask and online freelancing platforms.

Based on a sample of 1131 crowdworkers on 60 German and U.S. platforms, Krzywdzinski and Gerber (2020) find that slightly more crowdworkers in Germany are male and that they have a higher level of education than the general population. On microtask platforms, most crowdworkers are full-time or self-employed if they have a college degree. If crowdworkers only have a high school diploma, they are most often employed full-time or currently completing their university education. On platforms that require more creativity and professional knowledge, the majority of crowdworkers are self-employed, whether they have a high school diploma or college degree. Activities requiring professional knowledge are carried out significantly less often by students. Serfling (2018) reports that nearly two-thirds of crowdworkers are paid, and about 14% receive some form of voucher as remuneration. For a stratified sample of Germans over the age of 18, the average crowdworker earns 808 EUR per week, with a strong variation between microtasks and more complex tasks. While 40% of crowdworkers earn more than 1000 EUR per week, a quarter earn less than 25 EUR per week and around a third less than 100 EUR per week. An earlier study by Leimeister et al. (2016) finds that micro workers earn on average 144 EUR per month; on design platforms it is 660 EUR.

According to Belletti et al. (2021), around 8% of German companies in the information economy already use crowdwork; 6% in manufacturing. Around half of the companies see future access to specialized skills as a possible goal of using crowdwork. The usage rate of crowdsourcing has almost doubled since 2014 and, according to the companies, will continue to grow. Part of the increasing use of crowdsourcing is due to COVID-19-related adjustments in work organization and an increased need for specialists in IT and related areas (Erdsiek, 2021).

Hoang et al. (2020) examine a sample of 4579 U.S. adults who provided comprehensive information about their online earning activities. Overall, 24% of the respondents participated in some form of platform work. While most of them (20%) engaged in online sales activities, overall 9% participated in some form of online labor platform, and some participated in both. Online labor platforms include activities such as "'rideshare driving', 'delivery', 'online tasks' (e.g., coding, data entry, and taking surveys), 'house/laundry cleaning', or 'other platform work' (e.g., babysitting, mystery shopping, and legal services)" (Hoang et al., 2020, p. 687). The authors also find that slightly more women participated in platform work and that 41% of respondents who participated in platform work were aged between 18 and 29. The mean annual income (29,400 USD) was significantly lower for those who worked on some form of online labor platform than for those who did not participate in any platform work (34,700 USD) and those who participated in online selling (40,400 USD). They also find that those living in the South of the United States are more than twice as likely to participate in some form of online labor platforms as those in the Northeast. Interestingly, citizenship status was significant, with non-U.S. citizens being less than half as likely as U.S. citizens to participate in online selling activities. Examining time spent on the platform, Cantarella and Strozzi (2021) find that when only paid activities are considered, crowdworkers in the U.S. work 10 hours less than traditional workers per week. When considering the time spent on unpaid activities, it is only 3 hours less. However, most crowdworkers would actually like to work more in crowdwork or other forms of employment.

2.3   General Market Trends

The basic business model of crowdsourcing has hardly changed over the last decade. Howe's (2010) definition of the phenomenon still applies. However, in some sub-segments the speed with which the activities are to be carried out has increased. A general trend, which is particularly pronounced in China, is the move away from stationary computers and towards the use of mobile devices (Kemp, 2022). This development makes the work even more flexible and the possible execution of tasks faster than ever before. A striking example is the German company Gorillas, which was founded in 2020 and promised to deliver groceries and other supermarket goods at the same prices as in the supermarket. The goods were ordered via an app and delivered by around 14,000 bicycle couriers (Eckardt, 2022). There was a delivery price of 1.80 euros, but no minimum order value, and delivery to the customer took place within 10 minutes after receipt of the order. Although in December 2022 the Turkish competitor Getir bought Gorillas for 1.2 billion EUR, it remains to be seen whether such business models will continue to proliferate.

Just like with grocery delivery, the performance of crowdworkers will have to increase even with microtasks—which is the main focus of this book—in order to keep up with, for example, AI-based smart assistants like ChatGPT. Recent research has shown that chatbots could quickly catch up with even knowledge-intensive activities that would otherwise be reserved for academics, such as translation work, data analysis, research synthesis, statistical modelling, or defining specific phenomena like crowdfunding (Wenzlaff & Späth, 2022). While these systems are not yet perfect, the speed at which they learn is impressive, and the question therefore arises as to whether microtasks will not be completely replaced by chatbots and other intelligent AI-based systems, or whether crowdworkers will only serve to train these systems (Kittur et al., 2013). This development is contradicted by the fact that, due to international refugee movements and armed conflicts, there is an increasing demand for simple online activities that can be carried out from anywhere in the world without extensive training. An example of this is the increased demand for these tasks from Ukrainian women due to the armed conflict with Russia, which has severely impacted the traditional labor market in Ukraine (Bondarenko, 2022a; Bondarenko, 2022b).

References

Aloisi, A. (2015). Commoditized workers: The rising of on-demand work: A case study research on a set of online platforms and apps. *Comparative Labor Law & Policy Journal, 37*(3). Accessed from https://doi.org/10.2139/ssrn.2637485

Belletti, C., Erdsiek, D., Laitenberger, U., & Tubaro, P. (2021). Crowdworking in France and Germany. *ZEW-Kurzexpertise Nr. 21–09*. ffhal-03468022f. Accessed from https://ftp.zew.de/pub/zew-docs/ZEWKurzexpertisen/EN/ZEW_Shortreport2109.pdf

Bondarenko, A. (2022a, July 12). Portrait of a Ukrainian freelance developer during the war (Портрет українського розробника на фрилансі під час війни). *Feelancehunt Blog.* Accessed January 11, 2023, from https://freelancehunt.com/blog/portriet-ukrayinskogho-rozrobnika-na-frilansi-pid-chas-viini/

Bondarenko, A. (2022b, December 26). 2022 results: Freelancehunt in numbers (Підсумки 2022 року: Freelancehunt у цифрах). *Feelancehunt Blog.* Accessed January 11, 2023, from https://freelancehunt.com/blog/pidsumki-2022-roku-freelancehunt-u-tsifrakh/

Boudreau, K. J., & Lakhani, K. R. (2013). Using the crowd as an innovation partner. *Harvard Business Review, 91*(4), 60–69, 140.

Bonin, H., & Rinne, U. (2017). *Omnibusbefragung zur Verbesserung der Datenlage neuer Beschäftigungsformen.* Kurzexpertise im Auftrag des Bundesministeriums für Arbeit und Soziales. IZA Institute of Labour Economics. Research Report Series No. 80. Accessed from http://ftp.iza.org/report_pdfs/iza_report_80.pdf

Cantarella, M., & Strozzi, C. (2021). Workers in the crowd: The labor market impact of the online platform economy. *Industrial and Corporate Change, 30*(6), 1429–1458. https://doi.org/10.1093/icc/dtab022

Cappa, F., Oriani, R., Pinelli, M., & de Massis, A. (2019). When does crowdsourcing benefit firm stock market performance? *Research Policy, 48*(9), 103825. Accessed from https://www.sciencedirect.com/science/article/pii/S0048733319301453

CCTV. (2006). *The "Witkey" model: Breaking the geographical restrictions and impacting traditional industries* ("威客"模式:打破地域限制 冲击传统行业). Accessed February 16, 2022, from http://news.cctv.com/society/20060902/100707.shtml

Däubler, W., & Klebe, T. (2015). Crowdwork: Die neue Form der Arbeit – Arbeitgeber auf der Flucht*? Neue Zeitschrift für Arbeitsrecht, 2015*, 1032–1042.

Eckardt, L. (2022, May 24). Gorillas entlässt Mitarbeiter und erwägt weniger Auslandsgeschäfte. *Zeit Online.* Accessed January 10, 2023, from https://www.zeit.de/politik/2022-05/gorillas-lieferdienst-mitarbeiter-entlassung-startup

Erdsiek, D. (2021). Unternehmen setzen verstärkt auf Crowdworking. *Wirtschaftsdienst, 101*(11), 912–914. Accessed from https://doi.org/10.1007/s10273-021-3045-8

Huang, G. Q., & Wang, H. (2015). *Crowdsourcing and Wiktey.* China Remin University Press (黄国华、王强, 众包与威客, 中国人民大学出版社, 2015 年版).

Hara, K., Adams, A., Milland, K., Savage, S., Callison-Burch, C., & Bigham, J. P. (2018). A data-driven analysis of workers' earnings on Amazon Mechanical Turk. In *Proceedings of the 2018*

CHI Conference on Human Factors in Computing Systems (pp. 1–14). ACM. Accessed from https://doi.org/10.1145/3173574.3174023

Heiling, M., & Kuba, S. (2017). Die Ökonomie der Plattform. Strukturelle und empirische Befunde über die Plattformbranche und ihre PlayerInnen. In M. Risak & D. Lutz (Eds.), *Arbeit in der Gig-Economy – Rechtsfragen plattformbasierten Arbeitens* (pp. 28–43). ÖGB-Verlag

Hoang, L., Blank, G., & Quan-Haase, A. (2020). The winners and the losers of the platform economy: Who participates? *Information, Communication & Society, 23*(5), 681–700. https://doi.org/10.1080/1369118X.2020.1720771

Hornuf, L., & Vrankar, D. (2022). Hourly wages in crowdworking: A meta-analysis. *Business & Information Systems Engineering, 64,* 553–573. Accessed January 10, 2023, from https://doi.org/10.1007/s12599-022-00769-5

Howe, J. (2006). The rise of crowdsourcing. *Wired Magazine, 14*(6).

Howe, J. (2010). *Weblog von Jeff Howe.* Accessed January 10, 2023, from https://crowdsourcing.typepad.com

Huo, S., Zheng, C., & Tu, H. (2017). On the research of intelligent coupling and coordination between employers and Witkey on the crowd innovation network platform. *Journal of Xiangtan University, 41*(1), 94–101.

Huws, U., Spencer, N., & Joyce, S. (2016). *Crowd work in Europe FEPS studies preliminary results from a survey in the UK, Sweden, Germany, Austria and the Netherlands.* Accessed from https://euagenda.eu/upload/publications/untitled-88617-ea.pdf

iResearch. (2010). *2010 China Witkey industrial white paper (2010年中国威客行业白皮书).* Accessed February 16, 2022, from https://www.docin.com/p-186174144.html

Kemp, S. (2022). *Digital 2022: July global statshot report.* Accessed January 11, 2023, from https://datareportal.com/reports/digital-2022-july-global-statshot

Kittur, A., Nickerson, J. V., Bernstein, M., Gerber, E., Shaw, A., Zimmerman, J., Lease, M., & Horton, J. (2013). The future of crowd work. In *Proceedings of the 2013 Conference on Computer Supported Cooperative Work* (pp. 1301–1318). ACM. Accessed from https://doi.org/10.1145/2441776.2441923

Klebe, T., & Neugebauer, J. (2014). Crowdsourcing: Für eine handvoll Dollar oder workers of the crowd unite? *Arbeit und Recht, 2014,* 4–7.

Krzywdzinski, M., & Gerber, C. (2020). *Varieties of platform work: Platforms and social inequality in Germany and the United States. Weizenbaum Series, 7.* Accessed from https://www.weizenbaum-institut.de/media/Publikationen/Weizenbaum_Series/Weizenbaum_Series_7_Krzywdzinski_210412.pdf

Leimeister, J. M., & Zogaj, S. (2013). Neue *Arbeitsorganisation durch Crowdsourcing – Eine Literaturstudie. Düsseldorf: Arbeitspapier Nr. 287,* Hans-Böckler-Stiftung

Leimeister, J. M., Durward, D., & Zogaj, S. (2016). *Crowd worker in Deutschland: Eine empirische Studie zum Arbeitsumfeld auf externen Crowdsourcing-Plattformen, Study der Hans-Böckler-Stiftung,* 323. Accessed from https://www.econstor.eu/bitstream/10419/146407/1/867095172.pdf

Liu, F. (2008). *Principle of Witkey theories* (刘峰, 威客理论原理, 科学博客网, 2008年). Accessed March 12, 2022, from https://blog.sciencenet.cn/home.php?mod=space&uid=39263&do=blog&id=16862

Mrass, V., Peters, C., & Leimeister, J. M. (2020, March). Crowdworking platforms in Germany: Business insights from a study & implications for society. In *82. Jahrestagung des Verbands der Hochschullehrer für Betriebswirtschaft (VHB).* Accessed from https://ssrn.com/abstract=3926265

Newlands, G., & Lutz, C. (2021). Crowdwork and the mobile underclass: Barriers to participation in India and the United States. *New Media & Society, 23*(6), 1341–1361. Accessed January 10, 2023, from https://doi.org/10.1177/1461444820901847

Nierling, L., Krings, B. J., & Küstermann, L. (2020). *The landscape of crowd work in Germany: An overview of the scientific and public discourse. KIT Scientific Working Papers 133.* Accessed from https://publikationen.bibliothek.kit.edu/1000123935/88240435

Öhrler, B., & Spies, J. (2015). Crowdworking in der Automobilindustrie, Das Beispiel Daimler AG. In C. Benner (Ed.), *Crowdwork – zurück in die Zukunft? Perspektiven digitaler Arbeit* (pp. 43–60). Bund-Verlag

Online Labour Index. (2020). *The Online Labour Index 2020.* Accessed January 11, 2023, from http://onlinelabourobservatory.org

PEdaily. (2016). *Zhubajie platform disclosed ten years of trading data, and its trading volume is expected to be over 100 billion Yuan in next three years (*猪八戒披露十年交易大数据 预期未来三年交易额超千亿*).* Accessed February 16, 2022, from https://news.pedaily.cn/201612/201 61217406833.shtml

Pesole, A., Urzí Brancati, M. C, Fernández-Macías, E., Biagi, F., & González Vázquez, I. (2018). *Platform workers in Europe* (pp. 15–16). Publications Office of the European Union. Accessed from https://doi.org/10.2760/742789

Pongratz, H. J., & Bormann, S. (2017). Online-Arbeit auf Internet-Plattformen. Empirische Befunde zum Crowdworking in Deutschland. *Arbeits- und Industriesoziologische Studien, 10*(2) 158–181. Accessed from https://doi.org/10.21241/ssoar.64850

Rani, U., Dhir, K. R., Furrer, M., Gobel, N., Moraiti, A., Cooney, S., Manus, M. C., & Coddou, A. (2021). *World employment and social outlook: The role of digital labour platforms in transforming the world of work.* ILO. Accessed December 27, 2021, from https://www.ilo. org/global/research/global-reports/we-so/2021/WCMS_771749/lang–en/index.htm

Risak, M. (2015). Crowdwork – Erste rechtliche Annäherungen an eine neue Arbeitsform. *Zeitschrift für Arbeits- und Sozialrecht, 2015*(1), 11–19.

Schäfer, M. (2015). Fünf Fragen an Monika Schäfer, Mitglied des Betriebsrates IBM D EAS. In C. Benner (Ed.), *Crowdwork – zurück in die Zukunft? Perspektiven digitaler Arbeit* (pp. 61–66). Bund-Verlag.

Schriner, A., & Oerther, D. (2014). No really, (crowd) work is the silver bullet. *Procedia Engineering, 78*, 224–228. Accessed January 10, 2023, from https://doi.org/10.1016/j.proeng.2014. 07.060

Serfling, O. (2018). *Crowdworking Monitor Nr. 1.* Accessed from https://www.bmas.de/ SharedDocs/Downloads/DE/Meldungen/2018/crowdworking-monitor.pdf?__blob= publicationFile&v=1

Serfling, O. (2019). *Crowdworking Monitor Nr. 2.* Accessed from https://www.hochschule-rhein-waal.de/sites/default/files/documents/2019/05/08/discussion_papers_in_behavioural_sciences_and_economics_no5.pdf

Stephany, F., Kässi, O., Rani, U., & Lehdonvirta, V. (2021). Online Labour Index 2020: New ways to measure the world's remote freelancing market. *Big Data & Society.* Accessed from https:// doi.org/10.1177/20539517211043240

Teevan, J. (2016). The future of microwork. *XRDS Crossroads, 23*(2), 26–29. Accessed from https://doi.org/10.1145/3019600.

Twago. (2023). Accessed January 10, 2023, from http://www.twago.de

Van Delden, C. (2014). *Crowdsourced innovation: Revolutionizing open innovation with crowdsourcing.* innosabi Publishing.

Vandaele, K. (2018). *Will trade unions survive the platform economy? Emerging patterns of platform workers' collective voice and representation in Europe. Working Paper 2018.05.*

Wenzlaff, K., & Späth, S. (2022). *Smarter than humans? Validating how OpenAI's ChatGPT model ex-plains crowdfunding, alternative finance and community finance. WiSo-HH Working Paper Series, Working Paper No. 75.* Accessed from https://www.wiso.uni-hamburg.de/ forschung/forschungslabor/working-papers/pdfs-wp/wp75.pdf

Whiting, M. E., Hugh, G., & Bernstein, M. S. (2019). Fair work: Crowd work minimum wage with one line of code. In *Proceedings of the AAAI Conference on Human Computation and Crowdsourcing.* Stevenson (pp. 197–206). Accessed from https://ojs.aaai.org//index.php/ HCOMP/article/view/5283

World Bank. (2015, June). *The global opportunity in online outsourcing.*

Chapter 3
Data Protection Law in Germany, the United States, and China

3.1 Data Privacy and Crowdsourcing in Germany: Legal Instruments, Aspects of Contract Law, Consumer Protection, and Competition Law[1]

3.1.1 Legal Sources for Data Processing[2]

In Germany, the EU General Data Protection Regulation (GDPR) is the central regulatory instrument for the handling of personal data by crowdsourcing businesses. Platform companies are not specifically addressed by the EU legislation, but like any other data processor, they are subject to the legal requirements (Spiecker genannt Döhmann, 2019). On May 25, 2018, the GDPR became binding and applies by priority and directly (Art. 288 para. 2 TFEU[3]) in all EU member states. Its territorial scope of application is wide. According to what is called the "marketplace principle" (Art. 3 para. 2 GDPR), non-European companies offering goods and services to EU customers and website visitors must also observe the GDPR. As far as the supranational framework gives leeway for national regulations, the German Federal Data Protection Act (*Bundesdatenschutzgesetz*, BDSG)[4] remains applicable as a further relevant source of law. In their role as internet service providers, crowdsourcing platforms must also consider the requirements of the German Telecommunications Act (*Telekommunikationsgesetz*, TKG) and the Telemedia Act (*Telemediengesetz*, TMG) (Hetmank, 2016).

In practice, information on data processing on crowdsourcing platforms is often integrated into general terms and conditions. Such private autonomous regulations

---

[1] This subchapter was written by Sonja Mangold.

[2] This chapter covers only the most important sources of law.

[3] Treaty on the Functioning of the European Union

[4] Revised by the Data Protection Adaptation and Implementation Act EU - DSAnpUG- EU of June 30, 2017, Federal Law Gazette Part I No. 44, 2017.

© The Author(s) 2023
L. Hornuf et al., *Data Privacy and Crowdsourcing*, Advanced Studies in Diginomics and Digitalization, https://doi.org/10.1007/978-3-031-32064-4_3

must be measured against the abuse control provisions of the German Civil Code (*Bürgerliches Gesetzbuch*, BGB) for general terms and conditions (§§ 305 et seq. BGB). They must not deviate from the legal model—for example, the requirements of the GDPR—in a surprising or too far-reaching, disadvantageous manner. Insofar as platform users are consumers, particularly strict requirements apply to the pre-formulated data protection clauses (cf. § 308 et seq. BGB). Data protection violations can then also be prosecuted under civil law by consumer associations[5] under the Injunctive Action Act (*Unterlassungsklagengesetz*, UklaG).[6]

The use of personal data and the analysis of large datasets in digital business models can bring decisive competitive advantages. On the other hand, the notable trend in the crowdsourcing market towards the concentration of economic power and data resources through some large platforms harbors the risk of distortions of competition to the detriment of customers, consumers and smaller platforms (Schweitzer et al., 2018). Competition problems associated with the "data power" of companies are addressed by the European and German antitrust law. As the much-noticed case by the German Federal Cartel Office (*Bundeskartellamt*) against Meta-Facebook shows,[7] antitrust requirements can be a lever for enforcing data protection rights.

The GWB Digitization Act (*GWB-Digitalisierungsgesetz*),[8] which came into force in January 2021, contains specific regulations to limit platform power (von Wallenberg, 2020). The new regulatory framework expressly names access to competition-relevant data as a criterion for determining the market power of companies, which can be combated by means of antitrust abuse control (§ 18 para. 3 No. 3 GWB). The German Federal Cartel Office can prohibit anticompetitive behavior on the part of large platforms, such as denial of data portability (§ 19a para. 2 (1) No. 5 GWB). The regulation also provides for rights to data access over the objections of

---

[5] Consumer associations can assert injunctive relief due to the use of terms and conditions that violate data protection law (§ 1 UKlaG) and other violations of consumer data protection for commercial reasons (§ 2 para. 2 (1) no. 11 UKlaG). Another instrument for the collective enforcement of consumer rights is the "model declaratory action," which was introduced in the Code of Civil Procedure (*Zivilprozessordnung*, ZPO) in 2018 as a result of the "VW diesel scandal."

[6] A new instrument for collective private law enforcement of consumer and data protection rights is the EU collective action directive 2020/1828, which must be implemented and applied in the EU member states by 2023. For more information on the implications of the set of rules for the enforcement of data protection law, see e.g., Grewe and Stegemann (2021).

[7] The German Federal Cartel Office (*Bundeskartellamt*) had prohibited Facebook (now Meta) from collecting and merging data from third-party websites by means of general terms and conditions without the consent of the users. See Bundeskartellamt (2019), case report B6–22-16, online at: https://www.bundeskartellamt.de/SharedDocs/Meldung/DE/Meldungen%20News%20Karussell/2019/07_02_2019_Facebook.html (last accessed June 9, 2023). The Federal Court of Justice has confirmed the order of the Federal Cartel Office in an urgent procedure. Preliminary proceedings are currently pending before the ECJ.

[8] Act amending the Act against Restraints of Competition for a focused, proactive and digital competition law 4.0 and other provisions, Federal Law Gazette Part 1 No. 1, 2021.

powerful companies (§ 19 para. 2 No. 4, § 20 para. 1 (a) GWB) (see Schweitzer et al., 2018).[9]

German competition law also contains provisions that are relevant to issues of privacy. Platforms' data processing practices could be problematic from an unfair competition point of view.[10] For example, insufficient information about data collection and use can be assessed as anti-competitive and can be punished and prevented by associations and competing companies through the Unfair Competition Act (*Gesetz gegen den unlauteren Wettbewerb*, UWG) (Podszun & de Toma, 2016).

The EU regulation on the promotion of fairness and transparency for commercial users of online intermediation services (Regulation (EU) 1150/2019—Peer to Business (P2B) Regulation), which has been in force since summer 2020, is another important instrument that concerns platform businesses. The P2B Regulation contains contractual and competition law requirements to compensate for data-related market power asymmetries (Tribess, 2020). In particular, platforms are obliged to establish transparency towards their commercial users with regard to access to and processing of personal or other data (Art. 9 P2B Regulation). Customers can take action against non-transparent general terms and conditions through an internal complaint procedure to be created by the platforms (Art. 11 P2B Regulation). In addition, competition associations can prosecute violations of transparency obligations with regard to data processing (cf. Art. 14 P2B Regulation).[11]

The European Commission's new proposal for a directive on improving working conditions in platform work[12] deals specifically with privacy issues regarding crowdworkers. The planned legal framework contains restrictions on the processing of personal data of (self-employed and employed) platform workers in connection with algorithmic management (see Sect. 3.1.8, below).

The prospective ePrivacy Regulation[13] could bring new data protection standards in the EU member states with regard to the use of cookies and web tracking services. The ePrivacy regulation is expected to replace, expand and supplement the

---

[9]Using the criterion of data power, the Bundeskartellamt recently found that Alphabet/Google is subject to the extended abuse control for digital corporations (19 (a) GWB). See Bundeskartellamt, press release of January 5, 2022, online at: https://www.bundeskartellamt.de/SharedDocs/ Publikation/DE/Pressemitteilungen/2022/05_01_2022_Google_19a.html (last accessed June 9, 2023).

[10]See Wiedemann (2021) on the interplay between data protection and competition law.

[11]The current legislative initiative of the European Commission on the Digital Services Act (Regulation (EU) 2022/2065 of the European Parliament and of the Council of 19 October 2022 on a Single Market for Digital Services and amending Directive 2000/31/EC (Digital Services Act)) also includes new transparency and framework rules, especially for large platforms. For more details, see Berberich and Seip (2021).

[12]Proposal of the European Commission for a regulation of the European Parliament and of the Council on improving working conditions in platform work (COM (2021) 762 final).

[13]Proposal of the European Commission for a regulation of the European Parliament and of the Council on respect for private life and the protection of personal data in electronic communication and on the repeal of Directive 2002/58 / EC (regulation on privacy and electronic communication), 2017/0003 (COD).

information obligations and admissibility requirements set forth by the GDPR and
the German telecommunications law.[14] However, so far, no agreement has been
reached on the legislative proposal by the European Commission.

3.1.2   Data Security: At the Interface Between Data Protection and IT Security Law

Cyber attacks, the use of spyware, and identity theft are risks that are particularly
high in digital business models such as crowdsourcing. This results in new challenges for data security, which aims to protect against manipulation, loss or
unauthorized access to data (Spiecker genannt Döhmann, 2019). Data security is
legally guaranteed in Art. 5 para. 1 (f), Art. 32 GDPR. Although there are currently
no regulations that specifically take into account the security situation in platform
processes (Spiecker genannt Döhmann, 2019), various standards in German and
European law oblige companies to ensure IT security and to protect user data from
loss, destruction, theft or misuse. The general and area-specific German IT security
laws (BSI law, IT Security Act 2.0,[15] TMG, TKG) contain provisions on security
measures, information obligations and reporting obligations in the event of
malfunctions, which are also relevant for platforms. In addition, there are subordi-
nate legal regulations such as DIN standards and ISO standards. There are also
regulations in tax and commercial law that deal with the secure retention and storage
of data.

EU data protection law also contains specific regulations on data security.
According to Art. 32 GDPR, platform companies and their contract data processors
are obliged to carry out a risk analysis when processing personal data and to take
necessary technical and organizational security measures such as encryption. In
addition, Articles 33 and 34 GDPR provide for obligations in the event of data
breaches to report to authorities and those affected. Violations of data security can
result in official sanctions as well as contractual and liability consequences (Riehm
& Meier, 2020).

---

[14]The ePrivacy regulation is intended to replace the previous ePrivacy Directive and the Cookie
Directive (RL 2009/136/EG). According to the current legal situation German and European
privacy law (Sec. 25 (1) Telecommunications Telemedia Data Protection Act which implements
Art. 5 (3) ePrivacy Directive into national law) generally require that users give their voluntary,
specific, informed consent to the use of tracking and advertising cookies.

[15]For more information on the recently passed IT Security Act 2.0, which provides for changes and
extensions of the existing IT security law, see Kipker and Scholz (2020).

3.1.3   Protection of Personal and Sensitive Data

German and European data protection law only applies if platforms collect and process personal data. Such data are legally defined in Art. 4 para. 1 GDPR as "all information that relates to an identified or identifiable natural person." The information therefore does not have to explicitly identify a person; it is sufficient if a person can be identified by information such as date of birth and social security number.[16] Fixed and dynamic IP addresses can also represent personal data (on the latter, see ECJ, judgment of October 19, 2016—C-582/14—Breyer case).[17]

When processing data, platforms must consider that sensitive user information is particularly legally protected. For example, the processing of information about skin color, party and trade union membership, religious affiliation, or health data is principally prohibited according to Art. 9 para. 1 GDPR.[18] Data processing is only permitted in exceptional cases, for example if users have expressly consented to the processing of sensitive information for a specific purpose (Art. 9 para. 2 (a) GDPR).[19]

3.1.4   Particularities of Data Protection: Company Information, Consumer and Employee Data

German and European data protection law only relates to the personal information of natural persons (cf. Art. 1 para. 1, Art. 4 para. 1 GDPR). Insofar as crowdsourcing platforms collect and process company information, the existing data protection regulations are generally inapplicable.[20] Exceptions apply if business customer information allows direct conclusions to be drawn about individual natural persons (Ernst, 2021). Crowdworkers who are active as solo entrepreneurs on platforms can also rely on data protection law.

---

[16] According to Article 4 para.1 GDPR, identification may take place "in particular by reference to an identifier such as a name, an identification number, location data, an online identifier or to one or more factors specific to the physical, physiological, genetic, mental, economic, cultural or social identity of that natural person."

[17] For more detail on the controversial question of whether identifiability depends on the subjective perspective of the responsible data processor or objective criteria, see Spindler and Dalby (2019).

[18] Special categories of data in accordance with Article 9 para.1 GDPR include data on racial or ethnic origin; political opinions; religious, ideological or trade union beliefs; health data; genetic or biometric data; or information on a person's sex life or sexual orientation.

[19] Whether consent can justify the processing of sensitive data is problematic when there is a structural power imbalance between the responsible body and the user. See Spindler and Dalby (2019).

[20] Data of legal entities (e.g., limited liability companies, registered associations) such as company name, legal form or contact details are expressly not subject to the framework of data protection law (see Recital 14 GDPR).

Special data protection-related requirements must be observed if users of crowdsourcing platforms are consumers.[21] Website visitors and crowdworkers who occasionally work on platforms will regularly have to be classified as consumers (Däubler & Klebe, 2015). Therefore, under certain circumstances, stricter requirements apply to legitimizing consent to data processing (Ernst, 2017). Platform companies must also expect consumer associations to take legal action against possible data protection violations (see above). In the legal discussion in Germany, it is controversial whether crowdworkers are to be classified as employees (e.g., Walzer, 2019), which would interfere with regulations on employee data protection.[22] Most platform companies treat crowdworkers as self-employed. However, the Federal Labor Court (*Bundesarbeitsgericht*, BAG) recently classified a crowdworker who was active on a microtask platform as an employee in accordance with labor law (BAG, judgment of December 1, 2020–9 AZR 102/20). If crowdworkers fall under the concept of employee, the increased legality requirements for data processing in the employment relationship according to § 26 BDSG apply.[23] Accordingly, the collection and use of personal data are only permitted if they are necessary in view of the employment context. With regard to valid consent to data processing, strict assessment and documentation obligations apply (Düwell & Brink, 2017).

3.1.5   Basic Principles of Data Processing

Crowdsourcing platforms must observe some basic data protection principles. In contrast to the United States, the central principle in German and European data protection law is the principle of prohibition with reservation of permission. Accordingly, personal data may only be collected and processed if there is valid consent or another legal basis (Spiecker genannt Döhmann, 2019). The European Court of Justice (ECJ) has consistently held that any handling of personal data must meet the requirements of legal admissibility in accordance with Art. 6 GDPR and the principles regarding the quality of processing in accordance with Art. 5 GDPR (ECJ, case C-137/17 and C-507/17-Google France).

Art. 5 GDPR regulates some general data protection principles. In the event of non-compliance, the supervisory authority can impose a fine (cf. Art. 83 para. 5 (a) GDPR). Accordingly, platforms must deal with user data lawfully,

---

[21] For more about the concept of consumer in German and European private law, see Völker (2013).

[22] The concept of employee is legally defined in § 26 para. 8 of the German Civil Code (BDSG). Applicants are therefore also considered to be employees.

[23] Article 88 GDPR allows EU member states to adopt more specific rules on the protection of employees. In the course of adapting data protection law to the GDPR, the German legislature has made use of this in 2017 with the new regulation pursuant to § 26 of the German Federal Data Protection Act (BDSG).

transparently and fairly (Art. 5 para. 1 (a) GDPR).[24] Regarding the principle of transparency, Recital 39 GDPR states that data subjects must always be made aware of who is collecting the data, whether and to what extent personal data is being collected, and which data is stored and processed. It further states that any information and communication relating to the processing must be easily accessible and easy to understand, and that clear and plain language must be used. The principle of transparency is made more concrete in the detailed information obligations according to Art. 13 and Art. 14 GDPR. Accordingly, platforms that collect data directly or obtain data from third-party sources are obliged to specify the purposes and all legal bases of the processing, to name the recipients or recipient categories of the data, and to explain the storage period or the criteria for determining it. The data subject's rights according to Art. 15 et seq. GDPR—such as the right to access, deletion, and data portability—must also be listed in the privacy statement.[25]

Another central principle of data protection law is the requirement of purpose limitation (Art. 5 para. 1 (b) GDPR). Accordingly, personal information may only be collected and stored for specified, clear and legitimate purposes. Collection and storage of data without prior definition of the purpose is not permitted. If platforms continue to use collected data for changed purposes—such as marketing or claims management—this use requires a new justification.[26]

The principle of data minimization (Art. 5 para. 1 (c) GDPR) provides that the personal data collected must be adequate and factually relevant for the purpose. In addition, the processing must be limited to what is necessary for the purpose. Another key concern of data protection law is the principle of data accuracy (Art. 5 para. 1 (d) GDPR). This principle states that personal data must be factually correct and up-to-date. Platforms as controllers must take all reasonable steps to correct or delete incorrect personal data (Schantz, 2020). When creating individual user and personality profiles, for example for advertising purposes, it is important to ensure that the information is correct.[27] The principle of storage limitation (Art. 5 para. 1 (e) GDPR) is closely linked to the principles of data minimization and data accuracy. Accordingly, platforms are required not to store data longer than necessary. Outdated or incorrect data must be deleted. For this purpose, suitable test and deletion concepts must be developed. The principle of storage limitation also means

---

[24] Unfair processing—which at the same time infringes the principle of transparency—includes, for example, secret video and sound recordings (see Spindler & Dalby, 2019).

[25] Information obligations for platform companies operating websites in Germany may also arise from Article 5 TMG and Article 14 of the EU Regulation on the Online Settlement of Consumer Disputes.

[26] However, Article 6 para. 4 GDPR provides for unexplained facilitation of data processing for modified purposes; for more on the threat of solidifying data power and market power of platforms, see Spiecker genannt Döhmann (2019).

[27] Recital 71 para. 6 GDPR expressly calls for the use of professionally recognized methods and procedures in profiling in order to correct errors and minimize risks. However, it is controversial whether this results in a legal duty for companies to use such procedures (see Lorentz, 2020).

that personal data is anonymized or at least pseudonymized if possible (Schantz, 2020).

With Art. 25 GDPR, the concepts of data protection through "privacy by design" and "privacy by default" were established for the first time throughout the EU (see Baumgartner & Gausling, 2017). The rules on privacy by design and privacy by default specify the principles set out in Art. 5 GDPR, in particular the principle of data minimization. The obligation to privacy by design (Art. 25 para. 1 GDPR) means that platforms must take appropriate organizational and technical data protection measures before data processing, taking into account the state of the art and implementation costs. Thus, there is legal leeway for companies with regard to the selection of specific precautions. For example, anonymization, pseudonymization and encryption techniques come into consideration. Privacy by default (Art. 25 para. 2 GDPR) obliges companies to offer preselected privacy-friendly settings in programs, apps, and other applications. Users should thus be automatically protected against excessive data usage. If the obligations to privacy by design and privacy by default are violated, the supervisory authorities can impose fines of up to 10 million EUR or up to 2% of the company's worldwide annual turnover in the previous financial year, whichever is higher (Art. 83 para. 4 (a) GDPR). Platform companies can use data protection certifications to demonstrate compliance with the requirements set out in Art. 25 para. 1–3 GDPR.

3.1.6 Pseudonymization and Anonymization as Data Protection Measures

Pseudonymization and anonymization are central means of the European data protection framework (e.g., Voigt & von dem Busche, 2018). In Art. 25 para. 1 GDPR, pseudonymization is expressly mentioned as a way to implement privacy by design. Art. 32 para. 1 (a) GDPR describes pseudonymization as an instrument for establishing data security. Art. 4 para. 5 GDPR defines pseudonymization as "the processing of personal data in such a manner that the personal data can no longer be attributed to a specific data subject without the use of additional information, provided that such additional information is kept separately and is subject to technical and organizational measures to ensure that the personal data are not attributed to an identified or identifiable natural person." Successful pseudonymization thus makes it difficult to attribute data to a person; re-identification is only possible if certain additional information is known. If platforms process and use data in a pseudonymized form, for example when creating user profiles,[28] data protection risks can be significantly reduced. Successful

---

[28] Art. 15 para. 3 TMG entitles platforms as internet service providers to use pseudonymous user profiles, for example for the purposes of advertising and market research.

pseudonymization can be taken into account when justifying data processing (Art. 6, 9 GDPR) in favor of the platforms.

The anonymization of data guarantees even greater privacy protection. In the case of anonymized data, the personal reference is removed in such a way that re-identifiability is not possible or only possible with a disproportionately large amount of time and money. If platforms use user data in anonymous, aggregated form, for example for statistics and market research purposes, the requirements of data protection law do not apply.[29]

3.1.7   Consent as the Central Legitimation of Data Processing

In addition to legitimate business interests according to Art. 6 para. 1 (f) GDPR, crowdsourcing platforms will most often use the consent of the users (Art. 6 para. 1 (a), Art. 4 para. 11, Art. 7 et seq. GDPR) as the legal basis for their data processing. In the GDPR, consent[30] is a central concept of legitimizing data collection (Buchner, 2010). As a voluntary decision, it takes precedence over statutory provisions on admissibility. At the same time, statutory admissibility for platforms as responsible data processors is more legally certain (Frenzel, 2021). When obtaining consent, there are some legal requirements that must be observed. The consent must be given voluntarily, for the specific case and in an informed manner. Furthermore, platforms must be able to demonstrate that the user has consented to processing of data (Art. 7 para. 1 GDPR). If users as employees or consumers are in a power imbalance vis-à-vis the platform, the voluntary consent can be problematic (Recital 43 GDPR). In this case, consent can only freely be given if the data processing is in the interests of the user or if the user does not suffer any disadvantages by refusing to give consent (Stemmer, 2020). If platforms collect data that are not required for the provision of their services, the ban on "tying" (Art. 7 para. 4 GDPR) must also be observed. Accordingly, access to the service may not be made dependent on consent to an unnecessary use of data, in the sense of "take it or leave it." A voluntary decision is also doubtful if a large provider with a significant market share requires its users to consent to extensive data use as a condition for using the service (Ernst, 2017). If consent is obtained, as is often the case, through general terms and conditions, the consent to data processing section should be particularly emphasized (Art. 7 para. 2 GDPR). Informed consent cannot be assumed if the information on data processing is written in "legalese" (Ernst, 2017). A consent to excessive further use of personal data can be invalid if solicited through a surprise clause under

---

[29]Recital 26 para. 5 GDPR provides that the principles of data protection do not apply to anonymous information.

[30]Consent is legally defined in Article 4 para. 11 GDPR as "any freely given, specific, informed, and unambiguous indication of the data subject's wishes by which he or she, by a statement or by a clear affirmative action, signifies agreement to the processing of personal data relating to him or her."

general terms and conditions law (Spiecker genannt Döhmann, 2019). Likewise, pre-ticked boxes shall not constitute consent (Recital 32 GDPR).

According to German and European case law, the use of cookies to analyze user behavior and for advertising purposes also requires active consent in the sense of an opt-in[31] (see most recently ECJ, judgment of October 1, 2019, Az. C-673/17; BGH, judgment of May 28, 2020-I ZR 7/16).

3.1.8   Algorithm-Based Decision-Making: Risks of Discrimination, Solution Approaches

Crowdsourcing platforms use algorithm-supported, data-driven decisions in a variety of ways (see e.g. Hannák et al., 2017; Ivanova et al., 2018). For example, crowdsourcing platforms often use algorithms to select, place and evaluate the performance of crowdworkers. In addition, algorithm-based data mining and big data analysis methods can be used to create extensive customer and visitor profiles, for example for marketing purposes.

Existing studies show that algorithm-based decision-making and evaluation on crowdsourcing platforms can be associated with unlawful disadvantages for groups at risk of discrimination, for example because of their gender or ethnic origin (Hannák et al., 2017). Algorithmic risks of discrimination have not been comprehensively and specifically addressed in German and European data protection and anti-discrimination law. However, there are some starting points for regulating algorithmic discrimination (Orwat, 2020). Particularly noteworthy is the regulation in Art. 22 para. 1 GDPR, according to which data subjects generally have the right not to be subject to a "decision based solely on automated processing—including profiling."[32] If such a decision is permitted in exceptional cases (in the case of contract fulfillment or consent, Art. 22 para. 2 GDPR), affected persons have the right to contest the decision (cf. Art. 22 para. 3 GDPR). Even stricter requirements apply according to Art. 22 para. 4 GDPR if, within the framework of automated decisions, discriminatory data within the meaning of Art. 9 para. 1 GDPR are processed (Buchner, 2018).

In addition, the GDPR provides for extended information obligations and rights to information for those affected about the logic involved and the effects of automated decision-making (Art. 13 para. 2 (f), 14 para. 2 (g), 15 para. 1 (h) GDPR).

---

[31] The sending of a newsletter or promotional e-mails can be legitimized by checking the original consent of the user again via a final confirmation link sent to his or her e-mail address. With this double opt-in procedure, companies can obtain legally watertight proof of user consent.

[32] Profiling is legally defined in Article 4 para. 4 GDPR as any form of automated processing of personal data consisting of the use of personal data to evaluate certain personal aspects relating to a natural person, in particular to analyze or predict aspects concerning that natural person's performance at work, economic situation, health, personal preferences, interests, reliability, behavior, location or movements.

Accordingly, companies must provide information about the functionality and decision-making options of the algorithm (Orwat, 2020). Furthermore, Art. 35 para. 3 (a) GDPR obliges companies to carry out a data protection impact assessment if—in the case of algorithm-based, automated decisions—personal aspects of a person are comprehensively and systematically evaluated.

In addition, the German General Act on Equal Treatment (*Allgemeines Gleichbehandlungsgesetz*, AGG) offers individual and collective legal redress in order to take action against discriminatory decisions using algorithms (Orwat, 2020). With its current strategy on artificial intelligence, the European Commission[33] has proposed extensive new regulations to make algorithm-based decisions fair, transparent, and non-discriminatory. Also worth mentioning are the specifications regarding algorithmic management of the planned EU directive on improving working conditions in platform work, mentioned above. In particular, the proposed directive stipulates that platform companies shall not automatically process any personal data relating to the psychological state, health status, or private conversations of platform workers (cf. Art. 6 para. 5).

3.1.9 Rights of Data Subjects

Art. 15 et seq. GDPR delineates the rights that users can assert against platforms as responsible data processors. According to Art. 15 para. 1 GDPR[34] (right of access), platform companies must provide information on processing purposes, categories of data, recipients, storage duration and rights of appeal to a supervisory authority on request. Art. 15 para. 3 sent. 1 GDPR obliges organizations to provide a free copy of the personal data that is being processed, upon request by the data subject. According to Art. 16 para. 1 GDPR, users can immediately request the correction of incorrect information concerning them. Art. 17 GDPR defines the right to erasure of the data or to be forgotten. A deletion of data must be carried out in particular if the data is no longer required or the person concerned has revoked their original consent. The question of whether companies can legally fulfill their obligation to data deletion by anonymizing the data is legally controversial (e.g., Stürmer, 2020).

A central right of data subjects in the platform economy is the right to data portability according to Art. 20 GDPR (Ciotti et al., 2021; Schweitzer, 2019). This pursues a consumer protection and antitrust law objective and is intended to prevent lock-in effects in the sense of customer retention to one provider. Users are therefore entitled to receive all of their personal data in a commonly used and machine-readable format (Art. 20 para. 1 GDPR). In addition, those affected have the right to port their data to third parties, provided that the rights and freedoms of third parties

---

[33] European Commission, Proposal for a regulation laying down harmonized rules on artificial intelligence, COM (2021) 206 final.

[34] § 34 BDSG foresees some national limitations of the right of access.

are not affected (Art. 20 para. 4 GDPR). However, the exact scope, technical design and practical significance of the right to data portability are still unclear (Schweitzer, 2019).

Art. 21 GDPR grants users the right to object to lawful data processing under certain conditions. Platforms may then no longer be allowed to process the data in question. In Art. 21 para. 1 GDPR, the right is standardized to object to individually unreasonable processing—including profiling—on the basis of Art. 6 para. 1 (f) GDPR. In addition, data processing for the purpose of direct advertising can be prevented by the affected users asserting their right to object (see Art. 21 para. 2, para. 3 GDPR). In the event of violations of the rights of users according to Art. 15 et seq. GDPR, platforms must reckon with claims for damages and fines (Art. 82, Art. 83 para. 5 (b) GDPR).

3.1.10   The Data Protection Impact Assessment: Self-Evaluation in the Case of High-Risk Data Processing

In those cases of data processing that might result in elevated risk to the rights and freedoms of natural persons, companies must carry out a data protection impact assessment (Art. 35 et seq. GDPR), evaluating the consequences of data processing in advance and then selecting and taking adequate security and data protection measures. As part of the data protection impact assessment, risks for the protection of personal data must be identified and assessed. The recommendations of the German Federal Office for Information Security on protection needs can be helpful in this regard. Furthermore, a risk treatment plan must be drawn up (Friedewald, 2017).

A self-evaluation according to Art. 35 GDPR may be necessary for crowdsourcing for various reasons. In particular, platform companies can be obliged to carry out a privacy impact assessment if they use web tracking technologies, carry out big data analyses, or otherwise engage in profiling. There is also an obligation in accordance with Art. 35 GDPR if a large amount of highly sensitive data is processed (Hansen, 2020). If the data protection impact assessment shows that there is a high risk potential, the competent data protection supervisory authority must be consulted before data processing (Art. 36 para. 1 GDPR). A violation of the requirements according to Art. 35 et seq. GDPR can be punished with fines of up to ten million EUR or up to 2% of the company's worldwide annual turnover in the previous financial year (Art. 83 para. 4 (a) GDPR).

3.1.11   Internal and External Data Protection Controls

A central element of corporate self-monitoring in privacy issues is the company data protection officer (Art. 37 GDPR, § 38 BDSG), whose main tasks are advising, monitoring compliance with standards, training, cooperation with supervisory authorities, and responding to inquiries from those affected (cf. Art. 39 GDPR, § 7 BDSG). Platforms may be obliged to appoint a company data protection officer if they use GPS tracker apps or process large quantities of sensitive data in accordance with Art. 9 GDPR (cf. Art. 37 para. 1 (b), (c) GDPR). A designation requirement can also pertain under German law if a data protection impact assessment is required for crowdsourcing services (§ 38 para. 1 sent. 2 BDSG).[35] In addition, it may be advisable for platforms to voluntarily appoint a data protection officer in order to better meet their data protection obligations.

Private self-monitoring under data protection law within a company is flanked by state-level and national supervisory mechanisms. According to Art. 51 et seq. GDPR, each EU member state must set up one or more independent data protection authorities. In Germany, data protection supervision is organized on a federal basis with the Federal Data Protection Commissioner and the State Data Protection Commissioner. The national data protection authorities have extensive control responsibilities and powers. Their primary tasks include monitoring and enforcing the GDPR, making companies aware of their obligations under data protection law, and processing inquiries and complaints from those affected (cf. Art. 57 para. 1 GDPR). The supervisory authorities are also responsible for questions relating to employee data protection. Art. 58 GDPR regulates powers of investigation, remedial action and approval. For example, the data protection supervisory authorities can prohibit illegal data processing, have personal data deleted, and prevent data transfers to non-EU countries. According to Art. 58 para. 5 GDPR, the EU member states must grant the supervisory authorities the right to "engage in legal proceedings." Additional powers of the federal data protection officer and the state data protection officer according to national law, such as access rights, are regulated in §§ 16, 40 BDSG.

3.1.12   Sanctions

For the prosecution and sanctioning of data protection violations, the GDPR regulates, among others, fines, claims for damages, and the right to collective actions (e.g., Körner, 2017). In the event of violations of data protection obligations, the

---

[35] Pursuant to § 38 para. 1 BDSG, there is also an obligation to designate an officer if more than twenty persons are engaged in the automated processing of personal data. As many crowdsourcing platforms are small and medium-sized enterprises (SMEs), this threshold is typically unlikely to be reached.

supervisory authorities can impose fines of up to 10 million EUR or up to 2% of the company's total worldwide annual turnover of the previous financial year, whichever is higher (Art. 83 para. 4 GDPR). In the case of particularly serious data protection violations, even more severe fines can be imposed. In the event of violations of the processing principles of the GDPR, including the conditions for lawful consent, violations of the rights of the data subjects and disregard of the instructions of the supervisory authorities, the fine can even be up to 20 million EUR or 4% of annual sales. In addition, the GDPR provides for claims for compensation for material and immaterial damages against the person responsible or the contracted data processor in the event of data protection violations (Art. 82 GDPR).

3.2 Data Privacy in Digital Business in the United States: Fragmented Rules, State Pioneers and the Prominent Role of the Federal Trade Commission[36]

3.2.1 Patchwork of Privacy Regulation

The United States is home to a complicated patchwork of state and federal statutes and case law on data protection[37] (Barrett, 2019). Unlike in the EU, there is no general national privacy legislation.[38] However, numerous sector-specific laws on data use have been passed, some of which may also affect crowdsourcing platforms. For example, the Children's Online Privacy Protection Act (COPPA)[39] regulates requirements for operators of websites that collect personal data from children under the age of 13 (Ritvo et al., 2013). The Electronic Communications Privacy Act,[40] which addresses both public and private bodies, imposes restrictions on the use of electronic communication (Determann, 2016). When crowdsourcing platforms ask for, receive, and use background checks or credit information from users and customers, the requirements of the Fair Credit Reporting Act (FCRA)[41] may be

---

[36]This subchapter was written by Sonja Mangold.

[37]The term "data protection" is preferred in European law. The term "privacy" is commonly used in the U.S. "Data protection" rather refers to the protection process whereas "data privacy" is a more rights-based approach. In the following these two terms are used synonymously.

[38]The introduction of a uniform federal privacy law is currently being called for by various sides (tech industry, civil society); see Levine (2021), online at: https://www.politico.com/news/2021/0 6/01/washington-plan-protect-american-data-silicon-valley-491405 (last accessed: June 9, 2023).

[39]COPPA, available online at: https://www.ecfr.gov/cgi-bin/text-idx?SID=4939e77c77a1a1a08c1 cbf905fc4b409&node=16%3A1.0.1.3.36&rgn=div5 (last accessed June 9, 2023).

[40]The Electronic Communications Privacy Act (1986) includes the Wiretap Act and the Stored Communications Act.

[41]FCRA, available online at: https://www.ecfr.gov/cgi-bin/text-idx?SID=2b1fab8de5438fc52f2 a326fc6592874&mc=true&tpl=/ecfrbrowse/Title16/16CIsubchapF.tpl (last accessed June 9, 2023).

relevant (Hoofnagle, 2013). The FCRA contains provisions on the accuracy and disclosure of financial information and aims to protect consumers from identity theft. Accordingly, platforms can only obtain consumer reports, that is, the collections of documents that a prospective employer may use to evaluate a potential employee, for legally permissible purposes. Consumer reports include, for example, information from credit agencies about creditworthiness, general reputation, and personal characteristics of consumers. Background checks on crowdworkers can also be considered as consumer reports (Hoofnagle, 2013). If platforms have taken adverse action based on such reports, they must notify the affected persons.

As is practice in other countries, American crowdsourcing platforms often integrate privacy clauses into their general terms of use. There is no abuse control of standardized terms and conditions comparable to German law in the U.S. However, under certain circumstances, it is possible to proceed against privacy violations in terms of use under competition law (Munz, 1992).

Several antitrust bills were recently introduced in the U.S. Congress which are intended to limit the market and data power of large platform companies. The American Choice and Innovation Online Act[42] would prohibit data access restrictions on business users. The Augmenting Compatibility and Competition by Enabling Service Switching (ACCESS) Act[43] would require platforms to guarantee some minimum standard of interoperability and data portability. However, it is still uncertain whether these laws will ultimately be passed.

The Federal Trade Commission (FTC) plays a prominent role in enforcing data privacy in the U.S. (Solove & Hartzog, 2014). The FTC is an independent federal agency responsible for competition and consumer protection. Violations of consumer privacy can be pursued by the FTC as unfair competition on the basis of 15 Code of Laws of the United States of America (U.S.C.) § 45 (= Section 5 FTC Act). The FTC could take action against misleading or incorrect information in the privacy statements of crowdsourcing platforms. In the past, the FTC has repeatedly raised objections to the data protection practices of powerful digital corporations like Google or Meta-Facebook.[44] Data protection violations by crowdsourcing platforms and their representatives could also be sanctioned via U.S. tort law (Determann, 2016).[45]

Moreover, almost all U.S. states have specific data protection laws for residents that platform companies should consider. California has played a pioneering role in

---

[42] Available online at: https://www.congress.gov/bill/117th-congress/house-bill/3816/text?r=43& s=1 (last accessed June 9, 2023). This bill was not enacted. However, its provisions could still become binding law through inclusion in another bill.

[43] Available online at: https://www.congress.gov/bill/116th-congress/senate-bill/2658/text (last accessed June 10, 2023).

[44] All FTC Cases and Proceedings concerning consumer privacy are available online at: https://www.ftc.gov/enforcement/cases-proceedings (last accessed June 9, 2023).

[45] In most states there are four common law privacy torts, namely the offenses of intrusion upon seclusion, public disclosure of private matters, appropriation of names or likeness or false light publicity.

privacy legislation. With the California Consumer Privacy Act (CCPA) of 2018, which has been in force since January 2020, a data protection standard comparable to the GDPR has been established.[46] Other states are increasingly following the Californian example (Newell et al., 2021). In 2021, Virginia and Colorado passed new privacy laws, and legislation similar to the CCPA is planned in other states such as New York, Washington, Florida, and Minnesota.

Unlike in the EU, the voluntary self-regulation of companies is crucial for the U.S. data protection regime (e.g., Kranig & Peintinger, 2014). Examples of self-regulation in the internet economy are the privacy seal programs TRUSTe, BBBOnline and the Online Privacy Alliance Guidelines (Rodrigues & Papakonstantinou, 2018). Some U.S. crowdsourcing platforms expressly advertise on their website that they are TRUSTe and/or BBBOnline certified.[47] By using such privacy seals, the platforms apparently seek to stand out from the competition and create a positive image with customers and business partners.

The Privacy Shield Agreement, which was negotiated between the European Commission and the U.S. Department of Commerce, is an example of government-initiated self-regulation. Since 2016, U.S. companies have been able to participate in the Privacy Shield data protection framework and thus to be certified as recipients of legitimate data transfers from the EU. Many U.S. crowdsourcing providers still point out in their privacy policies that they have joined the Privacy Shield. With its judgment in the "Schrems II" case (ECJ judgment of July 16, 2020-C-311/18), the European Court of Justice has now declared the European Commission's decision on the adequacy of the level of protection offered by the EU–U.S. Privacy Shield invalid. This has raised concerns that the judgment would cause legal uncertainty for companies with regard to international data transfers (Botta, 2020). This uncertainty could be remedied in the near future by the new Trans-Atlantic Data Privacy Framework, which the European Commission and U.S. President Biden have agreed on in principle.[48]

3.2.2   Data Security: Numerous Legal Sources

There are numerous laws in the U.S. that impose data security obligations on private companies (Determann, 2016; McGeveran, 2019). At the federal level, the FTC, as the nation's consumer protection agency, often takes action against inadequate data security practices. All fifty states have adopted data breach notification laws, which

---

[46]The CCPA has been modified and extended by the CPRA which entered into force in January 2023. For more information, see: https://oag.ca.gov/privacy/ccpa; https://privacyrights.org/resources/california-privacy-rights-act-overview (last accessed June 9, 2023).

[47]See, for example, the website of Survey Monkey, online at: https://www.surveymonkey.com/ (last accessed June 9, 2023).

[48]For further information, see the press release of the European Commission: https://ec.europa.eu/commission/presscorner/detail/en/ip_22_2087 (last accessed June 9, 2023).

require companies that have exposed certain personal information to notify the affected data subjects and sometimes also a regulatory authority. Some states have passed additional standards on data security, data disposal, and cybersecurity.[49] For example, the state security-specific regulation of Massachusetts requires that companies covered by the legislation develop and implement a comprehensive information security program (McGeveran, 2019). California statutory law requires digital businesses to "implement reasonable security procedures and practices" to protect the personal data of California residents from unauthorized or illegal access, destruction, use, modification, or disclosure.[50]

There are also broad voluntary industry standards for data security. One of these standards is the Cybersecurity Framework, which was established by the National Institute of Standards and Technology (NIST)[51] and has proven to be highly influential on private companies (McGeveran, 2019). The NIST Framework, which relies *inter alia* on the ISO/IEC 27000 family of standards for information security management systems,[52] includes concrete cybersecurity measures in five phases: "Identify, Protect, Detect, Respond, Recover." Many statutory and private frameworks also encourage risk assessments, staff training, access controls for potentially vulnerable data, and multifactor authentication or encryption of data (McGeveran, 2019).

3.2.3   Protection of Personal and Sensitive Information: No Single Definition

Unlike in the EU, there is no single definition of the term "personal information" in the U.S. The U.S. approach to personal data includes various definitions and is rather inconsistent (e.g., Schwartz & Solove, 2014). COPPA, for example, which may be relevant for digital crowdsourcing, defines personal information as "individually identifiable information about an individual collected online," including name, address, username, phone number, video, photograph, location data or social security number.[53] Some privacy laws define personal information as something other than publicly accessible or aggregate, statistical data. Many state-level data breach notification laws contain lists of types of data that constitute personal information

---

[49]Data security protects personal information, whereas the term cybersecurity relates to the protection of the network's infrastructure (McGeveran, 2019).

[50]California Civil Code § 198.100, available online at: https://leginfo.legislature.ca.gov/faces/codes_displaySection.xhtml?sectionNum=1798.100.&nodeTreePath=8.4.45&lawCode=CIV (last accessed June 9, 2023).

[51]Available online at: https://www.nist.gov/cyberframework (last accessed June 9, 2023).

[52]For more information, see: https://www.iso.org/isoiec-27001-information-security.html (last accessed June 9, 2023).

[53]Children's Online Privacy Protection Rule § 312.2, available online at: https://www.ecfr.gov/cgi-bin/text-idx?rgn=div5&node=16:1.0.1.3.36#se16.1.312_12 (last accessed June 9, 2023).

(Schwartz & Solove, 2014). A more far-reaching approach adopts the standard set forth by the CCPA (Determann, 2018), whose definition even goes beyond the GDPR in some respects. Personal data are broadly defined as all information that relates to a particular consumer[54] or household. In contrast to the GDPR, household and device data are also classified as personal information. Among other items, the CCPA lists as personal information[55] name, address, account name, passport information, social security number, driver's license and signature. Personal information also includes commercial information, data on consumption and buying behavior, biometric data, browsing history, search history, IP address and geolocation data. The CCPA may apply to U.S. American and foreign crowdsourcing platforms doing business in California.[56]

Unlike in the EU, no legally binding concept of sensitive data that receive stronger protections than other types of data exists as a general matter of U.S. law. There is also no general express obligation to give consent for the processing of such data (King & Raja, 2012; Schwartz & Solove, 2014). However, crowdsourcing platforms that collect certain types of user information may be required to meet certain legal eligibility criteria. For example, COPPA imposes certain information privacy requirements for websites that collect personal data from children under the age of 13 years. Moreover, the FTC has provided in its guidelines and investigations clear examples for identifying sensitive consumer information (King & Raja, 2012). These include financial data, data about children, health information, precise location data and government-issued identification numbers such as social security numbers. The FTC has also advised digital businesses to obtain express consent from consumers to receive behavioral advertising before collecting or using sensitive information for this purpose.[57] At the state level, the California Privacy Rights Act (CPRA) provides a broad definition of sensitive data, which includes consumer financial information, geolocation data, the contents of a consumer's mail, health data, union membership, racial or ethnic origin, and religious or philosophical beliefs. The CPRA stipulates special information obligations and data subject rights with regard to the processing of such data (Spies, 2020). Consumers in California will therefore have the right to decide on the collection of sensitive data beyond the contractual relationship through opt-out. This can be done, for example, by including a button on the website that says, "Limit the Use of My Sensitive Personal

---

[54] Consumer means a natural person who is a California resident, CCPA, Cal. Civ. Code 1798.140 (i).

[55] CCPA, Cal. Civ. Code 1798.140(v) (1).

[56] The companies concerned must cross one of the following thresholds: have a gross annual revenue of over 25 million USD; buy, receive or sell personal information of 50,000 or more California residents, households or devices; or derive 50% or more of annual revenue from selling California residents' personal information.

[57] Federal Trade Commission (2009). Staff Report: FTC Report on Self-Regulatory Principles of Online Behavioral Advertising, available online at: https://www.ftc.gov/sites/default/files/documents/reports/federal-trade-commission-staff-report-self-regulatory-principles-online-behavioral-advertising/p085400behavadreport.pdf (last accessed June 9, 2023).

Information." Other states such as Colorado also have special legal requirements for the processing of sensitive information (Spies, 2021). However, it can be stated that U.S. statutory laws, unlike Art. 9 GDPR, generally allow the processing of sensitive data and do not require affirmative express consent. As we will see later in this book (Sect. 4.1), this is evidently reflected in extensive data collection practices among U.S. platforms.

3.2.4 Protection of Consumer and Employee Data

If users purchase goods or services on platforms primarily for personal purposes, they are classified as consumers. Crowdworkers who work occasionally on platforms and who are classified as individuals rather than business entities may also fall within the broad definition of consumers under U.S. laws (Delisle & Trujillo, 2010; Solove & Schwartz, 2020). If users are consumers, platforms must observe a patchwork of specific rules at the federal level and the state level. For example, the FCRA prescribes purpose limitations for the collection of consumer financial information.[58] Meanwhile, the FTC has a broad scope of power to enforce the privacy and security of personal consumer data (Hartzog & Solove, 2015). For example, the FTC can proceed as part of an administrative procedure against deceptive privacy policies or inadequate security practices of companies. FTC proceedings are typically terminated by consent decrees specifying remedial actions such as fines, corrective actions, or third-party monitoring of data usage practices. Otherwise, the FTC can enter after a formal procedure a cease-and-desist order demanding that the recipient stop the challenged illegal activity. In addition, the FTC may seek an injunction before the ordinary courts. Consumer data protection requirements can also be enforced by means of class actions, which have a considerable risk potential of punitive damages for companies (Determann, 2016).

Similar to German and European law, the legal classification of crowdworkers either as employees or independent contractors is highly controversial in the U.S. (e.g., Cherry & Poster, 2016).[59] In cases where employee status is affirmed, platforms must consider various scattered regulations with regard to employment privacy (Kim 2019; Otto, 2016). For example, the FCRA and numerous state laws regulate background checks by requiring the consent of potential employees. The Electronic Communications Privacy Act (ECPA) and the National Labor Relations Act also contain certain standards on the protection of employees' privacy interests.

---

[58] Permissible purposes include use for employment purposes or legitimate business use in connection with a business transaction that is initiated by the consumer.

[59] Especially in California there have been a large number of class actions filed by platform workers, almost all of which revolve around the question of whether platform workers are in fact dependent employees. These lawsuits often end with a settlement in which the platforms pay millions of dollars to the workers, thus avoiding a court decision on the question of dependent employment (Cherry & Poster, 2016).

Furthermore, in the case of privacy infringements and inadmissible crowdworker surveillance, platform companies may be liable under tort law. However, it should be noted that, unlike in Germany, U.S. law does not contain any general standards that limit the collection and use of personal information of workers. There are also no regulations that correspond to the specificity of the employment context with its power asymmetries (Otto, 2016).

3.2.5   Main Principles of Data Processing: Sector-Specific and State-Specific Approaches

In contrast to Europe, the U.S. generally allows the processing of personal data. The free flow of information and its benefit to free enterprise historically plays a significant role in the U.S. (Pardau, 2018). There is no omnibus regulation on basic principles of data processing such as transparency, purpose limitation, data minimization, accuracy, and storage limitation comparable to the GDPR. Nevertheless, key privacy requirements are partly reflected in U.S. sector-specific and state-specific privacy law (Rustad & Koenig, 2019) and can thus be relevant for crowdsourcing practices. For example, the FCRA incorporates norms of transparency, accuracy, and collection limitation. At the state level, California's privacy laws in particular have adopted principles closely resembling the European approach (Pardau, 2018; Spies, 2021). The CCPA incorporates comprehensive transparency and information duties. Accordingly, businesses are required to post in their privacy policies, *inter alia*, information about the categories of data collected, the purposes of processing, categories of personal information sold or disclosed, and a description of consumers' privacy rights such as the right to opt out of the sale of data and the right to request deletion of personal information. The CPRA contains data minimization and storage limitation rules similar to the GDPR.[60] However, it must be noted that California privacy laws don't reflect all European core privacy principles. For example, lawfulness and fairness requirements are absent from the California regulation.

As noted above, the concepts of privacy by design and privacy by default, which take a proactive approach to data privacy, are new key elements of the GDPR. U.S. regulators also have embraced the principle of privacy by design. Even before the GDPR adopted this strategy, the FTC established its privacy by design rules.[61]

---

[60] The CPRA states that a "business's collection and use" of a consumer's personal information shall be "reasonably necessary and proportionate to achieve the purposes for which the personal information was collected or processed." The CPRA further states that a business "shall not retain a consumer's personal information or sensitive personal information (...) for longer than is reasonably necessary" for the purpose for which it was collected; CPRA, Cal. Civ. Code 1798.100.

[61] Privacy By Design and the New Privacy Framework of the U.S. Federal Trade Commission (2012), available online at: https://www.ftc.gov/public-statements/2012/06/privacy-design-and-new-privacy-framework-us-federal-trade-commission (last accessed June 9, 2023).

The FTC framework calls on companies to implement various preventive techniques like reasonable security, SSL encryption and cookie blocking by default.

Worth mentioning in this context is that the FTC has set guidelines for fair information practices regarding internet privacy.[62] The FTC has identified five core principles of data protection that should be implemented primarily by company self-regulation: "Notice/Awareness," "Choice/Consent," "Access/Participation," "Integrity/Security," and "Enforcement/Redress" (Li et al., 2012). The American Law Institute (ALI), a leading independent scientific organization in the U.S., has also recently adopted a framework of data privacy principles that are aligned with the GDPR (Rustad & Koenig, 2019).[63] These instruments, however, are characteristically non-binding recommendations.

3.2.6 Anonymization and Pseudonymization

Some U.S. crowdsourcing platforms state in their privacy policy that they anonymize or pseudonymize personal information (see Sect. 4.1). Similar to Europe, U.S. privacy laws and FTC guidelines encourage practices of anonymization or encryption of data (Brasher, 2018). The FTC has clarified that anonymized data are exempt from the data protection legislation, provided that a company: (1) takes reasonable measures to ensure that the data is de-identified; (2) publicly commits not to try to re-identify the data; and (3) contractually prohibits third parties from trying to re-identify the data.[64] New state privacy laws such as the CCPA explicitly promote the pseudonymization of personal consumer information.

Compared to the GDPR, the U.S. approach to anonymization and pseudonymization has some shortcomings (Brasher, 2018). In Europe, only fully anonymized data falls outside the scope of data protection laws. Whereas pseudonymous data are protected by the GDPR, the U.S. law does not generally differentiate between anonymization and pseudonymization in such a way that those data categories are subject to different legal requirements based on their relative risk of re-identification. Threats to consumer privacy in the age of big data, for example through the commercial exploitation of immense amounts of behavioral data, which is also being discussed in the U.S., are thus not adequately addressed.

---

[62] Available online at: https://www.ftc.gov/reports/privacy-online-fair-information-practices-electronic-marketplace-federal-trade-commission (last accessed June 9, 2023).

[63] For more information, see: https://www.ali.org/news/articles/now-available-principles-law-data-privacy/ (last accessed June 9, 2023).

[64] FTC (2012), Protecting consumer privacy in an era of rapid change: Recommendations for businesses and policy makers, available online at: https://www.ftc.gov/reports/protecting-consumer-privacy-era-rapid-change-recommendations-businesses-policymakers (last accessed June 9, 2023).

3.2.7   Consent for Data Processing: Limited Legal Requirements

In the U.S., unlike in the EU, there is no general need to obtain an individual's consent for data collection and processing. There is no requirement of a legal justification for the processing of personal data. Nevertheless, the principle of consent is a relevant concept in U.S. privacy laws (Rustad & König, 2019; Schwartz & Peifer, 2017). Statutory laws make use of consent in the form of opt-in and opt-out mechanisms. In cases of opting-in, data processing cannot take place unless the person concerned gives their affirmative consent. Opt-out means that data processing takes place unless the data subject objects. These permission requirements can also affect crowdsourcing platforms. The FCRA contains one of the strongest opt-in mechanisms, requiring clear notice to and written authorization from a consumer before a potential employer can use a consumer credit report for employment purposes (Schwartz & Peifer, 2017). An example of opt-out consent can be found in the California privacy legislation. As mentioned above, the CCPA enshrines the right of consumers to object to the selling of their data. Moreover, the FTC advocates the concept of free and informed consent ("Notice and Choice") to companies' online data collection practices and has provided guidelines for its implementation (Sloan & Warner, 2013).

In sum, the consent requirements in U.S. law are limited and less restrictive than the EU provisions (Determann, 2016; Schwartz & Peifer, 2017). For example, U.S. statutory law does not concern itself with the possibility of power imbalances in employment or other relationships. Unlike the European context, when using web cookie technologies, implied consent is sufficient.[65] In addition, the mere use of a website is seen as implicit consent for data processing via general terms and conditions (Determann, 2016).

3.2.8   Regulation of Algorithmic Decision-Making: Steps and Gaps

Algorithmic decision-making may be used throughout the crowdsourcing process. Matching, selection, and performance ratings of crowdworkers are often based on algorithms. Algorithms can also be used for customer profiling. Nevertheless, algorithmic decision-making in crowdsourcing can be opaque and subject to error, bias, and discrimination (Hannák et al., 2017; Kaminski, 2019).

Platforms that use algorithms in their business should consider various privacy and equal opportunity laws that may apply to such processes. For example, the

---

[65]There are first approaches in U.S. law to limit tracking via cookies. For example, the California privacy legislation requires websites to inform in their privacy policies how they respond to "do not track" mechanisms exercised by consumers.

FCRA comes into play in certain circumstances where an algorithm denies people employment or other benefits. Section 5 of the FTC Act may be applicable when data analytics are used in a deceptive or unfair way, such as when algorithms are gender- or racially biased (Federal Trade Commission, 2016). In a much-noticed order for violations of COPPA, the FTC recently required WW International, formerly known as Weight Watchers, to destroy any algorithms trained with illegally collected data from children.[66] Some privacy statutes at the state level contain accountability and transparency rights around automated decision-making and profiling, similar to the GDPR. California privacy laws call for opt-out rights with respect to the use of automated decision-making, which also includes profiling. In addition, they require businesses to disclose information about the logic underlying such decision-making processes as well as their envisaged consequences for the consumer. Similar rules can be found in Virginia's new privacy law (Spies, 2021). Platforms that make use of algorithms should also consider U.S. anti-discrimination legislation, which primarily focuses on employment contexts, such as the Civil Rights Act of 1964 and the Genetic Information Nondiscrimination Act (FTC, 2016).

Overall, the risks of discrimination through algorithms have so far not been specifically and sufficiently addressed by U.S. laws (Ebers, 2020; Kaminski, 2019). For example, equal opportunity laws focus on human decision-makers without taking into account unintentional discrimination by algorithms. In contrast to European law, the few specific rules on algorithmic accountability and transparency in U.S. privacy laws are limited to state statutes and thus have a comparatively narrow scope.

3.2.9 Individual Rights: Scattered Rules

There is no comprehensive national regulation in the U.S. comparable to Art. 15 et seq. GDPR, which enshrines individual rights of data subjects vis-à-vis data processors. After all, the FTC's non-binding fair information practice principles include a limited set of consumer rights, such as access provisions, and rights of correction and deletion.[67] The recently adopted ALI's privacy recommendations additionally address data portability.[68] Sector-specific statutes that may be relevant

---

[66]More detailed information is available at: https://www.ftc.gov/news-events/news/press-releases/2022/03/ftc-takes-action-against-company-formerly-known-weight-watchers-illegally-collecting-kids-sensitive (last accessed June 9, 2023).

[67]Federal Trade Commission (2000). Privacy online: Fair information practices in the electronic marketplace: A Federal Trade Commission Report to Congress, available online at: https://www.ftc.gov/reports/privacy-online-fair-information-practices-electronic-marketplace-federal-trade-commission (last accessed: June 9, 2023).

[68]For more information, see: https://www.ali.org/news/articles/now-available-principles-law-data-privacy/ (last accessed June 9, 2023).

for digital crowdsourcing such as COPPA[69] or FCRA[70] also establish certain rights such as notification or erasure rights over data. The California privacy legislation echoes individual rights from the GDPR and even goes beyond them in some respects (Determann, 2018). Other states have followed the Californian standard, but merely mimic it. The CCPA allows individuals to make access requests for personal data, providing a high degree of transparency with respect to data processing in the private sector.[71] It partially prescribes disclosures and communication channels such as toll-free phone numbers that are not required to comply with GDPR. The CCPA also gives consumers a data portability right—namely, the right to access a copy of their personal information.[72] In addition, companies must honor requests for correction and deletion of data under certain circumstances.[73] In some respects, however, the CCPA provisions fall short of the GDPR standards. For example, there are more exceptions to the right to erasure. Companies are given a long period of 45 days to respond to consumer requests. Overall, the U.S. approach to individual rights towards data processing companies is less consistent and ambitious than the European law (Barrett, 2019).

3.2.10   Requirements for Data Protection Risk Assessments

A credible privacy impact assessment can help crowdsourcing platforms to proactively assess and manage privacy risks and to reduce customer concerns in this area. The FTC has repeatedly required companies to establish risk assessment procedures in its jurisprudence (Hoofnagle, 2016). At the state level the new CPRA prescribes that businesses conduct annual cybersecurity audits and to submit to the Privacy Protection Agency regular risk assessments if the "processing of consumers' personal information presents a significant risk to privacy or security."[74] Other state security laws also require companies to conduct periodic risk assessments (McGeveran, 2019). It is thus reasonable to conclude that the legal requirements for the implementation of a privacy impact assessment in the private sector are limited (Friedewald et al., 2016). Risk assessments are rarely required by law. Relevant regulations often only consist of recommendations and lack control and enforcement mechanisms.

---

[69] COPPA, §312.6.

[70] For more information, see: https://www.consumer.ftc.gov/articles/pdf-0096-fair-credit-reporting-act.pdf (last accessed June 9, 2023).

[71] CCPA, Cal. Civ. Code 1798.110.

[72] CCPA, Cal. Civ. Code 1798.130.

[73] CCPA, Cal. Civ. Code 1798.105.

[74] CPRA, Cal. Civ. Code 1798.185.

3.2.11 Internal and External Enforcement

It can be useful for platforms, as part of a compliance strategy, to appoint a data protection officer or chief privacy officer who has overall internal responsibility regarding matters of data privacy and data security. In a few cases, U.S. federal privacy laws require companies to appoint dedicated data protection officers. Some state security regulations establish a duty to name an employee or an outside provider specifically responsible for the management of data security (McGeveran, 2019). However, unlike in Germany and Europe, there is no general legal obligation to appoint internal or external data privacy or security officers. The creation of such positions is nevertheless a widespread practice in the business world, and a large proportion of U.S. companies have nominated chief privacy officers assessing and ensuring privacy compliance within their organizations (Determann, 2016).

Data protection authorities are a fundamental pillar of German and European data protection law. In contrast, there are no comparable special federal enforcement authorities in the U.S. (Determann, 2016). Data protection violations are primarily punished by the FTC as unfair competition. On the state level, state attorneys general play an essential role with respect to data privacy compliance within the scope of consumer protection. The CPRA establishes the new California Privacy Protection Agency. This is the first time that an authority will have been created in the U.S. for the sole purpose of protecting the privacy rights of a state's citizens. The California Privacy Protection Agency will have functions of rulemaking, interpretation, education, and enforcement.

3.2.12 Sanctions

U.S. privacy laws are enforced relatively rigorously by authorities and private plaintiffs, with high penalties and fines, and claims for damages often reaching millions if not billions of U.S. dollars in class actions (Determann, 2016). The FTC has already imposed high penalties against large platform companies, of a severity that is unheard of in the German legal system. For example, in 2019, in a historic settlement order the FTC issued a 5 billion USD penalty against Facebook for violating consumers' privacy. The FTC had challenged Facebook for using misleading privacy settings and sharing data with third parties in disregard of user preferences.[75] After Google bypassed Apple's Safari privacy settings, the FTC fined the company more than 22 million USD (Solove & Hartzog, 2014). Apple agreed to pay more than 32 million USD to settle an FTC complaint because of in-app

---

[75] For more information, see: https://www.ftc.gov/news-events/press-releases/2019/07/ftc-imposes-5-billion-penalty-sweeping-new-privacy-restrictions (last accessed June 9, 2023).

purchases by children without parental consent.[76] As mentioned above, the scope of fines under the GDPR is in the range of millions of euros. In Europe, too, high fines have recently been imposed on digital corporations such as Google for privacy violations.[77] Overall, the enforcement of privacy laws in the U.S., with penalties that can reach billions of U.S. dollars, is much stronger.

3.3   Data Privacy and Crowdsourcing in China

3.3.1   *Various Sources of Law for Data Processing: A Brief Overview*

Although China still lags behind the EU and U.S. in terms of data protection (Pernot-Leplay, 2020), China has seen rapid development in legislation protecting personal data.[78] Chinese legislators have recently adopted a number of legal norms to counter the increasing data abuse in the information age, drawing on relevant legal sources worldwide, most notably the GDPR.

In general, the Chinese legal framework in the field of data protection today is complex, diverse, and multi-layered.[79] Relevant legislation is defined as laws, regulations, rules, and other binding documents. Also worth mentioning are soft laws[80] such as national norms or guidelines, which are not strictly binding but have legal significance. Legislative authorities are organized hierarchically. Authorities that have passed such regulations include, for example, the National People's Congress (NPC),[81] the Standing Committee of the National People's Congress

---

[76]For more information, see: https://www.ftc.gov/news-events/news/press-releases/2014/01/apple-inc-will-provide-full-consumer-refunds-least-325-million-settle-ftc-complaint-it-charged-kids (last accessed June 9, 2023).

[77]In France, a record fine of 50 million EUR was imposed on Google. Recently, the French data protection authority announced that it would fine Google and Facebook millions of dollars for making it difficult for users to opt out of cookie tracking. For more information, see: https://netzpolitik.org/2022/frankreich-210-millionen-euro-strafen-gegen-google-und-facebook/ (last accessed June 9, 2023).

[78]In China, the term "personal information" is more common than "personal data," which is often used in Europe. As their definitions do not have any difference according to relevant data protection law, "data" and "information" are used interchangeably in this section of the book.

[79]For a detailed introduction to the Chinese legal system, see Chen (2011).

[80]The definition of soft law is controversial. Here it is used in reference to "normative provisions contained in non-binding texts." See Oxford Bibliographies, Accessed March 12, 2022, from https://www.oxfordbibliographies.com/view/document/obo-9780199796953/obo-9780199796953-0040.xml

[81]According to the Chinese Constitution (Art. 62 and Art. 64) and the Legislation Law (Art. 7), the NPC is the highest legislative organ that has the unique power to enact "basic laws" and amend the Constitution.

(SC-NPC),[82] the State Council,[83] the Ministry of Industry and Information Technology (MIIT),[84] and the Cyberspace Administration of China (CAC).[85] Chinese legislators use both cross-sectoral and unified approaches, with data protection requirements existing not only in the Personal Information Protection Law (PIPL) as a unified and comprehensive data protection instrument, but also scattered across some sectoral laws such as the Criminal Law, or the Law on Protecting Consumers' Rights and Interests. Legislation at the national level takes precedence; local-level privacy legislation in provincial-level Chinese administrative regions must always comply with national legislation, although the former may enact more detailed regulations that apply only within the respective regions.[86]

Crowdsourcing platforms are neither explicitly nor specifically regulated under the Chinese system. Currently, crowdsourcing platforms as defined in this book are not explicitly mentioned in any relevant legal norm. However, this does not mean

---

[82] According to the Chinese Constitution (Art. 67) and the Legislation Law (Art. 7), the SC-NPC is the second-highest legislative organ that can enact "laws" other than those that shall be promulgated by the NPC and amend "laws" made by the NPC, but the amendment cannot violate the basic principles of the corresponding laws.

[83] According to the Chinese Constitution (Art. 89) and the Legislative Law (Art. 9 and Art. 65), the State Council (central government) is the highest administrative authority. The NPC or the SC-NPC can empower the State Council to adopt "administrative regulations" to specify matters that have not been specified by "laws." Administrative regulations are legally enforceable, but they cannot conflict with "laws." Administrative rules are commonly referred to as "regulations" or sometimes "provisions" or "measures."

[84] According to the Chinese Constitution (Art. 90) and the Legislative Law (Art. 80), the ministries and commissions of the State Council, the People's Bank of China, the State Auditing Administration, and departments directly under the State Council may, in accordance with the laws as well as the administrative regulations, decisions, and orders of the State Council and within the limits of their power, formulate "department rules." Such rules are legally enforceable, but they cannot conflict with "laws" and "administrative regulations." They are commonly referred to as "provisions" or "measures."

[85] The Office of the Central Cyberspace Affairs Commission or the Cyberspace Administration of China (CAC) was established in 2011 as a department directly under the State Council that is responsible for coordinating the protection of personal information and relevant supervisory and administrative work. The CAC has the power to adopt "department rules." For more details, see its official website http://www.cac.gov.cn/index.htm.

[86] For example, the Standing Committee of the 15th Shanghai People's Congress adopted the Shanghai Data Regulation on November 25, 2021. Art. 1 of the Shanghai Data Regulation refers to the Data Security Law and the PIPL as its legal basis. The original text is available on the official website of the Shanghai government https://www.shanghai.gov.cn/nw12344/20211129/a1a38c3dfe8b4f8f8fcba5e79fbe9251.html. There are in total 34 provincial-level administrative regions in China, including 23 provinces, 5 ethnic autonomous regions, 4 municipalities directly governed by the State Council, and 2 special administrative regions. Each provincial-level administrative region has its own legislature. Except for Hong Kong, Macao, and Taiwan, according to Art. 72 and Art. 82 of the Legislation Law, people's congresses and their standing committees of the provincial-level administrative regions can, in according with the constitution, the laws and the administrative regulations, formulate "local regulations." The provincial-level governments can, in accordance with laws, administrative regulations, and the corresponding local regulations, formulate "local rules."

that the existing provisions do not apply to platform companies. Because crowdsourcing platforms collect and process personal data, they fall within the scope of legally regulated subjects such as "personal information processors" under the PIPL, "network operators" under the Cybersecurity Law, or even more broadly, "[a]ny organization that relies on the accessing of personal data of others," as stipulated in Art. 111 of the Civil Code.

Although privacy-related provisions can be found in the Chinese Constitution, promulgated by the NPC in 1982,[87] the first piece of legislation that explicitly established the protection of personal data was Art. 253(a), extended by the Seventh Amendment to the Criminal Law adopted by the SC-NPC in 2009.[88] Subsequently, on December 28, 2012, the SC-NPC adopted the 2012 SC-NPC Decision on Strengthening Information Protection in Networks, which focused on protecting the electronic information of individuals in networks on the internet.[89] It applies to "network service operators and other enterprises and institutions that collect or use citizens' personal electronic information in their business activities" and prohibits these entities from illegally acquiring and disclosing the collected information. In particular, principles of legality, appropriateness, and necessity set out in this decision, as well as the requirement to obtain the consent of the data subjects, have been adopted in subsequent legal texts. One such legal text is the Provisions on Protecting the Personal Information of Telecommunications and Internet Users (2013 MIIT Provisions), adopted by the MIIT in 2013. In addition, we find three central laws in the area of civil law, which contain provisions on data privacy. The first is the Civil Code, which was promulgated by the NPC and became binding on January 1, 2021. The unified Civil Code has a separate chapter entitled "Right to privacy and protection of personal data."[90] The second law that is central to data

---

[87] Art. 40 of the 1982 Constitution protects Chinese citizens' right to freedom and privacy of correspondence, which has been unchanged in the present version of the Constitution (2018 Amendment). For details on that matter see Greenleaf (2014, pp. 196–197).

[88] For a detailed introduction to the Seventh Amendment see Greenleaf (2014, pp. 197–198). In particular, the Seventh Amendment has been amended by the Ninth Amendment to the Criminal Law adopted by the SC-NPC in 2015. There are two main changes from Article 253(a) of the Criminal Law: (1) The subject of crime has been become broader, from "a state organ or an entity in such a field as finance, telecommunications, transportation, education, or medical treatment and one of its employees" to "whoever" (namely, any organization or individual); (2) the prison sentence has become longer, from "up to 3 years" to "up to 7 years."

[89] Although this text is referred to as a "decision" and not a "law," its legal effect is not affected as it is adopted by SC-NPC.

[90] In the first draft of the Civil Code, this chapter was entitled "Right to Privacy and Personal Information." In the second draft and the final version it was changed to "Right to Privacy and Protection of Personal Information." This change shows that the legislator wants to emphasize data protection. Before the promulgation of the Civil Code, the General Provisions of the Civil Code (GPCL) applied. Art. 111 of the GPCL provided that "the personal information of a natural person shall be protected by law. Any organization or individual shall legally obtain others' personal information and ensure the safety of such information, and shall not illegally collect, use, process or transmit, trade, provide or make public others' personal information." With the entry into force of the Civil Code, the GPCL is no longer applicable.

privacy is the Law on Protecting Consumers' Rights and Interests (CPL).[91] Shortly after the adoption of the 2012 SC-NPC Decision, the SC-NPC amended the CPL in 2013 to include provisions to protect consumer information. Basic principles regarding the collection and use of personal data are completely consistent with the 2012 SC-NPC decision. The third law that is central to data privacy is the E-Commerce Law (ECL). To protect the rights and interests of everyone involved in e-commerce, in January 2019 the SC-NPC passed the ECL, which governs internet-based "e-commerce businesses," including "e-commerce platform businesses." Under the ECL, platforms are required to comply with personal information protection provisions of any law or regulation when collecting personal data from users (Art. 23 ECL).

In addition, there are three comprehensive and specialized data protection laws. First, the Cybersecurity Law (CSL) became binding on November 7, 2016, and is the first law that comprehensively regulates cyberspace data security in China for the purpose of "guaranteeing cybersecurity, safeguarding cyberspace sovereignty, national security and public interest, protecting the lawful rights and interests of citizens, legal persons and other organizations, and promoting the sound development of economic and social informationization." Accordingly, "network operators," including "owners, administrators of the network and network service providers" are obliged to "not collect personal information irrelevant to the services provided by them" and "strictly keep their users' information confidential." Second, the Data Security Law (DSL) was passed in June 2021, and aims to "regulate the handling of data, ensure data security, promote the development and exploitation of data, protect the legitimate rights and interests of individuals and organizations, and preserve state sovereignty, security and development interests." According to Art. 2 of the DSL, it applies to both "data processing activities within the territory of PRC" and "extraterritorial data processing activities that would be detrimental to PRC's national interests, public interests or the legitimate rights and interests of individuals and organizations." Third and most important is the PIPL, which was promulgated on August 20, 2021, and went into effect on November 1, 2021. The PIPL is the first unified, comprehensive, and systematic data protection law in China and marks the establishment of the basic legal framework in the field of personal information protection (Jiang, 2021). It is therefore often referred to as the "Chinese GDPR." The purpose of the PIPL is to "protect the rights and interests of personal information, regulate the processing of personal information and promote the reasonable use of personal information." It prohibits "any organization or individual" from infringing upon rights and interests of natural persons' information.

Aside from the legal documents mentioned above, there exist several soft laws that—while legally unenforceable—still guide the behavior of crowdsourcing platforms. In 2013, the National Information Security Standardization Technical

---

[91] Whether users or crowd workers of crowdsourcing platforms can be defined as "consumers" (and thus whether the CPL is applicable to platform companies) is discussed below.

Committee (NISSTC)[92] released the Information Security Technology-Guidelines for Personal Information Protection within Public and Commercial Services Information Systems (2013 NISSTC Guidelines). This is the first national standard for the protection of personal information, and contains basic principles for handling personal data.[93] Another important national standard formulated by the NISSTC is the GB/T 35273-2020 Information Security Technology-Personal Information Security Specification (GB/T 35273-2020 PI Specification), which applies to "personal information activities carried out by all kinds of organizations" and specifies many aspects of the PIPL in a very detailed way.[94] In addition, there are self-regulatory codes in online commerce that have been adopted by the Internet Society of China (ISC).[95] Some of these codes are related to the protection of platform users' personal information, such as the T/ISC-0011-2021 Evaluation Method of Data Security Governance Capability. Such legally unenforceable standards can nevertheless provide detailed data protection guidelines for crowdsourcing platform companies.

As a unique approach, the Supreme People's Court (SPC) and the Supreme People's Procuratorate (SPP) are entitled to issue judicial interpretations for the consistent application of legal provisions.[96] Such interpretations have a quasi-legislative function as courts at all levels must refer to them when deciding cases (Chen, 2011). With regard to data protection, at least two judicial interpretations are applicable. One is the interpretations of the SPC and the SPP on Several Issues concerning the Application of Law in the Handling of Criminal Cases Involving Infringement for Citizens' Personal Information (2017). The other interpretation is the Provisions of the SPC on Several Issues concerning the Application of Law in the Trial of Cases Involving Civil Disputes over Infringements upon Personal Rights and Interests through the Information Networks (2021).[97] Both interpretations play an important role in ensuring data subjects' right to privacy in civil and criminal judicial practice.

---

[92] The NISSTC (also known also TC260) is a technical working organization engaging in information security standardization work. The establishment of the NISSTC was approved by the Standardization Administration of China (SAC) as a governmental department in 2002. For more relevant national standards see the official website of the NISSTC. Accessed March 12, 2022, from https://www.tc260.org.cn/.

[93] For a brief introduction to the 2013 NISSTC Guidelines, see Greenleaf (2014, pp. 209–210).

[94] The GB/T 35273–2020 PI Specification is an updated version of the GB/T 25273–2017 Information Security Technology-Personal Information Specification released by the NISSTC in 2017.

[95] The ISC was founded on May 25, 2001. It is a nationwide and non-profit social association established by the Chinese internet industry and internet-related enterprises and institutions. For further details see the official website of the ISC https://www.isc.org.cn/.

[96] According to the Legislation Law (Art. 104), the interpretations made by the SPC and SPP must refer to concrete provisions and be in compliance with the purpose, principle and intention of the legislation.

[97] According to Art. 6 of the Provisions of the SPC on the Work of Judicial Interpretation (Fafa [2007] No. 12), judicial interpretation is divided into four types, namely "interpretation," "provision," "reply" and "decision." Thus, although the text is referred to as "provisions," it belongs to what is known as "judicial interpretation."

Another relevant field for data protection is competition law. Platform companies that have collected large datasets can have competitive advantages and acquire a dominant market position (Li, 2021). In the age of big data, the competition problems caused by data monopolies among companies pose challenges to traditional Chinese competition law (Ding, 2021b). In 2021, the State Council issued the Anti-Monopoly Guidelines of the Anti-Monopoly Committee of the State Council on the Platform Economy (2021 Anti-Monopoly Guidelines). Accordingly, "the ability to control and process relevant data" is one of the factors determining whether a platform has a dominant market position. Meanwhile, in response to some data breach cases and other issues relating to the platform economy, China published a draft amendment (Draft) to the Anti-Monopoly Law (AML) in October 2021. Art. 10 of the AML Draft explicitly provides that "operators shall not eliminate or restrict competition by abusing data and algorithms, technology, capital advantages or platform rules etc." Art. 22 para. 2 of the AML Draft specifies that "it will be an abuse of a dominant market position for an operator with a dominant market position to set up obstacles or impose unreasonable restrictions on other business operators by using data and algorithms, technology, or platform rules etc." The data processing activities of Chinese platform companies are expected to be further regulated by the forthcoming updated AML (Ren, 2021).

In summary, the most relevant and comprehensive data privacy law that regulates crowdsourcing platforms in China is the PIPL, although data protection provisions can also be found in other legal sources. A more detailed introduction to the PIPL, other relevant legal norms, and non-mandatory national standards related to crowdsourcing platforms is provided below. In particular, some aspects of the PIPL that deviate from the GDPR are highlighted.[98]

3.3.2 Data Security

Data security is closely linked to data privacy, although they are fundamentally two different concepts. Data security mainly refers to protection of data from unauthorized accesses, modifications, or users. If data collected by platforms is not well protected against cyber attacks, the privacy of data subjects cannot be guaranteed (Bertino, 2016). As "processors of personal information" under the PIPL, crowdsourcing platforms are obliged to "take necessary measures to ensure the security of the processed personal information" (Art. 9 PIPL) and "prevent unauthorized access, leakage, alteration, and loss of personal information" (Art. 51 PIPL). In addition, the CSL prohibits internet platforms—deemed network operators under the CSL—from disclosing, manipulating or destroying collected personal data (Art. 42 para. 1 CSL). In the case that personal information has been or

---

[98] Given the limited scope of local rules and regulations, the following sections focus only on legal instruments at the national level.

is likely to be disclosed, destroyed or lost, crowdsourcing platforms shall remedy the situation immediately, promptly inform users, and report to the competent departments (Art. 42 para. 2 CSL). In addition, the DSL is a unified and comprehensive law to safeguard data security, which has an independent chapter setting forth the data security protection obligations of data processors (Chap. 4, DSL).

The specific measures taken by platform companies to ensure data security can be divided into technical measures and management measures (Liu, 2021a, pp. 25–26). The former include data encryption and de-identification. The latter measures include designing internal management systems and operating procedures, implementing categorical management of personal information, reasonably determining the operational authority of processing personal information and periodically conducting security education and training for workers, and formulating and organizing the implementation of emergency plans for cyber security incidents related to personal information (Art. 51 PIPL).

To clarify the provisions on data security under the PIPL, CSL and DSL, the Online Data Security Management Regulation was drafted by the CAC and published for comment in November 2021.

3.3.3 Protection of Personal Identifiable Information and Sensitive Data

In a legal sense, personal data is the information that directly or indirectly identifies a specific natural person (Xie, 2019, p. 138; Gao, 2019, p. 94; Zhang & Han, 2016, p. 128). A definition of personal data can be found not only in the recently published PIPL, but also in some earlier pieces of legislation. Art. 4 para. 1 of the PIPL defines personal information as "all kinds of information that identifies or can identify natural persons recorded electronically or by other means, but does not include anonymized information." This definition is almost identical to that under the CSL adopted in 2016, with the exception of two aspects: (1) the definition under the CSL does not specifically mention that the anonymized information is exempt from protection; and (2) several examples of personal identifiable information are available in the CSL, including "names, dates of birth, identification numbers, biometrics, addresses, and telephone numbers" (Art. 76 para. 5 CSL). Besides the examples given by the CSL, the Civil Code also lists "e-mail addresses, health information, and location tracking" (Art. 1034 para. 2 Civil Code) as examples of personal identifiable information. Further examples of personal identifiable information are available in the GB/T 35273-2020 PI Specification.

The PIPL has a specific section—(Section 2, Chapter 2), referred to as "Rules for Processing Sensitive Personal Information"—wherein sensitive personal data is legally defined as "personal data which, once leaked or used illegally, could easily lead to the detriment of an individual's dignity or damage to his person or property, including information on biometric identities, religious beliefs, specific identities and medical data, care and health, financial accounts and location tracking, and the personal data of minors under the age of 14" (Art. 28 para. 1 PIPL). The CSL, DSL and Civil Code do not address the definition of sensitive personal information; however, a similar definition of sensitive personal information can be found in the GB/T 35273-2020 PI Specification (also the 2017 version). In addition, the 2013 NISSTC Guidelines expressly state that personal information can be divided into sensitive personal information and general personal information. The former refers to "the information that once leaked or tampered with can cause adverse effects of data subjects, including identification numbers, telephone numbers, races, political opinions, religious beliefs, genes, fingerprints, etc." Apart from these examples, data on conversation records and content, property, credit, accommodation, sexual orientation and so forth are also listed as sensitive personal information in the GB/T 35273-2020 PI Specification. Unlike the GDPR, some information such as philosophical beliefs, trade union membership or data relating to a natural person's sex life (Art. 9 para. 1 GDPR) are not explicitly listed as sensitive personal data in either the PIPL or the relevant self-regulatory documents. By contrast, examples of sensitive personal data such as "financial accounts" and "location tracking" are found in Chinese law but not in the GDPR. In general, sensitive personal data are more strictly protected. According to Art 28, para. 29 of the PIPL, crowdsourcing platform enterprises as processors of personal information are only allowed to process sensitive personal data for specific purposes, but only when strictly necessary, and when strict safeguards are in place.

There is a related term for sensitive data in Chinese law, "important data," which is not addressed in the GDPR (Chen et al., 2020). The CSL requires platform companies to explicitly secure the important data they collect (Art. 21 para. 3 CSL). The DSL emphasizes that the relevant competent authority shall formulate a catalogue of important data and enhance its protection (Art. 21 para. 1 DSL). However, there is no definition of important data in these laws.

The obligations of platforms in terms of data protection run through all the activities of data processing, including the "collection, storage, processing, transmission, provision, disclosure, deletion, etc." of personal information (Art. 4 para. 2 PIPL).

3.3.4 Particularities of Data Protection: Company, Consumer, and Employee Data

Crowdsourcing platforms process not only personal data but also company data, especially that of crowdsourcers. This raises the question of whether Chinese data protection law also protects the data of the companies concerned. Like the GDPR, the PIPL only applies to the personal data of natural persons (Art. 2 PIPL), which means that company data collected by platforms is not protected by the PIPL. However, the DSL protects a broader range of data than the PIPL. The former defines data as "any record of information in electronic or other means" (Art. 3 DSL). Furthermore, Art. 7 of the DSL explicitly provides that "the State protects the rights and interests of individuals and organizations in relation to data." Accordingly, platforms seem to be obliged to fulfill corresponding obligations from the DSL if they process data from crowdsourcers. However, because the DSL is more relevant to data security than privacy, even where corporate data falls within the scope of the DSL, how and to what extent corporate data can be legally protected may well differ from that of personal information.

A related question is whether users of crowdsourcing platforms are consumers under the CPL. If platform users can be categorized as consumers, platforms as processors of personal information are obliged to protect current and potential users' data privacy and are, for example, not allowed to send them commercial messages without their consent (Art. 29 CPL). Furthermore, both the CPL and PIPL empower competent consumer associations to file lawsuits against violators of the rights and interests of consumers (Art. 47 CPL; Art. 70 PIPL). Although no specific study on this issue can be found in Chinese scholarly literature, we argue based on doctrinal legal research (McConville & Chui, 2007) that users of crowdsourcing platforms should be considered consumers for the purposes of the CPL. Even though the CPL does not provide a definition of the term "consumer," it states that the rights and interests of consumers who "buy or use commodities or receive services for daily needs" must be protected by the law (Art. 2 CPL) (Binding, 2014a). Users do utilize the services provided by the platforms, which allows them to meet their daily needs and to making a living. Thus, platform companies might also be confronted with lawsuits from consumer associations when they infringe on the rights and interests of platform users.

Finally, as in many other jurisdictions, the employment status of crowdworkers is disputed. Although the question of whether internet-based gig workers such as delivery drivers or ride-hailing drivers are "employees" protected by Chinese labor law[99] has been hotly debated in recent years, scant literature discusses the employment status of crowdworkers in China. Neither Chinese labor law nor labor contract law contain an explicit definition of employees. In practice, judges often use strict criteria to determine whether a worker is an employee, relying on the Notice on Issues Relating to the Determination of Employment Relations adopted by the Ministry of Labor and Social Security, which has been known as the Ministry of Human Resources and Social Security since 2005.[100] However, to our knowledge,

---

[99]For a comprehensive introduction to the system of Chinese labor and employment law, see Wang (2017).

[100]According to the Notice, "an employment relationship exists if an employer recruits a worker without a written labor contract, but there are the following circumstances: (1) The employer and the worker meet the subject qualifications stipulated by laws and regulations; (2) the labor rules formulated by the employer in accordance with law are applicable to the worker, and the worker is subject to the management of the employer and performs the paid work arranged by the employer; (3) the labor provided by the worker is an integral part of the employer's business." In practice, only if the three conditions are met at the same time, judges tend to determine an employment

there is not a single case in which a crowdworker has complained about not being recognized as an employee on a Chinese crowdsourcing platform. If a crowdworker were considered an employee in China, several special provisions regarding their data protection would theoretically apply.[101]

Some Chinese legal scholars have also pointed out that the protection of workers' personal information has its specificities and that the requirements of the PIPL are too general to achieve adequate protection for them (Wang, 2022; Xie, 2021). In particular, compared to the first and second drafts of the PIPL, its final version adds a provision as the legal basis for the processing of employee information: "necessary for the conduct of human resources management in accordance with lawfully formulated work regulation systems and lawfully concluded collective agreements" (Art. 13 para. 1(2) PIPL). Although these developments indicate advances in terms of data protection, they fall short of achieving the protection of workers' personal data in some important aspects. For example, in the context of the structurally weaker workforce, the requirement for informed consent often does not adequately address the position of powerful companies. In addition, the risk of monitoring and manipulating employees in the digitized workplace must be regulated more specifically (Wang, 2022).

3.3.5 Basic Principles of Data Processing

Crowdsourcing platforms as processors of personal information must observe some basic principles of data handling. These principles are currently set out primarily in the PIPL. Some can also be found in separate legal instruments that preceded the promulgation of the PIPL. However, the PIPL has integrated these previous provisions in a systematic and comprehensive manner.

The principles of the PIPL are broadly similar to those of the GDPR. First, crowdsourcing platforms must follow "the principles of lawfulness, reasonableness, necessity and creditworthiness" to process personal data, and methods that can be perceived as "misleading, fraudulent or coercive" may not be used (Art. 5 PIPL). Except for the principle of creditworthiness, which was added as part of the Civil Code reform, the principles of lawfulness, reasonableness and necessity had been introduced prior to the PIPL (Chen, 2021). They were first put forward in Art. 2 of

---

relationship exists between the worker and the employer. Self-employees or workers who cannot meet these requirements are often protected by civil law rather than labor law in China. For more details, see Wang (2016).

[101] For example, according to Art. 8 of the Labor Contract Law, employers are merely entitled to know the basic information directly relating to the labor contracts. Art. 13 of the Regulation on Employment Services and Employment Management provides that employers are obliged to keep the personal information of employees confidential. The disclosure of employees' information must be based on their written consent. For more details see Zhang (1996), Yang (2004), Wang (2011), and Wang (2019).

the 2012 SC-NPC Decision and subsequently laid down in other laws such as the CSL, CPL, and the Civil Code.

The principle of purpose limitation also applies in the PIPL. The processing of personal information must "have a clear and reasonable purpose, be directly related to that purpose and use means that affect the rights and interests of the individual as little as possible" (Art. 6 para. 1 PIPL). This principle is not available in laws such as the CSL or the Civil Code. However, the principle of necessity could, to a certain extent, already include the requirement of purpose limitation (Chen, 2021, pp. 9–13). Additionally, the principle of data minimization is set forth in Art. 6 of the PIPL. The collection of personal data must be "limited to the minimum necessary to achieve the purpose of the processing and excessive personal data shall not be collected" (Art. 6 para. 2 PIPL).

The principles of openness and transparency must also be considered by data processors. Crowdsourcing platforms are therefore obliged to disclose rules governing the processing of personal data and to clarify the purposes, methods and scope of processing (Art. 7 PIPL). These principles are based on the data subject's right to information under Art. 44 of the PIPL. Accordingly, users of platforms have the right to know the processing activities of their personal information and to decide to either accept or refuse the processing. The specific requirements of the principles of openness and transparency can also be founded in Art. 41 of the CSL and Art. 1035 of the Civil Code.

The principle of data correctness is also important for data processing. Data processors must ensure the quality of personal data in order to avoid negative impacts on the rights and interests of data subjects due to inaccurate or incomplete personal information (Art. 8 PIPL). If platform users, as data subjects, determine that the information they have provided is incorrect or incomplete, they have the right to demand corrections and additions from platforms in a timely manner (Art. 46 PIPL). Similarly, according to Art. 1037 of the Civil Code, natural persons are entitled to petition data processors to take necessary measures to correct or delete their inaccurate information. A similar requirement can also be found in Art. 24 of the ECL.

Crowdsourcing platforms must also take the principle of storage limitation into account. Art. 19 of the PIPL provides that that "the period of retention of personal data shall be the shortest time necessary to achieve the purposes of the processing, unless laws and regulations provide otherwise." This principle can also be found in Art. 6.1 (a) of the GB/T 35273-2020 PI Specification (also the 2017 version). Normally, platforms are required to delete or anonymize collected personal data after the specified retention period (Art. 6.1 (b) GB/T 35273-2020 PI specification). Although the PIPL does not provide a specific deadline, it lists several conditions under which platform companies are obliged to delete the relevant data (Art. 47 PIPL). By contrast, for reasons of data security, under certain circumstances it may be necessary for personal data to be available for a minimum period of time. For example, the CSL requires platform companies to retain the log files they collect for a minimum of 6 months (Art. 21 para. 3 CSL).

As noted above, data processors must take necessary measures such as encryption and de-identification to ensure data security and to protect personal information from unauthorized access, leaking, alteration, and loss (Art. 9 and Art. 51 PIPL). Such requirements can also be found in laws prior to the PIPL. For example, both the CSL and the ECL explicitly provide that the "integrity, confidentiality and availability" of network data must be maintained (Art. 10 CSL; Art. 31 ECL) and platforms are obliged to prevent personal information processed by them from being unduly disclosed, manipulated, or destroyed (Art. 42, para. 2 CSL).

Although the basic principles of data processing mentioned above under the PIPL correspond to those in Art. 5 of the GDPR, the Chinese PIPL does not maintain the concepts of privacy by design or privacy by default as under the GDPR.

3.3.6 Anonymization and de-Identification as Data Protection Instruments

Anonymization and pseudonymization are two important privacy protection measures. The latter term is called "de-identification" in Chinese legal texts.[102]

According to Art. 73, para. 4 of the PIPL, "anonymization" refers to "the process by which personal data is processed so that it cannot be used to identify a specific natural person and cannot be recovered after such processing." As mentioned above, anonymized data is not protected personal data under the PIPL (Art. 4 para. 1 PIPL). For example, if platforms use anonymized data for market research, the provisions of the PIPL do not apply.

Anonymizing personal data is also a way to protect the privacy of data subjects. Art. 73 para. 3 of the PIPL defines de-identification as "the operation of processing personal data that makes it impossible to identify a specific natural person without the help of additional information." De-identification as a technical measure to ensure data security is explicitly mentioned in Art. 51 of the PIPL. In contrast to anonymized data, however, de-identification cannot fully guarantee data protection, since the de-identified data could be re-identified with additional information. This means that the risk of identifying a specific data subject can only be ruled out to a certain extent. Thus, the PIPL does not fully exclude de-identified data from its scope. Even if platforms process users' information by de-identification, they still have to comply with the obligations under the PIPL.

The terms anonymization and de-identification and related rules are not found in other data protection laws but are available in the soft law document GB/T 35273-2020 PI Specification (also the 2017 version).

---

[102] According to Art. 4 para. 5 of the GDPR, "pseudonymization" refers to "the processing of personal data in such a manner that the personal data can no longer be attributed to a specific data subject without the use of additional information, provided that such additional information is kept separately and is subject to technical and organizational measures to ensure that the personal data are not attributed to an identified or identifiable natural person."

3.3.7   Consent as the Standard for Legitimation of Data Processing

As in the GDPR, the informed consent rule is at the heart of China's data protection laws. The importance of data subject consent is evident under many provisions of the PIPL. Although the relevant provisions do not specifically relate to crowdsourcing platforms, they are applicable as the platforms collect and process personal data of their users and are therefore "processors of personal information" within the scope of the PIPL.

Crowdsourcing platforms are only allowed to process users' personal data if they obtain their consent or certain exceptional conditions are met (Art. 13 para. 2 PIPL). According to Art. 13 para. 1 of the PIPL, these conditions include:

1. that the processing of personal data is necessary for the conclusion or performance of a contract to which the person is a party, or that it is necessary for the implementation of human resources management in accordance with lawfully formulated labor regulations and lawfully concluded collective agreements;
2. that it is necessary for the fulfillment of any legal obligation or obligations;
3. as necessary to respond to a public health incident or to protect the safety of life, health and property of individuals in an emergency;
4. to process personal data to a reasonable extent to carry out actions in the public interest, such as news reporting and public opinion monitoring;
5. for an appropriate level of processing of personal data disclosed by individuals or otherwise already lawfully disclosed under this law; and
6. other situations provided by laws or administrative regulations.

Accordingly, the consent of the persons concerned and the legal circumstances listed are the legal basis for platforms to process personal data of their users.

Unlike the GDPR, the PIPL does not provide a definition of the term "consent." However, it requires that consent from fully informed data subjects be voluntary and explicit (Art. 14 para. 1 PIPL). If the purposes or methods of processing personal data or the type of personal data to be processed change, platforms must again seek consent from data subjects (Art. 14 para. 2 PIPL).

Data subjects also have the right to withdraw their consent in a convenient and simple manner (Art. 15 para. 1 PIPL). Except where the processing of personal data is necessary for the provision of the services, platforms shall not refuse to provide services on the grounds that data subjects do not consent to the processing of their personal data or withdraw their consent (Art. 16 PIPL). In the event of, for example, a merger, demerger, dissolution or bankruptcy, users' personal data must be transferred to a third party, and the recipient party is obliged to continue to fulfill the obligations of the platform company. If the recipient changes the original purposes or methods of data processing, the consent of the data subjects must be obtained again (Art. 22 PIPL).

Unlike the GDPR, separate consent is an important term under the PIPL, although there is no legal definition for it. According to the PIPL, there are five situations in which processors of personal information need to obtain separate consent from data subjects (Liu, 2021b, p. 40). Among them are four cases related to crowdsourcing platforms[103]:

1. If platforms pass on the personal data they process to other processors of personal data, they must obtain the separate consent of the data subjects (Art. 23 PIPL).
2. Platforms are not allowed to publish personal data unless they have obtained the separate consent of the users (Art. 25 PIPL).
3. The processing of sensitive personal data must be based on the separate consent of the data subjects (Art. 29 PIPL).
4. If platforms transfer personal data to a foreign recipient outside the territory of the PRC, they are required to obtain separate consent from their users (Art. 39 PIPL).

In addition to the provisions of PIPL mentioned above, the requirement for informed consent was included in other laws that were in force before PIPL. The CSL stipulates that platforms must inform data subjects about the purpose, means and scope of the collection and use of personal data and obtain their consent (Part. 41 CSL), and platforms are not allowed to share personal data with others without the consent of the data subjects (Art. 42 CSL).

3.3.8 Automated Decision-Making

Algorithmic risks existed in practice even before the PIPL was passed. For example, automated decision-making might have violated platform users' right to privacy (Li, 2017). To respond to the fact that the algorithms used by a platform are supplanting human decision-making and putting pressure on them, leading to problems in human autonomy and masking platform culpability (Zhang, 2020, 2021), the PIPL restricts automated decision-making. Although the relevant provisions do not specifically relate to crowdsourcing platforms, they can be applied to them as the platforms are the processors of personal information regulated by the PIPL.

Platforms that use personal data for automated decision-making must ensure transparency of decision-making so that the results are fair and equitable, and shall not unreasonably discriminate between individuals on transaction terms such as price (Art. 24 para. 1 PIPL). With this provision, price discrimination based on algorithms can be countered, especially since pricing consumers differently for the same product or service has been a common economic phenomenon in practice in China (Zhao, 2020; Li, 2021, pp. 64–67). For example, there was a scandal

---

[103] The case, which seems most likely irrelevant for platforms, is mentioned in Art. 26 of the PIPL: "The installation of image capture and personal identification devices in public places must be done as necessary to ensure public safety, comply with relevant national regulations and have prominent warning labels. The collected personal images and identification information may only be used for the purpose of safeguarding public safety and may not be used for any other purpose unless the separate consent of the individual is obtained."

involving Chinese food delivery platform Meituan, which charged its paying members higher delivery fees than its free users (for more details, see Wang, 2020).

When decisions that significantly affect the rights and interests of platform users are made through automated decision-making, users have the right to request an explanation from the platforms and the right to oppose the decisions made by the platforms solely through algorithms (Art. 24 para. 3 PIPL). When information delivery and commercial marketing are carried out through algorithm-based decision-making, platforms are also obliged to offer users options that do not target their specific personal characteristics or to provide convenient means of opting out (Art. 24 para. 2 PIPL).

There are no automated decision-making provisions in other laws prior to the PIPL. However, relevant rules are available in the non-mandatory GB/T 35273-2020 PI Specification (also the 2017 version).

One way to reduce the algorithmic risks could be to conduct the data protection impact assessment before using automated decision-making (Liu, 2021b, p. 66). These are introduced in Sect. 3.3.10.

3.3.9 Rights of Data Subjects

The rights of data subjects are explicitly stated not only in the PIPL, but also in previously passed laws such as the CSL and the Civil Code. Compared to the previous legal instruments, the PIPL adds some new rights such as the right to data portability, and presents the rights of data subjects in a more comprehensive and systematic way. The PIPL has an independent chapter (Chap. 4) entitled "Rights of Individuals with Regard to the Processing of Personal Data," under which there are seven articles (Art. 44–Art. 50). In general, the specific data subject rights provided by the PIPL are very similar to those of the GDPR, although the wording is slightly different.

Platform users, as data subjects, generally have the right to know about the processing of their personal data and to make decisions about it, and have the right to restrict or refuse the processing of their data by others (Art. 44 PIPL). In particular, the PIPL requires platforms to inform data subjects "truthfully, accurately, and completely" about matters such as the name of the processing organization, the purposes and methods of processing personal data, the types of personal data processed, and the period for which data will be stored before it may be processed. The notice must be clearly visible and in clear and understandable language (Art. 17 para. 1 PIPL). If platforms draw attention to such issues by formulating rules for the processing of personal data, the rules must be made public and easy to read and store (Art. 17 para. 2 PIPL). Accordingly, crowdsourcing platforms are required to post their privacy statement, if they have one, on their websites to ensure that website visitors or users can know what data is being processed and how, and can opt in or opt out of the processing of their data.

Platform users also have the right to access and reproduce their personal data from platforms, except for some special cases[104] (Art. 45 para. 1 PIPL). If users exercise this right, platforms must provide them with relevant data in a timely manner (Art. 45 para. 2 PIPL). The right to access and reproduce is also found in Art. 1037 of the Civil Code, but not in the CSL before the promulgation of the PIPL.

As a newly added right in the final version of the PIPL (Greenleaf, 2021, p. 21; Liu, 2021a, b, p. 113), the right to data portability not only facilitates the transfer and reuse of personal information, but also places new demands on platforms (Wu, 2021). The right to transfer data is set out in Art. 45 para. 3 of the PIPL, which specifies that "when individuals request the transfer of personal data to other processors of personal information nominated by them and the conditions provided for by the CAC are met, the processors of personal information must provide channels for the transfer." In contrast to the right to data portability under the GDPR, the same right in the PIPL is much more general in two respects. First, the PIPL does not mention that the personal data requested must be in "a structured, commonly used and machine-readable format." Second, the PIPL does not specify exceptional cases, like under the GDPR, in which the exercise of this right could be restricted, for example when the transfer is not technically feasible or the rights and freedoms of others are affected. Instead, the PIPL only states that "conditions provided by the state Internet information departments" must be met. Chinese legislators tend to let the CAC or other competent authorities formulate departmental rules that may include specific conditions for the right to data portability. In fact, before the PIPL was passed, some Chinese legal scholars explicitly demanded that China's data protection law not duplicate the right to data portability under the GDPR.[105]

Platform users also have the right to correction. If users find that their personal information is inaccurate or incomplete, they have the right to request platforms to correct or supplement it (Art. 46 para. 1 PIPL). When users exercise this right, platforms are obliged to check the personal data and make corrections or additions in a timely manner (Art. 46 para. 2 PIPL). The right of correction can also be found in Art. 43 of the CSL and Art. 1037 of the Civil Code.

---

[104] The exceptional cases are mentioned in Art. 18 and Art. 35 of PIPL, including but not limited to matters relating to the protection of life, health and property, and the fulfillment of statutory duties by state bodies.

[105] On the one hand, some scholars have noted that the right to data portability could enable a more efficient flow of data, allowing platform users not to be confined to one platform, thus promoting effective competition among companies. On the other hand, many scholars have opposed the right to data portability. Their main arguments include, among other things, that such a right may put more pressure on small and medium-sized enterprise (SMEs) to comply, thus hindering competition and innovation in the market; that the right to data portability seems to be inconsistent with the general principle of competition law, which does not require companies in the market to share their property; and that personal data collected by companies may be regarded as trade secrets, and allowing one business to have easy access to another business's trade secrets through the users' right to data portability may lead to unfair competition (for more details see Ding, 2021a, pp. 144–165).

Another important user right is the right to have data deleted. This right is referred to in the GDPR as the right to erasure and the right to be forgotten.[106] Prior to the enactment of the PIPL, such a right had long been advocated by legal scholars (e.g., Yang & Han, 2015), although some scholars have noted that it is impossible to completely erase personal data once it has been disclosed (e.g., Ju & Ling, 2016; Wan, 2016). Art. 47 para. 1 of the PIPL provides for several circumstances in which platforms are obliged to delete personal data proactively:

1. the purpose of the processing has already been achieved or cannot be achieved, or the data is no longer necessary to achieve the purpose of the processing;
2. platforms stop providing services or the retention period has expired;
3. users withdraw their consent;
4. platforms violate laws, administrative regulations or agreements when processing personal data; and
5. other situations provided for by laws or administrative regulations.

If platforms fail to delete information in the stated case, their users have the right to request its deletion. Compared to the provisions in place before the PIPL, such as Art. 43 of the CSL and Art. 1037 of the Civil Code, the content of the right to delete data under the PIPL has been expanded (Liu, 2021b, pp. 117–121). Art. 48 of the PIPL recognizes the right of users to ask platforms to explain their rules on the processing of personal information, for example, in their privacy statements. If a platform user is deceased, their close relatives[107] may exercise the rights to access, copy, correct and delete the personal data of the deceased, unless otherwise agreed by the deceased user during his lifetime (Art. 49 PIPL).

Finally, platform users have the procedural right to exercise their right and seek redress when their rights have been violated. The PIPL requires platforms to set up convenient mechanisms for accepting and addressing requests from users to exercise their rights (Art. 50 para. 1 PIPL). A similar requirement is also established in Art. 49 of the CSL. If platforms reject users' requests to exercise their rights, they must explain the reasons (Art. 50 para. 1 PIPL), and platform users can sue in court against the rejection (Art. 50 para. 2 PIPL).

3.3.10   Data Protection Impact Assessment

Assessing the impact that certain actions have on the protection of personal data is important for reducing or eliminating potential data privacy risks. Prior to the

---

[106] Before the adoption of the PIPL, some Chinese scholars argued that "the right to erasure" should be used instead of "the right to be forgotten" as the latter term is not a clear legal concept and the nature of this right is not clearly identifiable (Zheng, 2015).

[107] According to Art. 1045 para. 2 of the Civil Code, "close relatives" are "spouse, parents, children, brothers and sisters, paternal grandparents, maternal grandparents, paternal grandchildren, and maternal grandchildren."

promulgation of the PIPL, no law or regulation required platforms as processors of personal data to conduct a data protection impact assessment. However, such a requirement and related detailed norms can be found in some non-mandatory national standards, such as the GB/T 35273-2020 PI Specification (also the 2017 version) and the GB/T 39335-2020 Information Security Technology-Guidelines for Personal Information Security Impact Assessment (GB/T 39335-2020 IA Guidelines). Without mentioning whether a personal data security impact assessment should only be carried out in specific situations, the GB/T 39335-2020 IA Guidelines, for example, outline the value, purposes, responsible subjects, factors to be considered, and the content of the assessment reports when carrying out an impact assessment on the security of personal data.

With the adoption of the PIPL, conducting such an assessment in certain cases has become a legally enforceable requirement of a self-regulatory rule in China. According to Art. 55 of the PIPL, platforms must first carry out an assessment of the impact on the protection of personal data and record the circumstances of the processing in the following situations:

1. the processing of sensitive personal information;
2. the use of personal information for automated decision-making;
3. entrusting third parties to process personal data, sharing personal data with other processors of personal information and publishing personal data;
4. providing personal information abroad; and
5. other personal data processing activities that have a major impact on the rights and interests of users.

The PIPL further clarifies the content of the data protection impact assessment. The assessment must cover three aspects: first, whether the purposes and methods of processing personal data are lawful, adequate and necessary; second, the implications and security risks for the rights and interests of individuals; and third, whether the protective measures used are legal, effective, and appropriate to the degree of risk (Art. 56, para. 1 PIPL). The personal data protection impact assessment reports and processing records must be stored for at least three years (Art. 56 para. 2 PIPL).

3.3.11 Internal and External Data Protection Supervision

Before the PIPL was adopted, some provisions regarding internal and external supervision of data protection could be found in laws such as the CSL. However, the previous provisions are much less specific, comprehensive, and systematic, and appear to be more relevant to data security than data privacy.

As processors of personal information, platform companies are obliged to self-regulate to ensure users' data privacy. When platforms process personal data to the extent specified by the CAC,[108] they must designate a person in charge of personal data protection who is responsible for overseeing the processing of personal data and any protection measures taken (Art. 52 para. 1 PIPL). The contact information of the nominated person must be made public and their names and contact information must be communicated to the competent authorities responsible for the protection of personal data (Art. 52 para. 2 PIPL). The designated person is thus very similar to the data protection officer under the GDPR. Furthermore, foreign platforms that process personal data within the territory of the PRC must set up special institutions or designated representatives in China responsible for handling privacy matters and report their names and contact information to the relevant authorities (Art. 53 PIPL). Finally, the PIPL requires platforms to regularly check whether their personal data processing activities comply with laws and administrative regulations (Art. 54 PIPL).

In addition to internal monitoring, external monitoring is required to protect the privacy of data subjects. In general, administrative departments of the government play an important role in data protection as supervisory authorities (Jiang, 2021). The PIPL has a separate chapter (Chap. 6) entitled "Departments that Perform Personal Data Protection Obligations," which contains 6 articles (Art. 60–Art. 65). The PIPL specifies what "departments performing personal information protection duties" refers to (Art. 60 para. 3 PIPL). These include the CAC and relevant departments of the State Council (Art. 60 para. 1 PIPL), and relevant departments of local governments at or above the county level (Art. 60 para. 2 PIPL). All these departments are obliged to perform duties such as carrying out public relations and education on personal data protection, directing and monitoring platforms to protect personal information, receiving and processing complaints and reports relating to personal information protection, the organization of personal data protection assessments and publication of the results, and investigating and combating illegal personal data processing activities (Art. 61 PIPL). In particular, the CAC, as the national internet information office, is responsible for planning and coordinating relevant departments to promote work on personal information protection, such as formulating specific rules and standards for the protection of personal information (Art. 62 PIPL). The PIPL empowers regulators to take certain actions to carry out their duties, including:

1. questioning the relevant parties and investigating the circumstances relating to the processing of personal data;
2. accessing and reproducing contracts, records, business books and other relevant materials relating to the processing of personal data;
3. conducting on-site inspections and investigations into suspected illegal personal information processing activities;
4. checking the equipment and objects relating to personal data processing activities and, for the equipment and objects for which there is evidence of use in illegal

---

[108] The specific scope remains to be specified by the CAC.

personal data processing activities, making a written report to the person in charge of the department and, after approval, ensuring that the materials are sealed or confiscated (Art. 63 para. 1 PIPL).

Platforms must provide support and cooperate, rather than preventing or impeding a competent authority from fulfilling its tasks (Art. 63 para. 2 PIPL). If the relevant departments determine that the processing of personal information poses a relatively high risk or that incidents related to the security of personal data have occurred, they can speak to the legal representative or the person responsible for the platform or request that the platform appoint a professional to conduct a compliance audit (Art. 64 para. 1 PIPL). To facilitate the supervisory authorities in receiving complaints or reports of illegal activities related to the processing of personal data from organizations and individuals (Art. 65 para. 1 PIPL), these authorities must publish their contact information (Art. 65 para. 2 PIPL).

As in the EU, the supervisory authorities are given the opportunity under the PIPL to take legal action against illegal activities involving the processing of personal data. According to Art. 70 para. 1 of the PIPL, should crowdsourcing platform companies violate relevant regulations when processing personal data and harm the rights and interests of a large number of individuals, the organizations designated by the CAC can file a lawsuit in court.[109]

Finally, the PIPL potentially exposes some platforms to public oversight. According to Art. 58 para. 4 of the PIPL, if platforms provide important internet platform services and have a large number of users or a complex business model,[110] they are obliged to publish regular social responsibility reports on the protection of personal data and accept social oversight. Accordingly, the crowdsourcing platforms concerned are obliged to include matters of data protection in their corporate social responsibility (CSR) reports or to publish independent data protection CSR reports.[111] Before the adoption of the PIPL, the T/ISC 003-2020 Guidelines on Compiling CSR Reports of Internet Enterprises issued by the ISC merely suggested that internet-based platform companies include the data protection and data security measures they have taken in the CSR reports.

---

[109] In addition to the organizations designated by the CAC, this article also authorizes "the People's Procuratorate" and "consumer organizations designated by law" to file a lawsuit against the illegal processing of personal data in court. According to Art. 58 of the Civil Procedure Law, such proceedings initiated by competent bodies are often initiated for reasons of public interest, for example to protect the environment or the rights and interests of consumers.

[110] What is meant by "important internet platform services," "a huge number of users," or "a complex operational model" is currently unclear and remains to be further specified by relevant authorities such as the CAC.

[111] The CSR reports are often freely available on the websites of the respective companies.

3.3.12   Sanctions

When a platform company unlawfully processes the personal information of its users, it is legally liable for its actions. Prior to the promulgation of the PIPL, various laws such as the CSL, the Civil Code and the Criminal Code already regulated platforms' liability for data breaches. However, compared to the previous provision, the PIPL provides for stricter, more specific, and more comprehensive sanctions.

Three types of liability for data breaches can be distinguished, namely administrative, civil and criminal liability. Regarding administrative penalties, the PIPL introduced three innovative regimes. First, platform applications that process unlawful personal data will be sentenced to suspend or discontinue their services and a fine will be imposed (Art. 66 para. 1 PIPL). Although in practice there are some cases where platforms have been ordered to suspend services due to data breaches, the PIPL provides for such a sanction in law for the first time (Liu, 2021b, p. 171). Second, the size of the fines is much greater. If the illegal personal information processing activities carried out by platform companies are serious, they can be fined up to 50 million CNY[112] or up to 5% of the previous year's business income (Art. 66 para. 2 PIPL). The maximum fine under the CSL is only 1 million CNY[113] (Art. 64 CSL). Notably, this penalty is even higher than under the GDPR, which has a limit of 2%. Third, the PIPL provides that the platform companies' directly liable managers and other directly liable persons may also be prohibited from serving as directors, supervisors, officers or persons responsible for the protection of personal data in relevant companies for a specified period of time (Art. 66 para. 2 PIPL) (Liu, 2021b, pp. 170–175). Apart from the three new sanctions, the PIPL, like the CSL, provides that if platform companies violate the provisions of the PIPL, the supervisory authorities are authorized to order corrections, issue warnings, confiscate unlawful profits, and report to the responsible supervisory authorities for the lifting of business permits or licenses (Art. 66 PIPL). Privacy violations by platforms can also be recorded in the credit register and may be publicly disclosed (Art. 67 PIPL). A similar provision can also be found in Art. 71 of the CSL. Thus, the violation of personal rights can seriously affect the business of the liable platforms.

The platforms that violate the data protection rights of their users can also be held liable for damages under civil law, more precisely in tort, if they cannot prove that they are not at fault (Art. 69 para. 1 PIPL). Liability for damages should be based on the damage suffered by the persons concerned or the benefits obtained from the liable platforms (Art. 69 para. 2 PIPL). As mentioned earlier, when platforms violate the provisions of the PIPL when processing personal data and harm the rights and interests of a large number of data subjects, the People's Procuratorate, consumer protection organizations designated by law, and organizations designated by the CAC can file a lawsuit in the courts (Art. 70 PIPL). In practice, there are many cases

---

[112] Based on an average exchange rate in 2021 of 7.6369 CNY per 1 EUR, 50 million CNY is approximately 6.5 million EUR.

[113] Accordingly, one million CNY is approximately 131,000 EUR.

in which the public prosecutor's office has sued internet-based platforms that have unlawfully processed personal data of users in order to protect the personal rights of data subjects (Liu, 2021b, pp. 185–186). As a result, some platforms have effectively been sanctioned for their data privacy violations. For example, in *Shanghai Baoshan District People's Procuratorate v. H Technology Ltd. and Han et al.*, the court held that the platform company, as the defendant, illegally sold users' personal information; the liable company and several managers directly responsible had to pay damages, the affected website had to be closed, and the personal information collected had to be deleted.[114]

Finally, Art. 71 of the PIPL mentions that if violations of this law constitute a criminal offence, criminal liability must be pursued under the law. This provision relates to Art. 253(a) of the Criminal Law. Accordingly, any organization or individual that illegally sells or provides to others the personal information of citizens will be subject to fines, detention, or up to seven years in prison if the circumstances are serious. As organizations, crowdsourcing platforms are subject to this provision.

3.4 Similarities and Differences in Regulatory Approaches

This subchapter[115] summarizes results from the above analysis of the data protection laws in Germany, the United States and China. As the following synoptic overview demonstrates, the legal frameworks for data protection on crowdsourcing platforms in the three countries show considerable differences, but also some similarities.

3.4.1 Particularities of Norm-Setting in the Field of Data Privacy

In Germany, the EU GDPR provides a comprehensive mandatory framework for handling of personal data by crowdsourcing businesses. Since going into effect in 2018, the GDPR applies automatically to EU member states without needing to be transposed into national laws. As far as the EU regulation gives national legislators leeway, platform companies must also obey the Federal Data Protection Act and sector-specific privacy regulations. New rules in German and European competition and antitrust law address the market and data power of large platforms. The proposed

---

[114]For more details see the official website of the Supreme People's Procuratorate of the PRC. Accessed March 9, 2022, from https://www.spp.gov.cn/spp/jcgyssljgrxxbh/202104/t20210422_52 7823.shtml.

[115]This subchapter was written by Sonja Mangold.

EU directive on improving working conditions in platform work specifically deals with privacy issues pertaining to crowdworkers.

China started developing its privacy legislation much later than Germany and the U.S. The Chinese approach is characterized by the different protection regime of privacy rights vis-à-vis private actors and privacy rights vis-à-vis the state government. While data protection rights in the private sector have been expanded, threats to privacy from state actors remain relatively neglected in Chinese law (Pernot-Leplay, 2020). The creation of China's Social Credit System, which uses digital technology to monitor and assess the behavior of citizens and companies, has raised serious concerns about negative privacy implications among Western scholars and commentators (e.g., Karpa et al., 2022; Calzada, 2022). It is argued that Chinese data protection vis-à-vis private actors could further increase data access and surveillance by the state. For the purpose of this book, we have limited ourselves to describing data protection legislation relevant to platforms.

Legal requirements for data protection and data security in crowdsourcing actually exist under Chinese law. Relevant privacy provisions which may affect platform businesses are found in various acts, sector-specific laws and executive rules. As formal norm-setting bodies, China's National People's Congress, its Standing Committee and Local People's Congresses are active in the field of data privacy. In addition, administrative regulations by the State Council and other executive bodies are of great importance (Binding, 2014b). In recent years, the Chinese legislature has made efforts to unify the incoherent, fragmented legal framework for data protection and data security. The new PIPL, which came into effect in 2021, lays out for the first time a comprehensive set of rules for the protection of personal data in the digital economy. The PIPL is seen to have many similarities with the GDPR. Furthermore, similar to Europe, antimonopoly reforms have recently been undertaken to limit market power due to data control by big tech platforms.

In the United States, there isn't (yet) a federal omnibus regulation regarding personal data protection. U.S. legislatures traditionally tend to emphasize the benefits of the free flow of information and of free enterprise over individuals' privacy rights. Privacy provisions relevant to crowdsourcing businesses are scattered across numerous sectoral and state privacy laws. The state of California has recently passed consumer protection legislation that is comparable to the GDPR. Unlike in Germany and Europe, voluntary industry self-regulation (e.g., through privacy seals or the spontaneous adoption of privacy-enhancing technologies) plays an important role in the U.S. data protection regime. U.S. lawmakers generally tend to favor rather minimal regulation in the field of data privacy. However, compliance with consumer privacy rules is backed by strong public enforcement. The FTC as the nation's principal consumer protection agency has already taken legal action against powerful digital platforms. Additionally, the threat of class actions in the U.S. implies high financial risks for platform businesses.

3.4.2   Data Security Standards

Various norms in German and European law oblige platform companies to ensure IT security and to protect user data from loss, destruction, theft or misuse. According to Art. 32 GDPR, platform companies are expected to implement appropriate technical and organizational security measures such as encryption. Furthermore, the GDPR contains rules for notifying victims and authorities in the event of data breaches.

In China, provisions relating to data security are found in the Cybersecurity Law (CSL), in the Data Security Law (DSL) and in the Personal Information Protection Law (PIPL). Accordingly, platform companies "shall adopt the necessary measures to safeguard the security of the personal information they handle" (Art. 9 PIPL) and "prevent unauthorized access as well as personal information leaks, distortion, or loss" (Art. 51 PIPL). Chinese law promotes a variety of concrete data security measures, including encryption, staff training and personal information security incident response plans.

In the United States, all fifty states have enacted data breach notification laws. These laws require companies to notify customers when their personal information has been exposed. Some states, like California, have passed additional prescriptive data security regulations. At the federal level, consumer protection regulation plays a dominant role in the data security framework. The FTC has taken a number of enforcement actions against companies for failure to adopt reasonable security practices. In addition, voluntary industry standards such as the Cybersecurity Framework released by the National Institute of Standards and Technology (NIST) have proven to be highly influential on business practice.

3.4.3   Protection of Personal and Sensitive Data

The GDPR broadly protects all data related to an identified or identifiable natural person. The new Chinese data protection legislation contains a definition of personal information that is similar to that in the GDPR. In contrast, the U.S. approach to personal information is rather inconsistent, differing between sector-specific and state-specific laws and lacking in overarching definitions.

European data protection law contains specific requirements as additional safeguards to protect sensitive data. The main legal basis for the processing of such data is express consent. Sensitive data are clearly listed. China's PIPL also requires higher protection for sensitive information. Platforms must obtain separate explicit consent from internet users before handling such information. In contrast to the GDPR, the PIPL contains a non-exhaustive list of sensitive data. The Chinese definition is comparatively broad. For example, financial data and location tracking data are also classified as sensitive information. The U.S. law does not have an overarching principle providing higher protection for sensitive data. However, it should be noted that California privacy law advances a broad concept of sensitive information. Additional safeguards are provided to protect consumers' financial information, email contents or geolocation data.

3.4.4 Collection of Company Information and Consumer and Employee Data in the GDPR Broadly

When crowdsourcing platforms collect business information from their customers, the data protection regimes in Germany, China and the U.S. generally do not apply. German and European data protection law only pertain to natural persons, not corporate entities. Similarly, company data collected by platforms are not protected under China's PIPL. However, when platforms process information about a small company that enables conclusions about natural persons, this information falls within the data protection regime. Crowdworkers active as solo entrepreneurs can thus rely on data protection law.

When platforms collect information about consumers, they must comply with specific legal requirements. The European, Chinese and U.S. privacy laws all provide specific provisions for protecting consumer data. Under German and Chinese law, consumer associations can take legal action against violations of consumer privacy rights. In the United States, class actions and proceedings of the FTC are powerful tools for protecting consumer privacy.

When platforms collect and use personal information of crowdworkers, specific rules on employee data protection may apply. Whether crowdworkers are self-employed or employees is a highly controversial issue. German, Chinese and U.S. laws all contain specific privacy provisions in the employment context. However, only German law contains adequate rules and strict consent requirements that address power imbalances between platform companies and workers.

3.4.5 General Principles of Data Processing, Privacy by Design and by Default

The key feature of the European data protection framework is the principle "prohibition unless permission." Art. 5 GDPR contains a number of core data protection principles such as lawfulness, purpose limitation, transparency of processing, data minimization and data accuracy. Platform companies must observe these general requirements of data processing. If they don't comply with the principles laid down in Art. 5 GDPR they can be fined. Some of these principles and requirements also exist in U.S. sectoral and state-specific privacy laws, but some principles are simply absent. In contrast to the GDPR, U.S. laws generally allow the processing of personal data. The European approach is therefore stricter and more stringent. China's PIPL includes several core data protection principles similar to the GDPR such as legality, necessity, purpose limitation, transparency of processing and data accuracy. With regard to fundamental data protection principles that apply to private actors and companies, China thus appears to be moving closer to European law.

According to Art. 25 GDPR, platform companies must comply with the principles of privacy by design and default. For example, anonymization, pseudonymization, and encryption techniques are protective measures that fall under privacy by design. Privacy by default means that data processors pre-select the least privacy-invasive choice. China's PIPL lacks provisions for data protection by design and default. In the United States, privacy by design is not a binding rule and is limited to consumer privacy protection.

3.4.6 Anonymization and Pseudonymization

The data protection laws in all three countries encourage companies and crowdsourcing platforms to anonymize and pseudonymize personal data of their users. Anonymization and pseudonymization are central instruments of the European data protection framework. The GDPR clearly defines anonymous and pseudonymous data. Pseudonymization techniques are expressly mentioned by the EU legislator as a way to implement data security and privacy by design. The concepts of anonymization and pseudonymization are also anchored in Chinese and U.S. privacy laws. Compared to the GDPR, however, the Chinese and the U.S. approaches show some shortcomings. Chinese law does not put forward any ways in which anonymization of personal information can be achieved. U.S. law does not impose any additional requirements for pseudonymization, where the risk of re-identification is much higher than with anonymization.

3.4.7 Consent for Legitimizing Data Processing

Informed consent represents the prime legal basis for processing personal data under the GDPR. The European law requires that consent must be freely given, explicit, specific, unambiguous and properly documented. If users are employees or consumers and therefore face a power imbalance vis-à-vis the platforms, voluntary consent can be doubtful. In China, the concept of data subject consent also exists. However, the requirements of Chinese law are relatively vague. China's PIPL does not contain a clear definition of "consent." In the United States, there is a rather liberal understanding of what constitutes consent. For example, implied consent is often considered to be a sufficient legal basis for the processing of personal data. Under U.S. privacy laws, visiting a website or the mere use of a platform service constitutes valid consent.

3.4.8   Regulation of Algorithmic Decision-Making

A coherent, special legal framework that addresses the risks of algorithmic management on crowdsourcing platforms is currently still lacking in all three countries. However, in Germany as well as in China and the United States there are accountability and transparency requirements and individual rights with regard to automated decisions including profiling. Art. 22 GDPR allows automated decision-making determined solely by machines only in exceptional cases. Furthermore, the GDPR severely restricts automated decision-making based on sensitive data. The proposed EU directive on platform work requires platform companies to inform workers about automated monitoring and decision-making systems (Art. 6). China's PIPL follows the GDPR in the restrictions on automated decisions, including profiling. In the United States, the FTC has already taken action against corporations for violations of consumers' and children's privacy in the context of algorithms.

3.4.9   Individual Rights

The GDPR codifies a number of individual rights which users and consumers can assert against crowdsourcing platforms. These include rights of access and correction and the right to delete data. The right to data portability (Art. 20 GDPR) pursues a consumer protection and antitrust law objective and is intended to prevent lock-in effects in the sense of customer retention to one platform. The new Chinese data protection legislation echoes the GDPR in terms of individual rights. However, a major difference from Germany and Europe is that, according to the Chinese understanding, individual data protection rights can primarily be asserted in the private sector and not against the state (Pernot-Leplay, 2020). In the United States, there is no comprehensive national legislation that enshrines individual rights of users against platforms. The U.S. approach to individual rights is less consistent and offers less protection than the GDPR.

3.4.10   Data Protection Impact Assessment

Crowdsourcing platforms may be required under the GDPR to carry out a formal data protection impact assessment. An obligation exists in high-risk cases such as the use of big data analytics and web tracking technologies. The data protection impact assessment can be divided into two different stages: prior analysis of the risks and consequences of data processing, and definition of the measures envisaged to address these risks. China's PIPL also requires a data protection impact assessment in certain defined high-risk situations, such as the processing of sensitive information or the use of personal information for automated decisions. In the United States, some state privacy laws require companies to carry out periodic risk assessments or cybersecurity audits. Taken together, however, U.S. laws are rather lax. Risk assessments are rarely required by law, and relevant provisions often only consist of non-binding recommendations.

3.4.11 Enforcement Mechanisms

Under European and German data protection law, platforms may be obliged to appoint a data protection officer responsible for compliance issues. The designation of a data protection officer is required of platforms if, for example, they process sensitive data to a large extent or use GPS trackers. Similarly, the Chinese PIPL requires that companies shall have data protection officers in cases of extensive processing of personal data. In the United States, on the other hand, there is no general legal obligation to appoint internal or external data privacy officers. The existence of data protection officers in companies is often on a purely voluntary basis. In all three countries, state data protection authorities can impose severe fines and penalties on platform companies for data protection violations. Overall, it can be said that U.S. privacy laws are enforced comparatively rigorously by authorities and private plaintiffs, with high penalties, fines and claims for damages often reaching millions, if not billions, of U.S. dollars in class actions. The FTC has already imposed high penalties against digital corporations such as Google and Meta-Facebook.

3.5 Interim Result and the Aspect of Regulatory Competition

Our comparative legal analysis has shown that there is currently no specific legal framework for the collection of personal data on crowdsourcing platforms in Germany, the United States and China. However, in all three countries, legal changes can be observed that selectively address privacy issues on the platform market. Problem-oriented norm-setting in this area has increased in recent years. In Germany, the EU GDPR provides comparatively strict legal standards to protect platform users' privacy. China recently adopted the PIPL, whose provisions are close to the requirements of the GDPR. In the United States, California can be considered a pioneer in privacy regulation in the digital era.

A much-discussed concept in the development of the globalized and digitalized economy is that of regulatory competition (Eidenmüller, 2011; Çapar, 2022). The far-reaching debate on this topic can only be touched upon here. Regulatory competition can be generally defined as the activity of public or private norm-setters who intend to produce novel legislation or alter existing legislation in response to competitive pressure from other norm-setters (Gödker & Hornuf, 2019). There have been extensive debates over whether globalization and regulatory competition may cause a "race to the top" or a "race to the bottom" in standard-setting (e.g., Deakin, 2006; Vogel & Kagan, 2004). The "race to the top" hypothesis suggests that under regulatory competition, lawmakers produce better and stricter laws. According to the "race to the bottom" argument, the pressures of competitive lawmaking may induce norm-setters to lower their regulatory standards.

In the area of digital privacy there are indications that regulatory competition among lawmakers actually exists and has the potential to induce a race to the top in public standard-setting (Çapar, 2022; Rustad & König, 2019). The EU GDPR, which also applies to crowdsourcing platforms, has influenced other countries to adopt similar laws. The broad extraterritorial scope of the EU privacy regime puts pressure on countries and firms outside Europe to make changes that are in line with the stricter EU standards. As discussed above, the norms of the European data protection framework have also diffused into Chinese and U.S. privacy laws. A growing number of studies have investigated the regulatory spillover effects of GDPR theoretically and empirically (see especially Bradford, 2020; Frankenreiter, 2022; Peukert et al., 2022). The "Brussels effect" could hence shape future privacy regulation of the platform economy.

In the United States, California has adopted GDPR-like privacy laws as part of its digital market regulation. Other states have followed California's example and passed stricter online privacy laws. California's pioneering privacy legislation has thus spread throughout the United States. This seems to further support the thesis of a race of the top in the field of data privacy.

The pressure from customers, workers and consumers could further promote a global upward harmonization of data protection standards. Data privacy awareness among digital users has increased worldwide over recent years. As existing studies have shown (e.g., Xia et al., 2017; Sannon et al., 2022), customers and workers also have high expectations of data privacy and data security in crowdsourcing businesses. Especially among crowdworkers, privacy concerns and fear of surveillance are widespread. The calls for stronger data protection measures on online platforms have become louder, giving us reason to expect that public lawmakers will enact further more specific and stricter privacy regulations in the area of crowdsourcing in the future.

References

Barrett, L. (2019). Confiding in con men: U.S. privacy law, the GDPR, and information fiduciaries. *Seattle University Law Review, 42*(3), 1057–1114.

Baumgartner, U., & Gausling, T. (2017). Datenschutz durch Technikgestaltung und datenschutzfreundliche Voreinstellungen. *Zeitschrift für Datenschutz (ZD), 2017*, 308–313.

Berberich, M., & Seip, F. (2021). Der Entwurf des digital services act. *GRUR-Prax-Praxis im Immaterialgüter- und Wettbewerbsrecht, 2021*, 4–7.

Bertino, E. (2016). Data security and privacy: Concepts, approaches, and research directions. In *Proceedings of the 40th IEEE Computer Software and Applications Conference (COMPSAC 2016)*.

Binding, J. (2014a). Consumer protection law in the People's Republic of China. *China-EU Law Journal, 3*, 223–352.

Binding, J. (2014b). Grundzüge des Verbraucherdatenschutzrechts der VR China. Leitfaden für die Praxis. *Zeitschrift für Datenschutz (ZD), 2014*, 327–336.

Botta, J. (2020). Zwischen Rechtsvereinheitlichung und Verantwortungsdiffusion: Die Prüfung grenzüberschreitender Datenübermittlungen nach "Schrems II". *Computer und Recht (CR), 2020*, 505–513.

Bradford, A. (2020). *The Brussels effect: How the European Union rules the world*. Oxford University Press.

Brasher, E. A. (2018). Addressing the failure of anonymization: Guidance from the European Union's general data protection legislation. *Columbia Business Law Review, 2018*(1), 209–253.

Buchner, B. (2010). Die Einwilligung im Datenschutzrecht – vom Rechtfertigungsgrund zum Kommerzialisierungsinstrument. *Zeitschrift Datenschutz und Datensicherheit (DuD), 34*, 39–43.

Buchner, B. (2018). In J. Kühling & B. Buchner (Eds.), *Datenschutz-Grundverordnung: Kommentar*. Beck. Art. 22 GDPR.

Bundeskartellamt. (2019). *Case report B6-22-16*. Accessed from https://www.bundeskartellamt.de/SharedDocs/Entscheid/DE/Fallberichte/Missbrauchsaufsicht/2019/B6-22-16.html; jsessionid=155FBEA9CB733450C12F077C9DD8FD72.2_cid381?Nn=3591568

Calzada, I. (2022). Citizens' data privacy in China: The state-of-the-art of the personal information protection law (PIPL). *Smart Cities, 5*(3), 1129–1150. https://doi.org/10.3390/smartcities5030057

Çapar, G. (2022). Global regulatory competition on digital rights and data protection: A novel and contractive form of Eurocentrism? *Global Constitutionalism, 2022*, 1–29. Accessed December 9, 2022, from https://papers.ssrn.com/sol3/papers.cfm?abstract_id=4064205

Chen, A. H. (2011). *An introduction to the legal system of the People's Republic of China* (4th ed.).

Chen, X. (2021). On basic principles of China personal international protection law. *Journal of National Prosecutors College, 5*, 3–20 (程潇, 论我国个人信息保护法的基本原则, 国家检察官学院学报, 2021年第5期, 第3–20页).

Chen, J., Han, L., & Kipker, D.-K. (2020). An introduction into the new Chinese data protection legal framework. *Datenschutz und Datensicherheit - DuD, 44*(1), 52–57.

Cherry, M. A., & Poster, W. R. (2016). *Crowdwork, corporate social responsibility, and fair labor practices. Saint Louis University of Legal Studies Research Paper No. 2016-8*. Accessed June 9, 2023, from https://papers.ssrn.com/sol3/papers.cfm?abstract_id=2777201

Ciotti, F., Hornuf, L., & Stenzhorn, E. (2021). *Lock-in effects in online labor markets. CESifo Working Paper No. 9379*. Accessed from https://papers.ssrn.com/sol3/papers.cfm?abstract_id=3953015

Däubler, W., & Klebe, T. (2015). Crowdwork: Die neue Form der Arbeit – Arbeitgeber auf der Flucht? *Neue Zeitschrift für Arbeitsrecht (NZA), 2015*, 1032–1042.

Deakin, S. (2006). Is regulatory competition the future for European integration? *Swedish Economic Policy Review, 13*, 71–95.

Delisle, J., & Trujillo, E. (2010). Consumer Protection in Transnational Contexts. *American Journal of Comparative Law, 58*, 135. Accessed June 10, 2023, from https://scholarship.law.tamu.edu/facscholar/802/

Determann, L. (2016). Datenschutz in den USA-Dichtung und Wahrheit. *Neue Zeitschrift für Verwaltungsrecht (NVwZ), 2016*, 561–567.

Determann, L. (2018). *Analysis: The California Consumer Privacy Act*. Accessed June 10, 2023, from https://iapp.org/news/a/analysis-the-california-consumer-privacy-act-of-2018/

Ding, X. D. (2021a). *Personal information protection: Principles and practice*. Law Press China (丁晓东, 个人信息保护:原理与实践, 法律出版社, 2021年版).

Ding, X. D. (2021b). Data monopolies: Jurisprudential reflections on antitrust in the view of big data. *Oriental Law, 3*, 108–133 (丁晓东, 论数据垄断:大数据视野下反垄断的法理思考, 东方法学, 2021年第3期, 第108–123页).

Düwell, F. J., & Brink, S. (2017). Beschäftigtendatenschutz nach der Umsetzung der Datenschutzgrundverordnung: Viele Änderungen und wenig Neues. *Neue Zeitschrift für Arbeitsrecht (NZA), 2017*, 1081–1085.

Ebers, M. (2020). Regulating AI and robotics: Ethical and legal challenges. In M. Ebers & S. Navas (Eds.), *Algorithms and law* (pp. 37–99). Cambridge University Press.

Eidenmüller, H. (2011). The transnational law market, regulatory competition, and transnational corporations. *Indiana Journal of Global Legal Studies, 18*(2), 707–749.

Ernst, S. (2017). Die Einwilligung nach der Datenschutzgrundverordnung. *Zeitschrift für Datenschutz (ZD), 2017*, 110–114.

Ernst, S. (2021). *Datenschutz-Grundverordnung. Bundesdatenschutzgesetz: DSGVO BDSG. Kommentar.* Beck. Art. 4 GDPR.

European Commission. (2017). *Proposal for a regulation on respect for private life and the protection of personal data in Electronic Communication and on the Repeal of Directive 2002/58 / EC (Regulation on Privacy and Electronic Communication), COM/2017/010 final – 2017/03 (COD).* Accessed from https://eur-lex.europa.eu/legal-content/DE/TXT/?uri=CELEX%3A52017PC0010&qid=1649428836228

European Commission. (2020). *Proposal for a regulation on a single market for digital services (digital services act) and amending Directive 2000/31/EC, COM (2020) 825 final.* Accessed from https://eur-lex.europa.eu/legal-content/DE/TXT/?uri=CELEX%3A52020PC0825&qid=1649428515875

European Commission. (2021). *Proposal for a regulation laying down harmonized rules on artificial intelligence, COM (2021) 206 final.* Accessed from https://eur-lex.europa.eu/legal-content/DE/TXT/?uri=CELEX%3A52021PC0206&qid=1649428455414

Federal Trade Commission. (2000). *Privacy online: Fair information practices in the electronic marketplace: A Federal Trade Commission Report to Congress.* Accessed June 9, 2023, from https://www.ftc.gov/reports/privacy-online-fair-information.practices-electronic-market-place-federal-trade-commission

Federal Trade Commission. (2009). *FTC report on self-regulatory principles of online behavioral advertising.* Accessed June 9, 2023, from https://www.ftc.gov/sites/default/files/documents/reports/federal-trade-commission-staff-report-self-regulatory-principles-online-behavioral-advertising/p085400behavadreport.pdf

Federal Trade Commission. (2012). *Protecting consumer privacy in an era of rapid change: Recommendations for businesses and policy makers.* Accessed June 9, 2023, from https://www.ftc.gov/reports/protecting-consumer-privacy-era-rapid-change-recommendations-businesses-policymakers

Federal Trade Commission. (2016). *Big data. A tool for inclusion or exclusion? FTC Report.* Accessed June 9, 2023, from https://www.ftc.gov/reports/big-data-tool-inclusion-or-exclusion-understanding-issues-ftc-report

Frankenreiter, J. (2022). The missing "California effect" in data privacy law. *Yale Journal on Regulation, 1068*, 2022. Accessed June 9, 2023, from https://papers.ssrn.com/sol3/papers.cfm?abstract_id=3883728

Frenzel, E. M. (2021). *Datenschutz-Grundverordnung. Bundesdatenschutzgesetz: DSGVO BDSG. Kommentar.* Beck. Art. 6 GDPR.

Friedewald, M. (2017). Datenschutz-Folgenabschätzung. In H. Hill, D. Kugelmann, & M. Martini (Eds.), *Perspektiven der digitalen Lebenswelt* (pp. 37–62). Baden-Baden.

Friedewald, M., Bieker, R. Obersteller, H., Nebel, M., Martin, N., Rost, M., & Hansen, M. (2016). *White Paper Datenschutz-Folgenabschätzung des Forums Privatheit.* Accessed February 16, 2022, from https://www.forum-privatheit.de/datenschutz-folgenabschaetzung/

Gao, F. P. (2019). On the purpose of personal information protection: A perspective of the protected interests on personal information. *Studies in Law and Business, 1*, 93–104 (高富平, 论个人信

息保护的目的——以个人信息保护法益区分为核心, 法商研究, 2019年第1期, 第93–104页).

Gödker, K., & Hornuf, L. (2019). Regulatory competition. In A. Marciano & G. Battista Ramello (Eds.), *Encyclopedia of law and economics* (Vol. 3, pp. 1787–1795). Springer.

Greenleaf, G. (2014). Asian data privacy Laws: Trade & human rights perspectives. *Oxford University Press*, 191–226.

Greenleaf, G. (2021). China's completed personal information protection law: Rights plus cyber-security. *Privacy Laws & Business International Report, 172*, 20–23.

Grewe, M., & Stegemann, L. (2021). EU – Verbandsklagerichtlinie. *Zeitschrift für Datenschutz (ZD), 2021*, 183–187.

Hannák, A., Wagner, C., Garcia, D., Mislove, A, Strohmaier, M., & Wilson, C. (2017). Bias in online freelance marketplaces: Evidence from TaskRabbit and Fiverr. In *Proceedings of the 2017 ACM conference on computer-supported cooperative work and social computing, CSCW 2017*, pp. 1914–1933. ACM. Accessed from https://dl.acm.org/doi/10.1145/2998181.2998327

Hansen, M. (2020). *Beck'scher Online-Kommentar Datenschutzrecht* (31st ed.). Art. 35 GDPR.

Hartzog, W., & Solove, D. L. (2015). The scope and potential of FTC data protection. *George Washington Law Review, 83*(6), 2230–2300.

Hetmank, S. (2016). *Internetrecht. Grundlagen. Streitfragen. Aktuelle Entwicklungen*. Springer.

Hoofnagle, C. J. (2013). *How the fair credit reporting act regulates big data (September 10, 2013). Future of privacy forum workshop on big data and privacy: Making ends meet.* Accessed June 9, 2023, from https://ssrn.com/abstract=2432955

Hoofnagle, C. J. (2016). *Federal trade commission privacy law and policy*. Cambridge University Press.

Ivanova, M., Bronowicka, J., Kocher, E., & Degner, A. (2018). The app as a boss? Control and autonomy in application-based management. In J. Koch, E. Kocher, & K. Weber (Eds.), *Europa-Universität Viadrina. ARBEIT/GRENZE/FLUSS.* Accessed June 9, 2023, from https://www.researchgate.net/publication/328606283_The_App_as_a_Boss_Control_and_Auton omy_in_Application-Based_Management

Jiang, H. Z. (2021). Administrative supervision in the Personal Data Protection Act. *China Law Review, 5*, 48–58 (蒋红珍, 《个人信息保护法》中的行政监管, 中国法律评论, 2021年第5期, 第48–58页).

Ju, Y., & Ling, X. D. (2016). Study on infringement and legal remedies of personal information of online consumers under big data era. *Hebei Law Science, 11*, 52–60 (鞠晔、凌学东, 大数据背景下网络消费者个人信息侵权问题及法律救济, 河北法学, 2016 年第11 期, 第52–60页).

Kaminski, M. E. (2019). The right to explanation, explained. *Berkeley Technology, Law Journal, 34*(1), 189–218.

Karpa, D., Klarl, T., & Rochlitz, M. (2022). Artificial intelligence, surveillance, and big data. In L. Hornuf (Ed.), *Diginomics research perspectives: The role of digitalization in business and society. Advanced studies in diginomics and digitalization.* Springer. https://doi.org/10.1007/978-3-031-04063-4_8

Kim, P. T. (2019). Data mining and the challenges of protecting employee privacy under U.S. Law. *Comparative Labor Law & Policy Journal, 40*(3), 405–420.

King, N., & Raja, V. T. (2012). Protecting the privacy and security of sensitive customer data in the cloud. *Computer Law & Security Review, 28*(3), 308–319.

Kipker, D.-K., & Scholz, D. (2020). Das IT-Sicherheitsgesetz 2.0 – Eine kritische Analyse. *Datenschutz und Datensicherheit (DuD), 2020*, 40–45.

Körner, M. (2017). *Wirksamer Beschäftigtendatenschutz im Lichte der Europäischen Datenschutz-Grundverordnung (DS-GVO)* (Vol. 18). HSI-Schriftenreihe.

Kranig, T., & Peintinger, S. (2014). Selbstregulierung im Datenschutzrecht. Rechtslage in Deutschland, Europa und den USA unter Berücksichtigung des Vorschlags zur DS-GVO. *Zeitschrift für Datenschutz, 1*(2014), 3–9.

Levine, A. S. (2021). A U.S. privacy law seemed possible this congress. Now, prospects are fading fast. *Politico*. Accessed June 9, 2023, from https://www.politico.com/news/2021/06/01/washington-plan-protect-american-data-silicon-valley-491405

Li, Y., Stweart, W., Zhu, J. & Ni, A. (2012). Online privacy policy of the thirty Dow Jones corporations: Compliance with FTC fair information practice principles and readability assessment, Communications of the IIMA: 12(3), Article 5. Accessed June 13, 2023, https://doi.org/10.58729/1941-6687.1194

Li, Q. (2017). Personality, privacy and data: Commercial practices and limits – And a review of the first Chinese cookie privacy dispute. *China Law Review, 2*, 122–138 (李谦, 人格、隐私与数据:商业实践及其限度——兼评中国cookie隐私权纠纷第一案, 中国法律评论, 2017年第2期, 第122–138页).

Li, Y. J. (2021). Internet data monopoly: Theoretical differences, governance practices and policy suggestions. *Frontiers, 21*, 56–66 (李勇坚,互联网平台数据垄断:理论分歧、治理实践及政策建议, 学术前沿, 2021年21第21期, 第56–66页).

Liu, X. Y. (2021a). *Data protection: Compliance guidelines and rule analysis* (2nd edn). China Legal Publishing House (刘新宇, 数据保护:合规指引与规则解析(第2版), 中国法制出版社, 2021年版).

Liu, X. Y. (2021b). *Key interpretation and case analysis of the personal information protection law of the People's Republic of China*. China Legal Publishing House (刘新宇, 中华人民共和国个人信息保护法重点解读与案例解析, 中国法制出版社, 2021年版).

Lorentz, N. (2020). *Profiling – Persönlichkeitsschutz durch Datenschutz*. Mohr Siebeck.

McConville, M., & Chui, W. H. (Eds.). (2007). *Research methods for law*. Edinburgh University Press.

McGeveran, W. (2019). The duty of data security. *Minnesota Law Review, 103*(3), 1135–1208.

Munz, M. (1992). *Allgemeine Geschäftsbedingungen in den USA und Deutschland im Handelsverkehr: eine rechtsvergleichende Untersuchung der richterlichen Kontrolle vorformulierter Vertragsklauseln*.

Newell, R. G., Meyer, C. D., O'Reardon, M. E., & Thoren-Peden, D. S. (2021). *Virginia's Consumer Data Protection Act and the coming wave of CCPA-like state privacy laws*. Accessed June 9, 2023, from https://www.pillsburylaw.com/en/news-and-insights/virginia-consumer-data-protection-act-ccpa-state-privacy-laws.html

Orwat, C. (2020). *Diskriminierungsrisiken durch Verwendung von Algorithmen. Antidiskriminierungsstelle des Bundes*. Accessed from https://www.antidiskriminierungsstelle.de/SharedDocs/Downloads/DE/publikationen/Expertisen/studie_diskriminierungsrisiken_durch_verwendung_von_algorithmen.pdf?__blob=publicationFile&v=6

Otto, M. (2016). *The right to privacy in employment: A comparative analysis*. Hart Publishing.

Pardau, S. L. (2018). The California consumer privacy act: Towards European-style privacy regime in the United States. *Journal of Technology Law & Policy, 23*(1), 68–114.

Pernot-Leplay, E. (2020). China's approach on data privacy law: A third way between the U.S. and the EU? *Penn State Journal of Law & International Affairs, 8*(1), 49–117.

Peukert, C., Bechtold, S., Batikas, M., & Kretschmer, T. (2022). Regulatory spillovers and data governance: Evidence from the GDPR. *Marketing Science, 41*(4), 746–768. https://pubsonline.informs.org/doi/10.1287/mksc.2021.1339

Podszun, R., & de Toma, M. (2016). Die Durchsetzung des Datenschutzes durch Verbraucherrecht, Lauterkeitsrecht und Kartellrecht. *Neue Juristische Wochenschrift (NJW), 2016*, 2977–3056.

Ren, W. D. (2021, November 2). Experts and scholars talk about the draft amendment of the anti-monopoly law. *The Democracy and Law Times*, 3. Accessed January 26, 2022, from http://e.mzyfz.com/paper/1735/paper_46095_9776.html (任文岱, 专家学者谈反垄断法修正草案, 民主与法制时报, 2021年11月2日, 第3版).

Riehm, T., & Meier, S. (2020). Rechtliche Durchsetzung von Anforderungen an die IT-Sicherheit. *Multimedia und Recht (MMR), 2020*, 571–576.

Ritvo, D., Bavitz, Ch., Gupta, R., & Obermann, I. (2013). Privacy and children's data - An overview of the children's online privacy protection act and the family educational rights and privacy act. Berkman Center Research Publication No. 23. Available at SSRN: https://ssrn.com/abstract=2354339.

Rodrigues, R., & Papakonstantinou, V. (Eds.). (2018). *Privacy and data protection seals.* Springer.

Rustad, M., & König, T. H. (2019). Towards a global data privacy standard. *Florida Law Review, 71*(2), 365–454.

Sannon, S., Sun, B., & Cosley, D. (2022). Privacy, surveillance, and power in the gig economy. In *Proceedings of the 2022 CHI Conference on Human Factors in Computing Systems*, Vol. 619, pp. 1–15. Accessed from https://doi.org/10.1145/3491102.3502083

Schantz, P. (2020). In H. A. Wolff & S. Brink (Eds.), *Beck'scher Online-Kommentar Datenschutzrecht* (31st ed.). Art. 5 GDPR.

Schwartz, P. M., & Peifer, K. (2017). Transatlantic data privacy law. *Georgetown Law Journal, 106*(1), 115–180.

Schwartz, P. M., & Solove, D. J. (2014). Reconciling personal information in the United States and European Union. *California Law Review, 102*(4), 877–316.

Schweitzer, H. (2019). Datenzugang in der Datenökonomie: Eckpfeiler einer neuen Informationsordnung. *Zeitschrift Gewerblicher Rechtsschutz und Urheberrecht (GRUR), 2019,* 569–580.

Schweitzer, H., Haucap, J., Kerber, W., & Welker, R. (2018). *Modernisierung der Missbrauchsaufsicht für marktmächtige Unternehmen.* Nomos.

Sloan, R. H., & Warner, R. (2013). Beyond notice and choice: Privacy, norms, and consent. *Journal of High Technology Law, 14*(2), 370–414.

Solove, D. J., & Hartzog, W. (2014). The FTC and the new common law of privacy. *Columbia Law Review, 114,* 593. Accessed June 9, 2023, from https://papers.ssrn.com/sol3/papers.cfm?abstract_id=2312913#

Solove, D. J., & Schwartz, P. M. (2020). *Consumer privacy and data protection.* Wolters Kluwer.

Spiecker genannt Döhmann, I. (2019). Digitale Mobilität: Plattform governance. *Zeitschrift Gewerblicher Rechtsschutz und Urheberrecht (GRUR), 2019,* 341–352.

Spies, A. (2020). USA: Neues kalifornisches Datenschutzgesetz (CPRA) vom Wahler gebilligt. *Zeitschrift für Datenschutz (ZD)-Aktuell, 2020,* 04407.

Spies, A. (2021). USA: Neues Datenschutzgesetz im US-Staat Virginia, *Zeitschrift für Datenschutz (ZD)-Aktuell, 2021,* 05047.

Spindler, G., & Dalby, L. (2019). In G. Spindler & F. Schuster (Eds.), *Recht der elektronischen Medien. Grauer Kommentar* (4th ed.). Beck. Art. 4, GDPR.

Stemmer, M. (2020). In H. A. Wolff & S. Brink (Eds.), *Beck'scher Online-Kommentar Datenschutzrecht* (31st ed.). Art. 7 GDPR.

Stürmer, V. (2020). Löschen durch Anonymisieren? *Zeitschrift für Datenschutz (ZD), 2020,* 626–631.

Tribess, A. (2020). Datenzugangsrechte in der Plattformökonomie. *Zeitschrift für Datenschutz (ZD), 2020,* 440–444.

Vogel, D., & Kagan, R. A. (Eds.). (2004). *Dynamics of regulatory change. How globalization affects national regulatory policies.* University of California Press.

Voigt, P., & von dem Busche, A. (2018). *EU-Datenschutz-Grundverordnung (DSGVO). Praktikerhandbuch.* Springer.

Völker, L. (2013). *Verbraucherschutz im Internethandel: Vertragsrechte und die Neukonzeption des Verbraucher-Acquis.* Diplomica Verlag.

Von Wallenberg, G. (2020). GWB-Novelle – Ordnungsrahmen zur Digitalisierung der Wirtschaft. *Zeitschrift für Rechtspolitik (ZRP), 2020,* 238–241.

Walzer, S. (2019). *Der arbeitsrechtliche Schutz der Crowdworker.* Nomos.

Wan, F. (2016). The right to be forgotten in the end: Reflections on the introduction of the right to be forgotten in China. *Law Review, 6,* 155–162 (万方, 终将被遗忘的权利——我国引入被遗忘权的思考, 法学评论, 2016 年第 6 期, 第155–162页).

Wang, Q. (2011). Restrictions on the employers' right to information at the recruitment stage: Also on the understanding and application of the second half of Article 8 of the Labor Contract Law.

Social Law Review, 5, 85–104 (王倩, 招聘阶段用人单位知情权的限制——也谈《劳动合同法》第八条后半句的理解和适用, 社会法评论(2011年第五卷), 第85–104页).

Wang, T. Y. (2016). Determination of employment relations for the provision of labor services based on internet platforms. *Legal Science, 6*, 50–60 (王天玉,基于互联网平台提供劳务的劳动关系认定, 法学, 2016年第6期, 第50–60页).

Wang, Q. X. (2017). *Labor law* (4th ed.). Law Press China (王全兴, 劳动法 (第四版), 法律出版社, 2017年版).

Wang, C. (2019). Selection of a model for civil law protection of personal information. *Social Sciences in China, 6*, 124–207 (王成, 个人信息民法保护的模式选择, 中国社会科学, 2019年第6期, 第124–207页).

Wang, G.F. (2020, December 20). Meituan played its members for a sucker, and how did big data-enabled price discrimination cheat users? *Tai Media App.* Accessed May 3, 2022, from https://baijiahao.baidu.com/s?id=1686581764335388622 (王古峰, 美团会员成"韭菜", 大数据杀熟是如何收割用户的?钛媒体APP, 2020年12月20日).

Wang, Q. (2022). Protection of personal information as labor standards. *Peking University Law Journal, 1*, 183–201 (王倩, 作为劳动基准的个人信息保护, 中外法学, 2022年第34卷第1期, 第183–201页).

Wiedemann, K. (2021). Data protection and competition law enforcement in the digital economy: Why a coherent and consistent approach is necessary. *IIC-International Review of Intellectual Property and Competition Law, 52*(7), 915–933.

Wu, X. L. (2021, August 25). Personal data can be taken away. *China Consumer News, 4.* Accessed January 25, 2022, from https://zxb.ccn.com.cn/shtml/zgxfzb/20210825/v4.shtml (武晓莉, 个人数据可以带着走, 中国消费者报, 2021年8月25日, 第4版).

Xia, H., Wang, Y., Huang, Y., & Shah, A. (2017). "Our privacy needs to be protected at all costs": Crowd workers' privacy experiences on Amazon mechanical Turk. In *Proceedings of the ACM on Human-Computer Interaction*, 1(CSCW), pp. 1–22. Accessed from https://doi.org/10.1145/3134748

Xie, Y. Y. (2019). Construction and rethinking on the regulations of "Informationelle Selbstbestimmung" in the draft of personal right chapter of Civil Code. *Modern Law Science, 6*, 133–148 (谢远扬, 民法典人格权编(草案)中个人信息自决的规范建构及其反思, 现代法学, 2019年第6期, 第133–148页).

Xie, Z. Y. (2021). Protection of employees' personal information: Value, principle and path. *Journal of Comparative Law, 3*, 25–39 (谢增毅,劳动者个人信息保护的法律价值、基本原则及立法路径,比较法研究,2021年第3 期,第25–39页).

Yang, B. (2004). Chinese labor law and the legal protection of workers' privacy. *Social Sciences in Guangxi, 2*, 112–115 (杨彪, 中国劳动法与劳动者隐私权的法律保护, 广西社会科学, 2004年第2期, 第112–115页).

Yang L. X., & Han, X. (2015). The localization and legal application of the right to be forgotten in China. *Journal of Law Application, 2*, 24–34 (杨立新、韩煦: 被遗忘权的中国本土化及法律适用, 法律适用, 2015 年第 2 期, 第24–34页).

Zhang, X. B. (1996). Protection and limitation of employees' privacy in the workplace *Modern Law Science, 5*, 4–14 (张新宝, 雇员在工作场所的隐私权保护与限制, 现代法学, 1996年第5期, 第4–14页).

Zhang, L. H. (2020). Automated decisions and human autonomy. *Renmin University Law Review, 2*, 20–48 (张凌寒, 自动化决策与人的主体性, 人大法律评论, 2020年第2辑, 第20–48页).

Zhang, L. H. (2021). Algorithmic accountability construction for online platform regulation. *Oriental Law, 3*, 22–40 (张凌寒, 网络平台监管的算法问责制构建, 东方法学, 2021年第3期, 第22–40页).

Zhang, L., & Han X. Z. (2016). The private law nature of personal information right in the big data era *Legal Forum, 3*, 119–129 (张里安、韩旭至, 大数据时代下个人信息权的私法属性, 法学论坛, 2016年第3期, 第119–129页).

Zhao, X. D. (2020). Big data and price discrimination. In *IEEE 5th International Conference on Cloud Computing and Big Data Analytics (ICCCBDA)* (pp. 471–475).

Zheng, Z. F. (2015). Study on the right to be forgotten in the network society. *Studies in Law and Business, 6*, 50–60 (郑志峰, 网络社会的被遗忘权研究, 法商研究, 2015 年第 6 期, 第50–60页).

Chapter 4
Privacy Statements in China, Germany, and the United States

4.1 Processing of Data

This sub chapter investigates how crowdsourcing platforms *de facto* handle matters of data protection. The primary sources of information regarding data protection practices are the respective privacy statements of the platform companies. Our empirical method of analysis is largely based on Dorfleitner and Hornuf (2019). Most importantly, we categorize the data that is actually mentioned in the privacy statements and not that which would be theoretically or legally conceivable. Our examination addresses the following research questions: Which user data is collected? And how is the data processed? For each data category, we study the differences between China, Germany, and the U.S. and relate them to the respective legal system. In line with the classification of Boudreau and Lakhani (2013), we also examine differences between crowd complementor, crowd labor market, collaborative community, and crowd contest platforms. Finally, for the German market, we investigate differences in the processing of data between crowdsourcing platforms and another innovative, technology driven industry: the fintech sector. This comparison allows us to work out the industry-specific characteristics of crowdsourcing.

In a first step, we identified the crowdsourcing platforms that are active in the respective country. We started the search for crowdsourcing platforms through intensive internet research. To qualify for inclusion in our analysis, the crowd labor market and crowd contest platforms had to mediate tasks for which virtually anyone could apply. In the case of crowd complementors, the platforms had to present a task such as a software program to whose improvement everyone could in principle contribute. Finally, on collaborative community platforms, users could offer their products to the public, for example photos or apps, and others must pay for use. We did not consider traditional recruitment websites such as Monster.com or Indeed.com in our analysis, because they do not correspond to the definition of crowdsourcing. Crowdsourcing platforms differ from traditional job portals in that they have a greater influence on the handling of work and business processes, for

© The Author(s) 2023
L. Hornuf et al., *Data Privacy and Crowdsourcing*, Advanced Studies in Diginomics and Digitalization, https://doi.org/10.1007/978-3-031-32064-4_4

example, by pre-selecting and rating the crowdworkers and crowdsourcers. Moreover, crowdworkers in our sample have frequently been self-employed and not employees. The platform often only acts as a mediator between the crowdworker and crowdsourcer. Crowdworkers can theoretically be employed by the crowdsourcer, but those in our sample have most often been self-employed. To qualify for inclusion in our sample, crowdworkers must also be paid by the crowdsourcer. Thus, we did not consider platforms where users posted ideas, opinions, evaluations, or solutions without any remuneration. Finally, to qualify for inclusion, the tasks on the platform have to be done online; that is, gig work platforms such as Uber Eats in the U.S. or Gorillas in Germany did not qualify for inclusion. In case the platform offered hybrid tasks that could be completed online and offline, we still considered these platforms in our sample.

For China, our main source for identifying crowdsourcing platforms is a list of such platforms from the 2010 China Witkey Industry White Paper, platforms referenced in academic literature, platforms covered by media such as China Central Television (CCTV), platforms mentioned on such websites as Baidu Zhidao or Zhihu, and platforms found through a systematic Baidu and Google search. We checked the platforms to ensure that only those that fit the definition of crowdsourcing in this book are included in our sample. For Germany, we extensively relied on the list by Mrass and Leimeister (2018), which was gathered as part of the project *Innovations for Tomorrow's Production, Services, and Work* and was supported by the German Federal Ministry of Education and Research. The crowdsourcing platform list for Germany was appended by other sources such as Crunchbase. The current status of platforms was updated, for example, if platforms had in the meantime merged and only the surviving platform was taken into account. For the U.S., we mostly relied on Crunchbase to compile a crowdsourcing platform list, but also considered other sources, for example, platforms that have been cited in the literature. For all countries, we also conducted a systematic Google search to identify crowdsourcing platforms.

As Fig. 4.1 shows, we have identified 145 crowdsourcing platforms for China that fall under the definition of crowdsourcing outlined above. Of these companies, 22 had no website and thus no privacy statement available. Another 22 had a website; however, despite an extensive search on the website, we could not find any privacy statement online. We have identified 47 crowdsourcing platforms in Germany and all of these platform companies had a website and privacy statement. For the U.S., we have identified 293 crowdsourcing platforms, of which 20 had a website but, despite an extensive search on the respective website, we could not find any privacy statement online. Another five of these platform companies had no website and thus no privacy statement available. In sum, we have identified 416 privacy statements that we can use for our empirical analysis. A list of all crowdsourcing platforms in our data sample is included in the Appendix.

The privacy statements in the three countries varied in their size and sophistication. On average, the privacy statements from China had 7171 words (standard deviation 5183 words). The shortest Chinese privacy statement had only 393 words and the longest 22,371 words. Assuming a reading speed of 250 words per minute

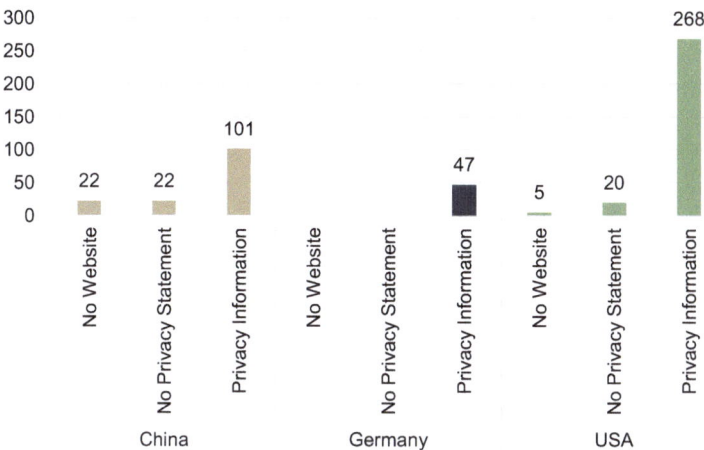

Fig. 4.1 Frequency of providing a privacy statement. Distinction by country. Number of privacy statements $N = 485$

(McDonald & Cranor, 2009), it took almost half an hour to read an average privacy statement from China. The average privacy statement from Germany had 4284 words (standard deviation 2836 words). The shortest privacy statement had only 891 words and the longest 13,699 words. Thus, the average reading time for a privacy statement from a German crowdsourcing platform was 16 minutes and thus almost as long as a privacy statement from a German fintech platform (Dorfleitner & Hornuf, 2019, p. 54). The reason for this similarity might be the development towards more standardization and boilerplate language in privacy statements as a result of the GDPR (Dorfleitner et al., 2023). Finally, the privacy statements from the U.S. were the shortest and had on average 2831 words (standard deviation 2485 words). The shortest privacy statement had only 30 words and the longest 16,065 words.

In line with the definition by Boudreau and Lakhani (2013) and the exclusion criteria outlined above, we have classified the crowdsourcing platforms into crowd complementors, crowd labor markets, collaborative communities, and crowd contest platforms. Crowdtesting refers to the testing of products and especially software by a group of testers over the internet and is assigned to crowd labor markets. As Fig. 4.2 shows, crowd labor markets are an important segment in all three countries, although crowd contests are even more important in China. In Germany and the U.S., crowd labor markets are the most important segment. Note that some platforms offer services that fall under several segments, hence the shares of the four segments do not add up to 100%. This overlap occurs most frequently in China, where platforms often operate services that are based solely on smart phone applications rather than websites, while in Germany and the U.S. websites are also common formats.

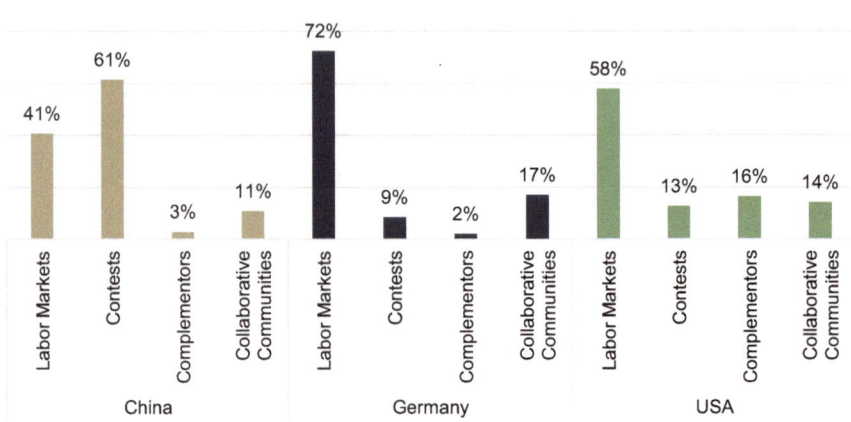

Fig. 4.2 Frequency of crowdsourcing segments. Distinction by country. Number of evaluated privacy statements $N = 416$

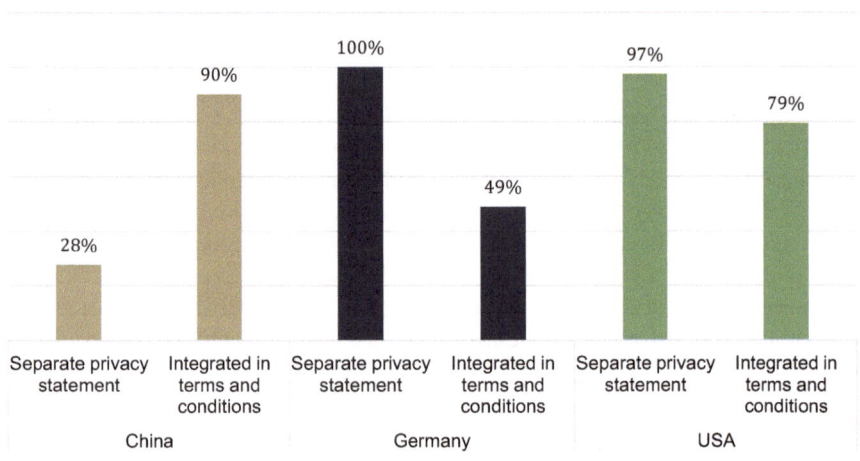

Fig. 4.3 Frequency of separate and integrated privacy statements. Distinction by country. Number of evaluated privacy statements $N = 416$

Even though companies are not required by law to have a privacy statement, they often comply with the requirement to inform their users (Art. 13–15 GDPR) by publishing such statements about the personal data they process. [1] As Fig. 4.3 shows, informing users about the personal data processed can take place in one of two ways: either the platform publishes a separate privacy statement that only contains information about how data is processed or the platform integrates information about the

---

[1] For alternative ways to inform users about the processing of their data, see Geminn et al. (2021).

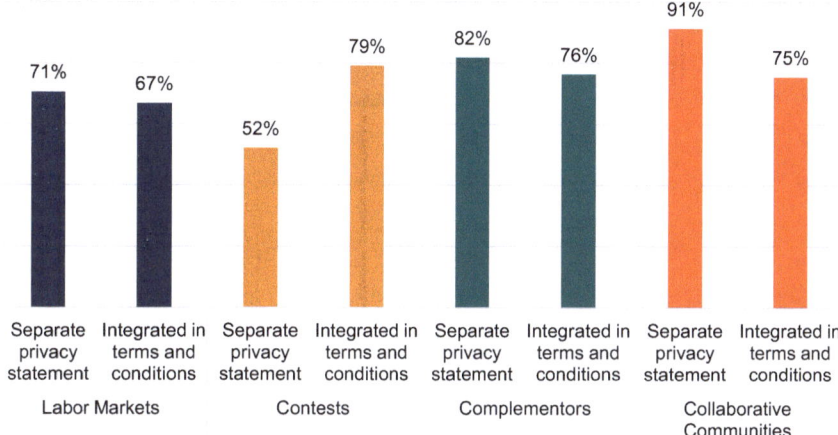

Fig. 4.4 Frequency of separate and integrated privacy statements. Distinction by crowdsourcing segment. Number of evaluated privacy statements $N = 416$

processing of user data into the general terms and conditions. We find that all German platforms made a separate privacy statement available to their users, while about half of the platforms integrated further information in the terms and conditions. The U.S. platforms behave very similarly. An absolute majority publish a separate privacy statement and 79% publish further information about privacy in the terms and conditions. For China, we observe the opposite picture. The majority of platforms integrate information about the processing of personal data in the terms and conditions, while only 28% publish a separate privacy statement. This result is most likely due to the fact that foreign users only rarely use Chinese platforms, which makes the GDPR barely applicable to Chinese platforms. By contrast, U.S. platforms might fall under the scope of the GDPR and the requirement to inform their users if European crowdworkers are active on their platform. Furthermore, China only recently passed the Chinese Personal Information Protection Law in 2021, which could indicate that the need for a separate and more sophisticated privacy statement did not previously exist on the platforms. Finally, the texts of Chinese privacy statements have been on average longer, which indicates that China simply took a different approach in informing their platform users by integrating the information into a single document, the terms and conditions.

When comparing the privacy practices of separate and integrated privacy statements across platform types, we do not find significant differences between crowd labor markets, crowd complementors, and collaborative communities. As Fig. 4.4 shows, crowd contest platforms seem to integrate the privacy information more often into the general terms and conditions.

Many platforms explicitly stated that the processing of personal data is based on a specific legislation. Very few pieces of legislation are mentioned in the privacy statements of German platforms. As Fig. 4.5 shows, 94% German platforms refer to the GDPR and to a much lesser extent also to the Federal Data Protection Act

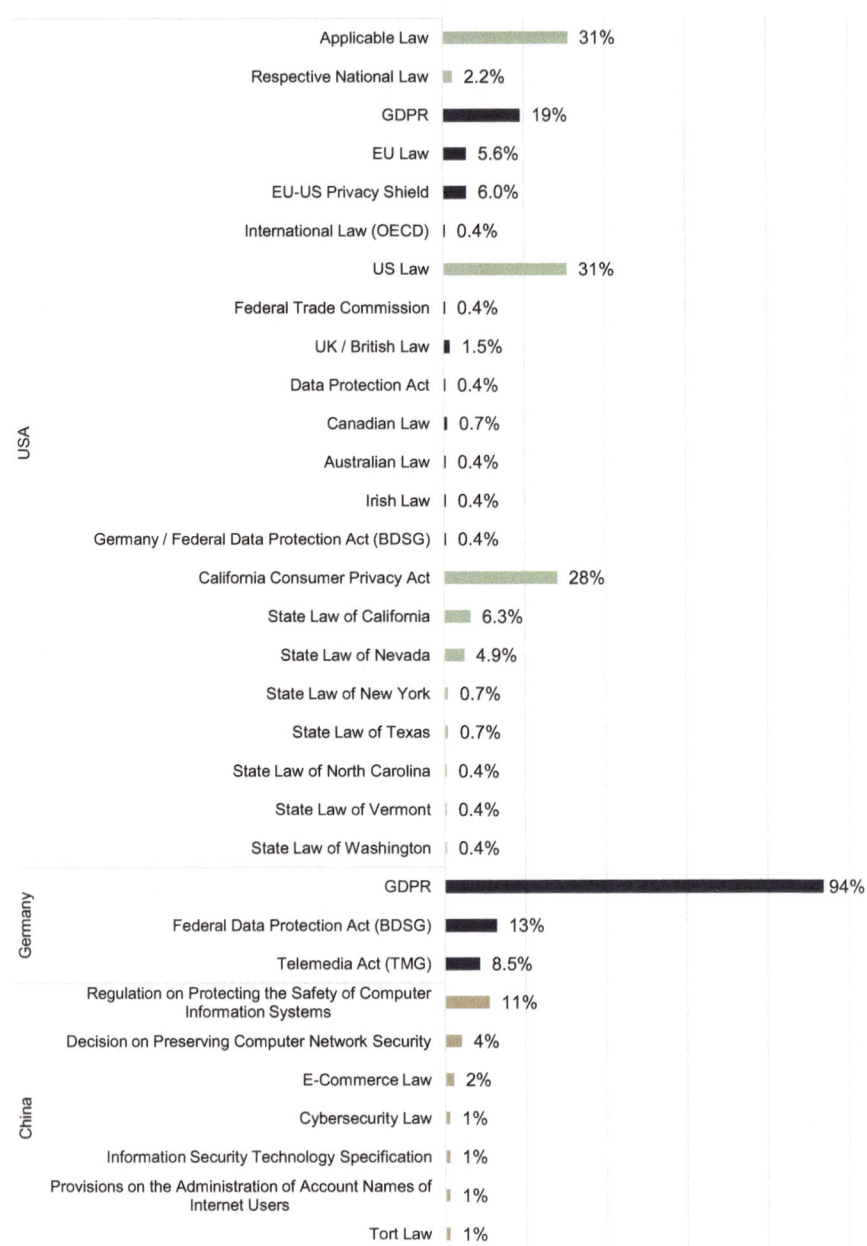

Fig. 4.5 Law applicable to data processing if a law was explicitly mentioned. Distinction by crowdsourcing segment. Number of evaluated privacy statements $N = 416$

(*Bundesdatenschutzgesetz*, BDSG) and the Telemedia Act (*Telemediengesetz*, TMG). The Federal Data Protection Act supplements and clarifies the GDPR, especially with regard to the processing of employee data, video surveillance, and the appointment of data protection officers and supervisory authorities. The Telemedia Act regulates the legal framework for services deemed *telemedia* in Germany, which include web shops, search engines, web mail services, information services, podcasts, and dating communities. Alongside the GDPR, the Telemedia Act is one of the central regulations in German internet law. When we compare the platforms that explicitly state that the processing of personal data is based on a different legislation than German law with a slightly older sample of the fintech industry, we find that references to the GDPR are now made much more frequently and references to specific foreign laws are no longer made.

Given that the Chinese Personal Information Protection Law (PIPL) was only passed in 2021 after our data collection ended, none of the Chinese platforms in our sample referred to the new law. Nevertheless, every tenth platform referred to the Regulation on Protecting the Safety of Computer Information Systems, which came into effect in 2011 and aims to promote the application and development of computers. Overall, 4% of the Chinese platforms refer to the Decision on Preserving Computer Network Security, which prohibits, among other things, the displaying of any online content that has not been approved by the government (Lee & Liu, 2012). Only 1% of the Chinese platforms refer to the Cybersecurity Law that came into effect in 2017 and for the first time comprehensively regulates data security in cyberspace in China. Chinese platforms do not refer to the GDPR. In general, the legal instruments mentioned in the privacy statements of Chinese platforms are more related to data security than to data privacy. In addition, some important and applicable legal sources related to the protection of personal data are not mentioned at all in privacy statements; for example, the General Provisions of Civil Law, or the Decision on Strengthening Information Protection on Networks. However, with the PIPL, the Data Security Law, and the Civil Code which came into effect in 2021, we expect Chinese platforms to update their privacy statements and also mention these new laws.

U.S. platforms refer to 22 different types of regulation. Most often, crowdsourcing platforms simply refer to the applicable law or U.S. law (each 31%). Second most important is the state law of California (28%), which is followed by the European GDPR (19%). In general, the types of regulation U.S. platforms refer to can be categorized into four types: (1) national law, (2) international law, (3) foreign law, and (4) state law. With regard to national law, besides mentioning U.S. law, platforms also mention the regulations of the Federal Trade Commission; however, such cases are rare. When mentioning international law, U.S. platforms often refer to the GDPR or EU law, the EU–US Privacy Shield, and OECD regulations. The EU–US Privacy Shield was negotiated by the U.S. Department of Commerce and the European Commission from 2015 to 2016 to provide companies with a mechanism for compliance with data protection requirements when transferring personal data. It consisted of a number of assurances from the U.S. federal government and an adequacy decision by the European Commission, but has been

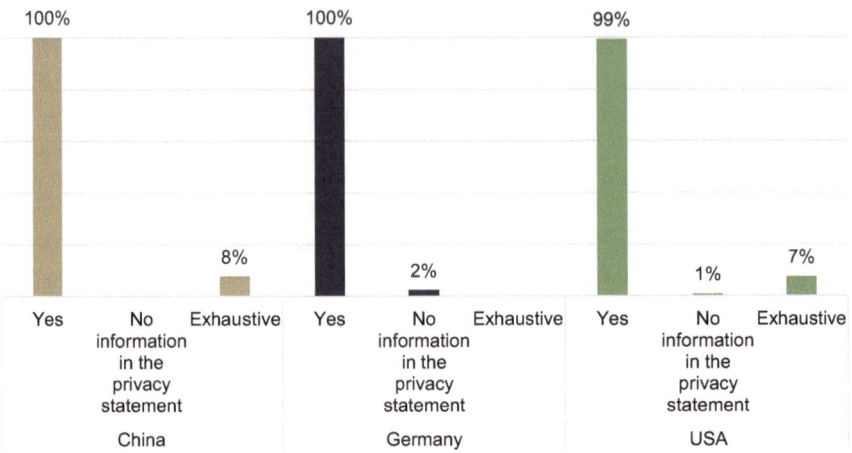

Fig. 4.6 Frequency of privacy statements indicating that personal or personally identifiable information is being processed. Distinction by country. Number of evaluated privacy statements $N = 416$

struck down by the Court of Justice of the European Union in 2020 (see Sect. 3.3 above for more details). As for foreign law, the U.S. privacy statements cite UK/British law, Canadian law, Australian law, Irish law, and German law. Finally, state laws explicitly mentioned are the California Consumer Privacy Act, followed by the State Law of California and the State Law of Nevada. Other state laws mentioned are those of New York, Texas, North Carolina, Vermont and Washington.

Overall, it appears that the aforementioned rights primarily reflect the international and federal nature of the U.S. and the predominant position of the GDPR in Germany. Data protection has only recently become more important in China and will continue to do so with the Chinese Personal Information Protection Law of 2021. The fact that foreign laws are not mentioned in Chinese privacy statements is again reflective of the fact that Chinese services are virtually still closed to foreigners.

As Fig. 4.6 shows, almost all crowdsourcing platforms state that they process personal data and no platform company explicitly mentioned in its privacy statement that it was not processing personal data. This pattern is identical for all three countries and four platform types. However, the majority of crowdsourcing platforms did not *exhaustively* list the types of personal data that were processed. In China and the U.S. respectively, 8% and 7% of the platforms provided an exhaustive list of the types of data being processed. None of the German platforms provided such an exhaustive list. The remaining platforms either provided examples of the data being processed or simply mentioned that personal data is processed by the platform. The fact that few platforms provide an exhaustive list of the personal data processed is in line with earlier findings for the German fintech industry (Dorfleitner

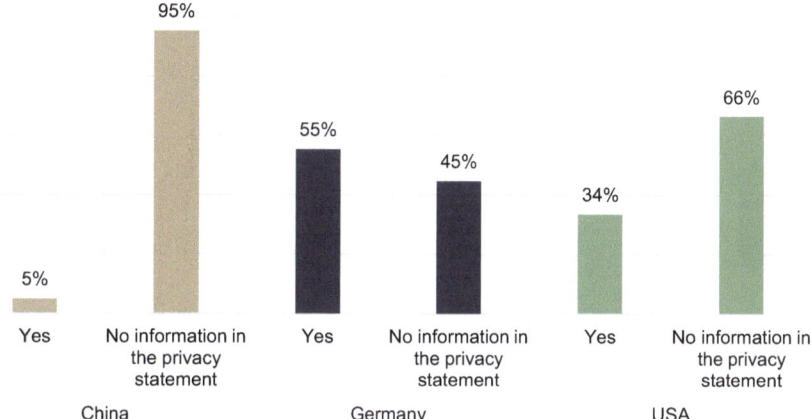

Fig. 4.7 Frequency of privacy statements that differentiate between data collected from crowdworkers and from other groups (clients, visitors to the website). Distinction by country. Number of evaluated privacy statements $N = 416$

& Hornuf, 2019) and most likely results from the fact that the GDPR led to more standardized and boilerplate privacy statements, which no longer address the specific privacy practices of a platform (Dorfleitner et al., 2023). Another reason why platform companies do not provide an exhaustive list of processed data is probably that the privacy statement has to be updated with each new cooperation with a third party, which leads to high transaction costs.

Crowdsourcing platforms are specific in their matching of crowdworkers with crowdsourcers. As Fig. 4.7 shows, especially German (55%), but also U.S. platforms (34%), make an explicit distinction between data processed from crowdworkers and data from other user groups, such as crowdsourcers, clients, and visitors to the website. Only 5% of the Chinese platforms make such a distinction. This result is most likely due to the fact that there is no data protection law specifically related to crowdworkers, or the existing provisions in the field of personal data protection do not refer to crowdworkers. When analyzing whether particular types of crowdsourcing platforms differentiate between the processing of data from crowdworkers and other user groups, we find little difference. As Fig. 4.8 shows, at the extreme, collaborative communities differentiate in 30% of the privacy statements between different user groups, while crowd contests do so in 22% of the privacy statements.

In the following analysis, we investigate the specifically listed types of data the crowdsourcing platforms process according to their privacy statement. As Fig. 4.9 shows, we find that most platforms specifically report which personal data are processed, even though the lists are seldom exhaustive. In a minority of cases (1–2%), it is not clear at all from the privacy statement which personal data is processed. In a more detailed analysis, as reported in Fig. 4.10, we find that most privacy statements list data such as the e-mail address (88%), name (82%), address (72%), phone number (68%), password (63%), and the IP address (62%). This is

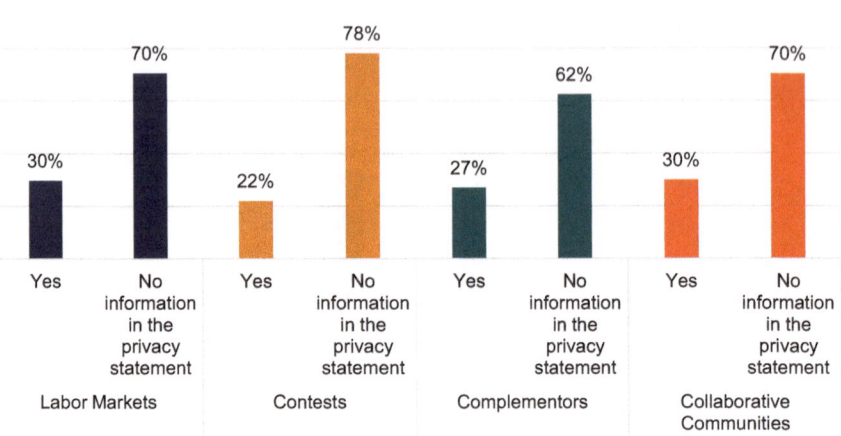

Fig. 4.8 Frequency of privacy statements that differentiate between the data collected from crowdworkers and from other groups (clients, visitors to the website). Distinction by crowdsourcing segment. Number of evaluated privacy statements $N = 416$

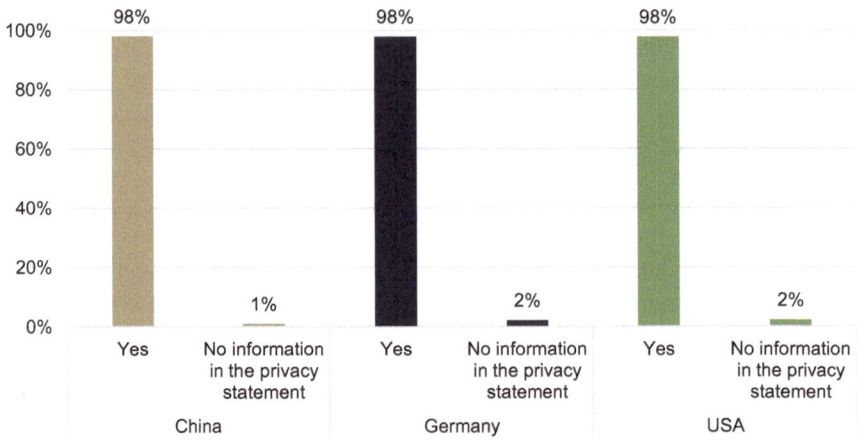

Fig. 4.9 Frequency of privacy statements reporting which personal data are processed. Distinction by country. Number of evaluated privacy statements $N = 416$

followed by bank account details (60%), gender (45%), date of birth (40%), passport and identity card data (36%), occupation and employment information (24%), and GPS and location data (23%). In less than 20% of the privacy statements, further data such as language, family status, or information on insurance were explicitly mentioned.

When comparing the three countries with regard to specific types of data processed, some differences become evident. Chinese privacy statements mention the processing of the email address, bank account details, and the IP address less often, but very frequently refer to the processing of passwords. According to the German privacy statements, the processing of passwords takes place comparatively

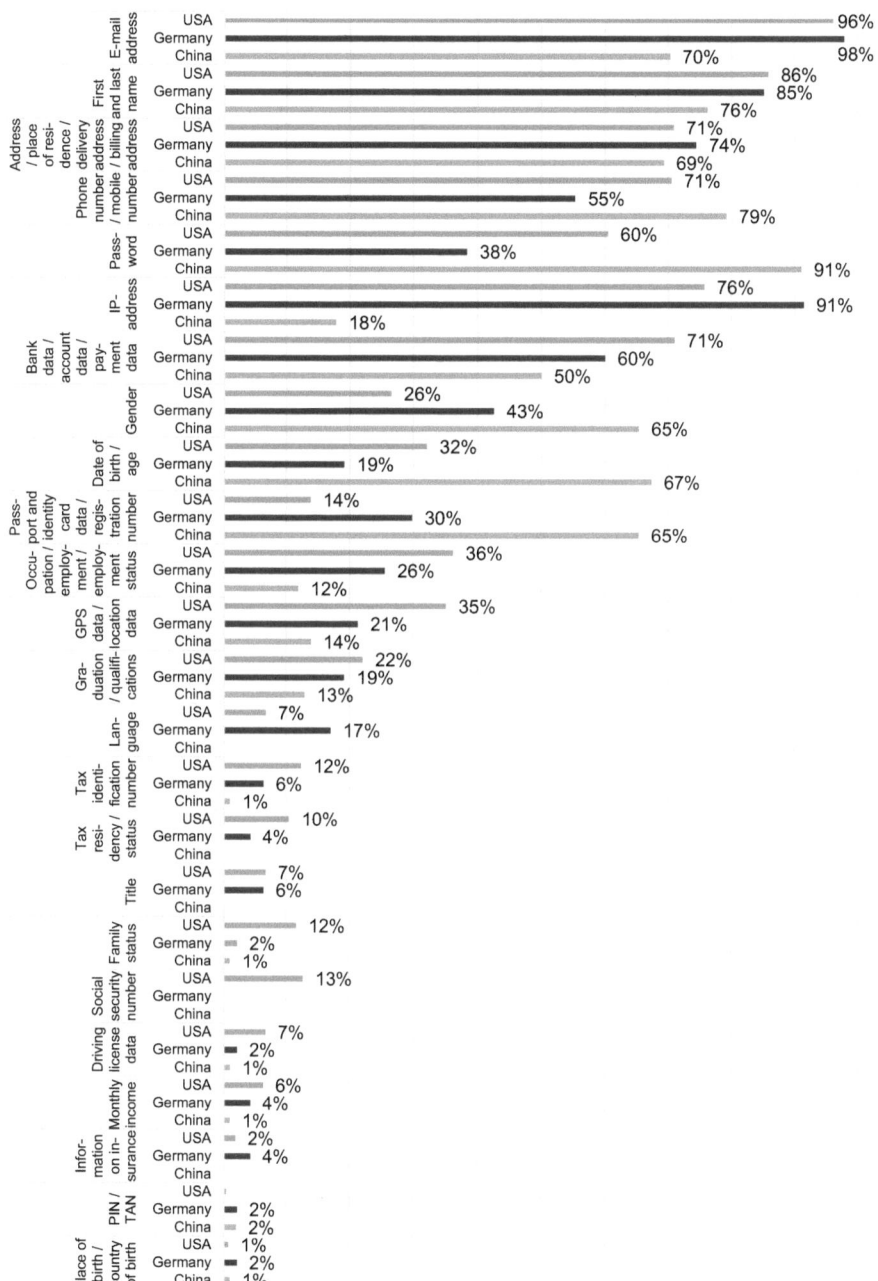

Fig. 4.10 Types of personal data processed according to the privacy statement. Distinction by country. Number of evaluated privacy statements $N = 416$

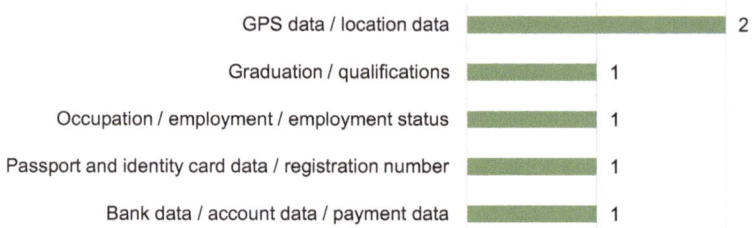

Fig. 4.11 Types of personal data not processed according to the privacy statement. All U.-S. platforms. Number of evaluated privacy statements $N = 268$

less often (38%), but the processing of the IP address significantly more often (91%). Interestingly, and as Fig. 4.11 shows, some U.S. statements report which type of personal data is not processed. Explicitly mentioned were GPS and location data, information about graduation, qualifications, occupation and employment, and passport and ID card data, which reflects that some platforms want to stand out positively from their competitors. For example, the platform Shutterstock emphasizes in its privacy statement that no location-based information is collected from users. The company also advertises that it has the TRUSTe privacy seal. Another reason for specifying which data is not processed is the strict California data privacy law. For example, the platform Ebates mentions in its privacy statement that information such as professional information or education information is generally not collected from California residents, in accordance with California law.

When comparing the listed types of data processed by crowdsourcing platforms across different platform categories, we find that crowd contest platforms report processing IP addresses significantly less often (38%), while they tend to process passport and identity card data more often (49%) relative to the other crowdsourcing platforms. As Fig. 4.12 shows, beside these data types, we do not observe particular differences across platform types. When comparing the listed types of data processed within the German fintech sector, we observe that, for example, bank account details (only 23% in the fintech sector), IP address (only 13% in the fintech sector), and password (only 7% in the fintech sector) are mentioned significantly more often by crowdsourcing platforms (Dorfleitner & Hornuf, 2019, p. 20).

In addition to personal data, the GDPR defined in Art. 9 special categories of personal data, stating that "Processing of personal data revealing racial or ethnic origin, political opinions, religious or philosophical beliefs, or trade union membership, and the processing of genetic data, biometric data for the purpose of uniquely identifying a natural person, data concerning health or data concerning a natural person's sex life or sexual orientation shall be prohibited." According to the privacy statements even of German crowdsourcing platforms, some of these data are nevertheless processed. After the GDPR became binding, processing of this data is only permitted by law in exceptional cases. This is the case, for example, if users have expressly consented to the processing of sensitive data for specific purposes or if the platform company processes data in compliance with its labor and social law obligations (Art. 9 (2) GDPR).

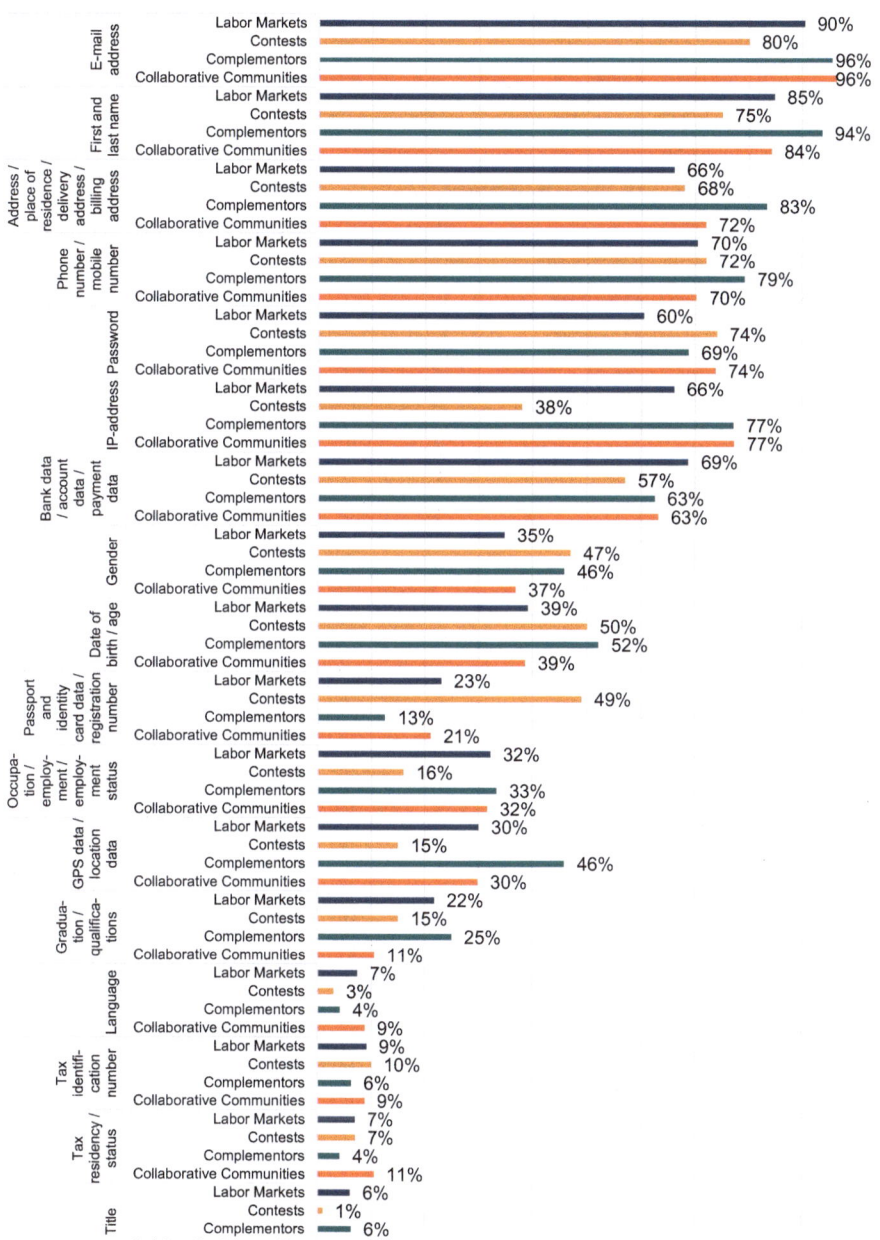

Fig. 4.12 Types of personal data processed according to the privacy statement. Distinction by crowdsourcing segment. Number of evaluated privacy statements $N = 416$

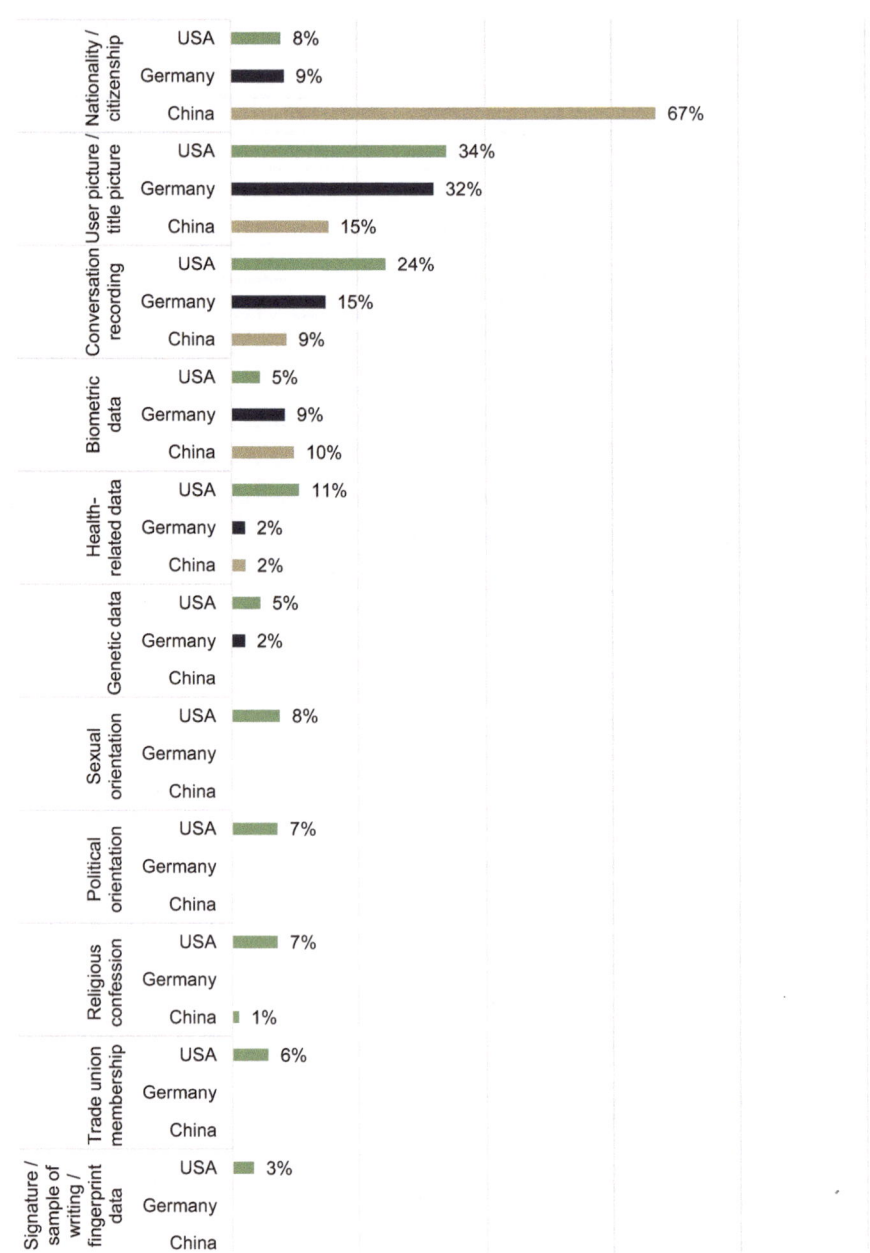

Fig. 4.13 Special categories of personal data processed according to the privacy statement. Distinction by country. Number of evaluated privacy statements $N = 416$

As Fig. 4.13 shows, Chinese crowdsourcing platforms frequently process data about nationality and citizenship (67%), while Germany (9%) and the U.S. (8%) do so much less frequently. All three countries are rather similar in the processing of

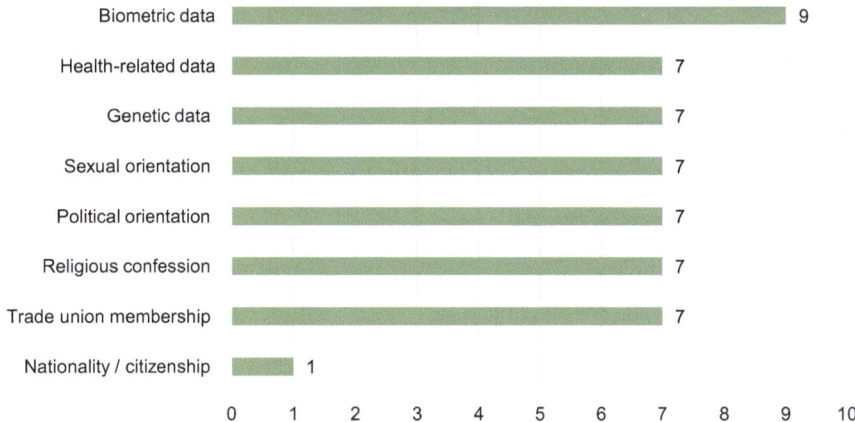

Fig. 4.14 Special categories of personal data not processed according to the privacy statement. All U.S. platforms. Number of evaluated privacy statements $N = 416$

pictures and biometric data, with China processing user pictures the least. However, the U.S. more frequently processes conversation recording data (24%) than the other two countries. In particular U.S. platforms (11%) report to process health-related data, while respectively only 2% of Chinese and German platforms mention in their privacy statements the processing of such data. Platforms from Germany and the U.S., however, note that they would also process genetic data (2% and 5%, respectively). Especially U.S. crowdsourcing platforms further indicate the processing of data related to sexual orientation (8%), political views (7%), religious affiliation (7%), trade union membership (6%), as well as signature, writing sample, and fingerprint data (3%).

Again, and as Fig. 4.14 shows, U.S. platforms explicitly mention which data is not processed by the platforms. Most frequently the privacy statements mention biometric data ($N = 9$), followed by health-related data, genetic data, sexual orientation, political orientation, religious confession, trade union membership (all $N = 7$), and nationality and citizenship ($N = 1$). Thus, while the U.S. platforms are again explicit in stating which data is not processed, they also mention a much larger variety of special categories of personal data that is processed. Chinese crowdsourcing platforms stand out for their processing of nationality and citizenship.

According to the GDPR, an enterprise is "a natural or legal person engaged in an economic activity, irrespective of its legal form, including partnerships or associations regularly engaged in an economic activity." Company data are not personal data and therefore are not subject to the GDPR. However, crowdsourcing platforms process various data related to particular companies and their employees. Moreover, a closer look revealed that some platforms in all three countries collect company information from crowdworkers as solo-self-employed (*Solo-Selbstständige*). As Fig. 4.15 shows, crowdsourcing platforms most often process data related to the

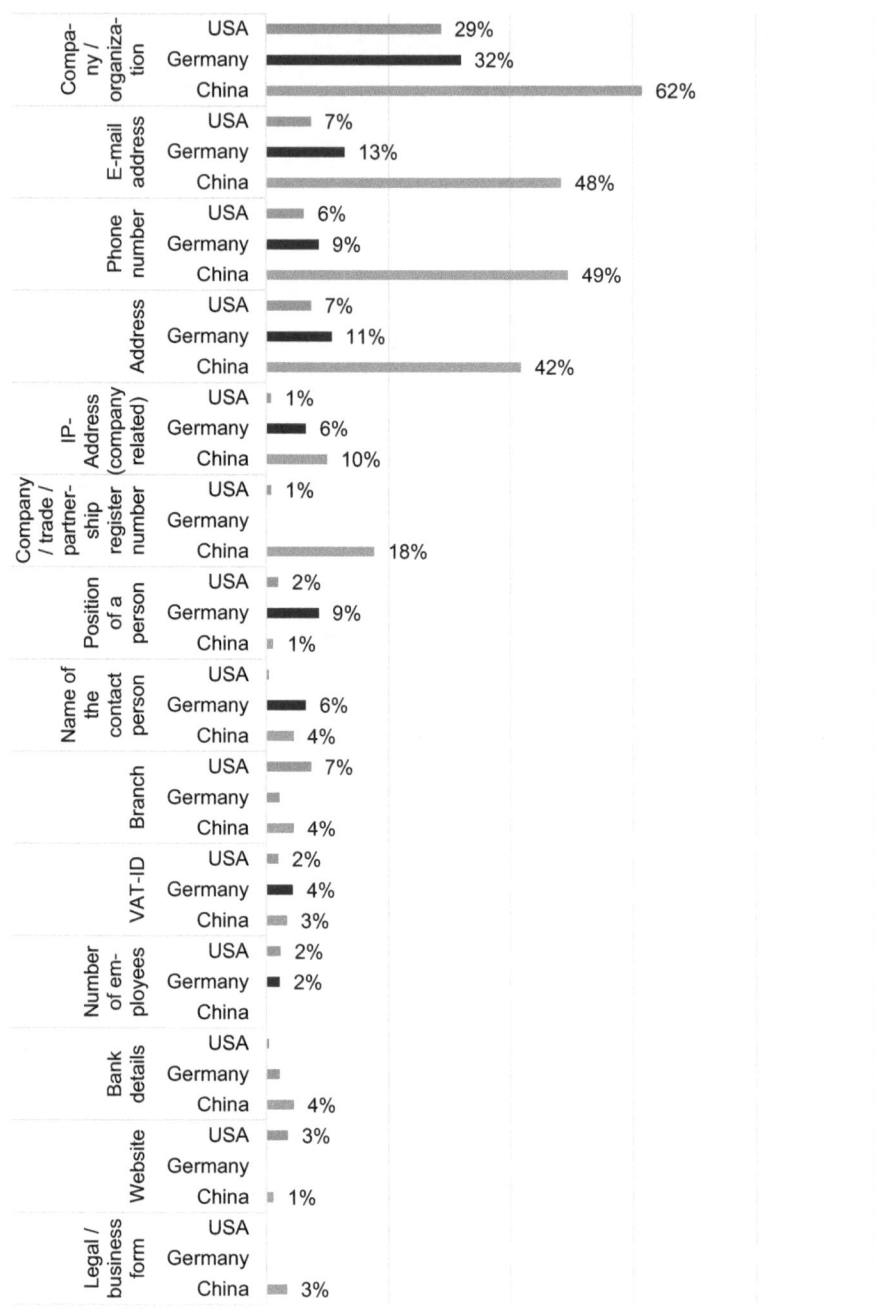

Fig. 4.15 Type of company-related data processed according to the privacy statement. Distinction by country. Number of evaluated privacy statements $N = 416$

company name (41%), e-mail address (23%), phone number (21%), and address (20%). All of these data types are most frequently processed by Chinese platforms and least frequently processed by U.S. platforms. The position of a person in the company and the name of a contact person are on average processed according to 4% of the privacy statements, most frequently by German crowdsourcing platforms. When we compare the processing of this data type, it is evident that this is reported more often by crowdsourcing platforms than by fintech companies in Germany. Only 10% of the privacy statements in the fintech sector reported processing the company name (Dorfleitner & Hornuf, 2019, p. 27).

Because the processing of the IP address was mentioned significantly more often than in the earlier fintech sample of Dorfleitner and Hornuf (2019), we investigate the context in which the IP addresses of the users are processed. As Fig. 4.16 shows, it is predominantly the privacy statements of German crowdsourcing platforms that provide reasons for the processing of the IP address. This finding might result from the fact that the European Court of Justice clarified in its Breyer judgment (C-582/14) that IP addresses are considered data that could be related to individuals and thus are personal data that fall under the scope of the GDPR (see Sect. 3.1 above for details). Similar to the German fintech sector, the German crowdsourcing platforms process the IP address mostly to be able to use web tracking services (62%), social plug-ins (49%), and cookies (45%), to send personalized newsletters (32%), to allow for comments or blog functions of the platform (15%), and to integrate third party content (21%), such as videos, maps, RSS feeds and graphics. If Chinese and U.S. platforms mention a reason for the processing of the IP address, they often name other reasons or refer generally to the storage of data. Often, crowdsourcing platforms argued that processing IP addresses is important for "the security of the company" or "the interest of the user," or mentioned the necessity to share data with law enforcement. Most Chinese and U.S. privacy statements did not specify any reasons for processing IP addresses.

Most of the privacy statements not only stated a reason for storing the IP addresses but also mentioned reasons for processing personal data. Figures 4.17 and 4.18 show that in most privacy statements across all three countries and four crowdsourcing platform categories, a reason was given for the processing of personal data. A mere 1% of the Chinese and 2% of the U.S. platforms did not provide a reason for the processing of personal data; all German platforms mentioned the reason for processing personal data. With respect to the crowdsourcing platform categories, we find that in the case of crowd complementors, a reason for the processing of personal data was given in every privacy statement; however, 9% of the crowd contest platforms did not explicitly mention the reason for processing personal data.

Very similar to the German fintech sector, privacy statements from all three countries and four crowdsourcing segments stated that the processing of data is vital for contractual purposes and the service delivery for users (94%). This could include the simple contacting of users. The second most common reason for the processing of personal data was for marketing, self-promotion, third-party advertising, and the sending of newsletters (74%). Of somewhat less importance was

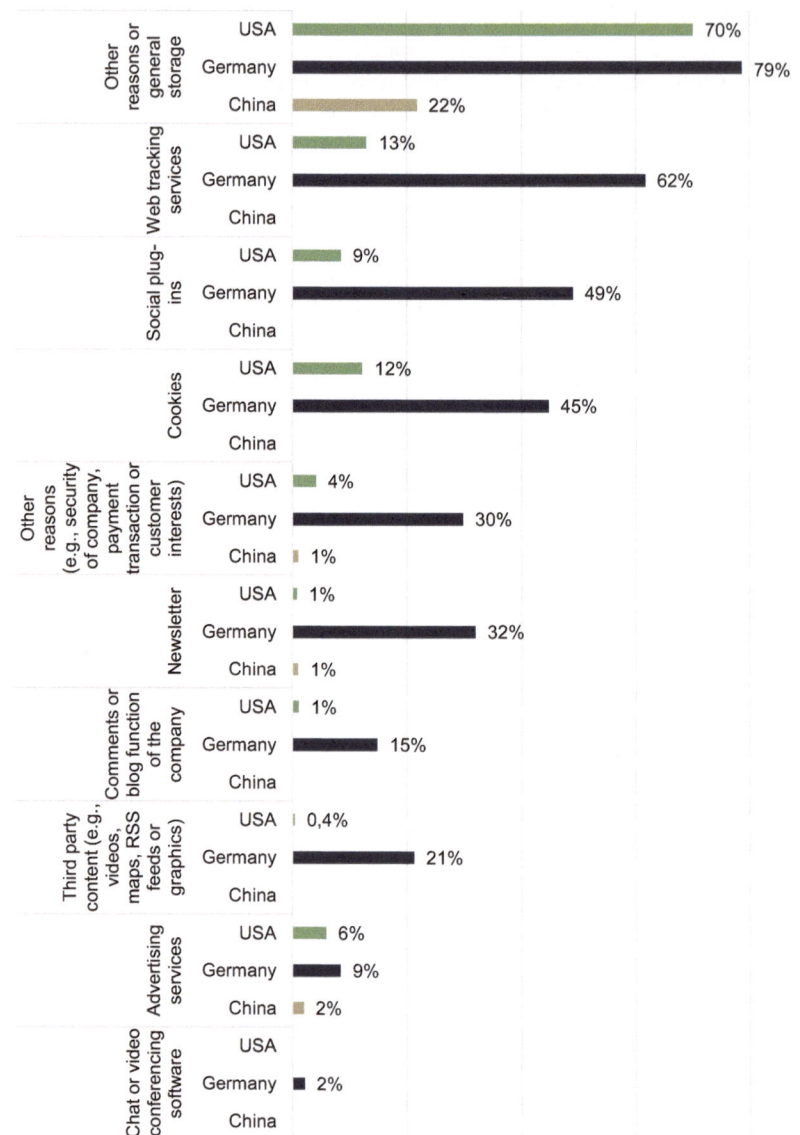

Fig. 4.16 In which contexts are the IP addresses of the users processed? Distinction by country. Number of evaluated privacy statements $N = 416$

customer security and the fulfillment of legal provisions (49%), as well as the creation of user profiles to improve offers (44%). Figures 4.19 and 4.20 provide an overview of the mentioned reasons for the collection of personal data.

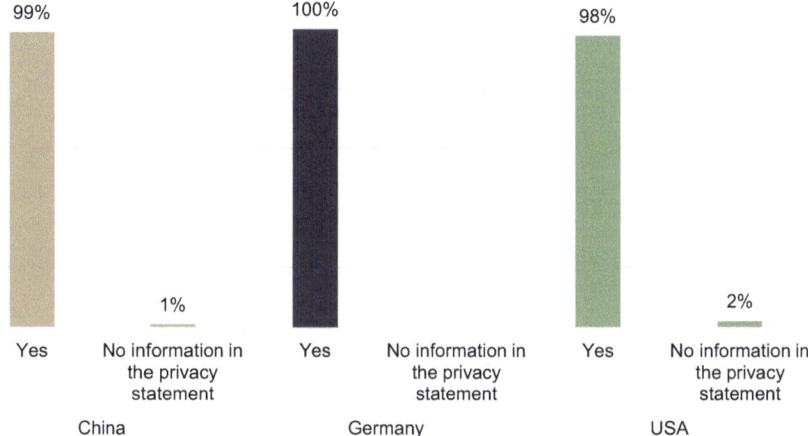

Fig. 4.17 Is a reason given for processing personal data? Distinction by country. Number of evaluated privacy statements $N = 416$

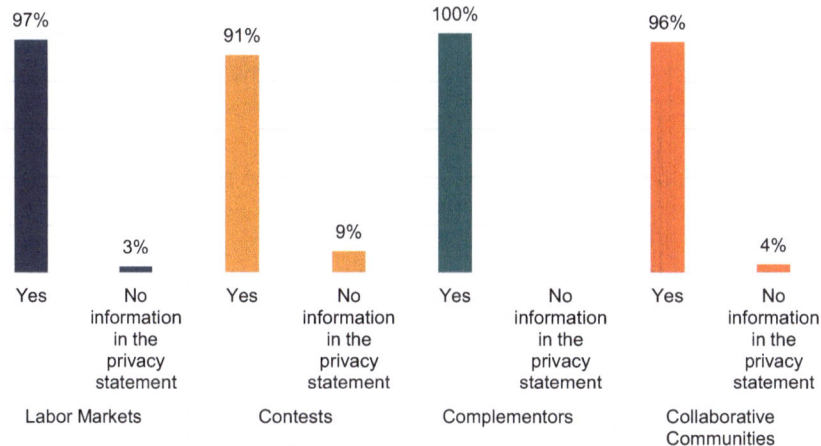

Fig. 4.18 Is a reason given for processing personal data? Distinction by crowdsourcing segment. Number of evaluated privacy statements $N = 416$

According to Art. 15 Sec. 1 GDPR, users have the right to obtain information about the planned period for which their personal data will be stored or, at least, the criteria used to determine that period. Platforms even have an active obligation to provide information regarding the storage period, or at least the criteria that determine the storage period (Art. 13 para. 2 (a), Art. 14 para. 2 (a) GDPR). As Fig. 4.21 shows, with a share of 49% and 60% respectively, around half of the Chinese and German crowdsourcing platforms stated how long they will store users' personal data. For China, this outcome is likely to be influenced by the provisions of relevant laws, such as the Cybersecurity Law or the E-Commerce Law, which require certain

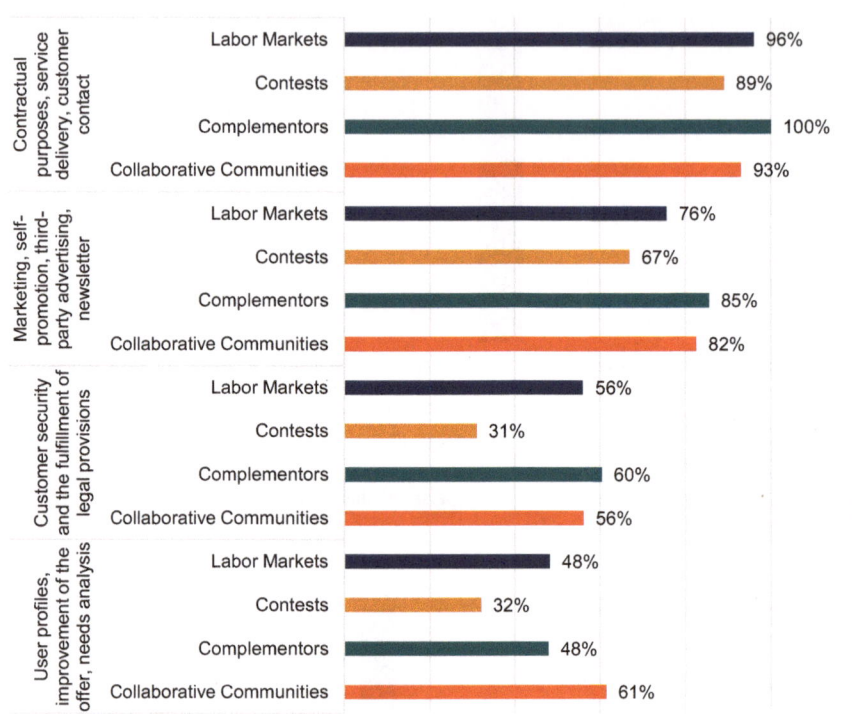

Fig. 4.19 Which reason is given for processing personal data? Distinction by crowdsourcing segment. Number of evaluated privacy statements $N = 416$

data such as log files to be stored for a certain period of time. At the same time, the privacy statements that mention the limited duration of storage periods seem to voluntarily comply with the 2017 version of the Information Security Technology-Personal Information Security Specification as a non-mandatory national standard. The results are more damning for U.S. platforms, which reported in only 10% of the privacy statements how long data are stored or when data are deleted. If we analyze the four crowdsourcing platform categories, crowd contests seem a bit more exemplary, given that 38% report how long they will store users' personal data, which is almost twice as long as any of the other three platform categories (Fig. 4.22). A comparison with the German fintech sector (Dorfleitner & Hornuf, 2019, p. 69) reveals that Chinese and German crowdsourcing platforms report with similar frequency how long data are stored or when data are deleted; however, the U.S. is not a role model in this regard.

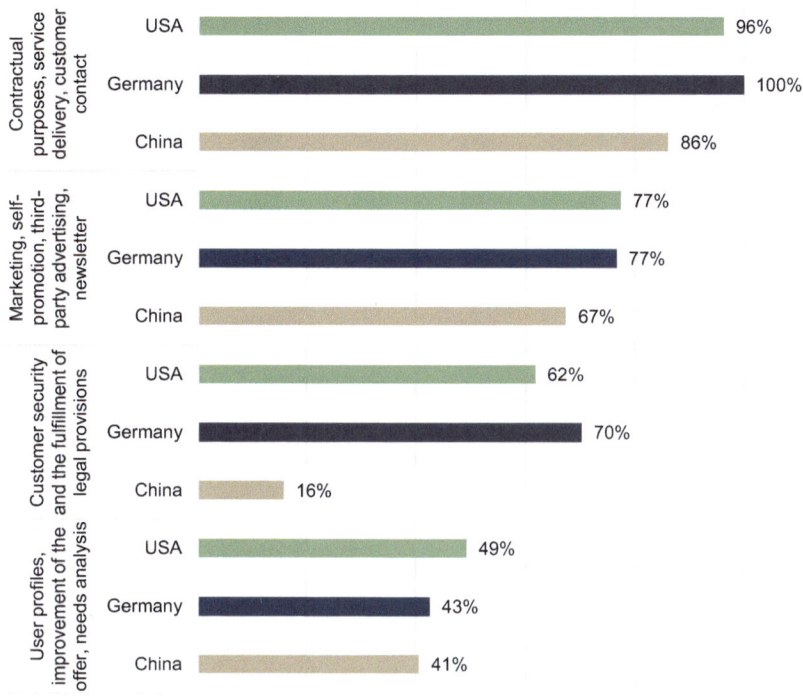

Fig. 4.20 Which reason is given for processing personal data? Distinction by country. Number of evaluated privacy statements $N = 416$

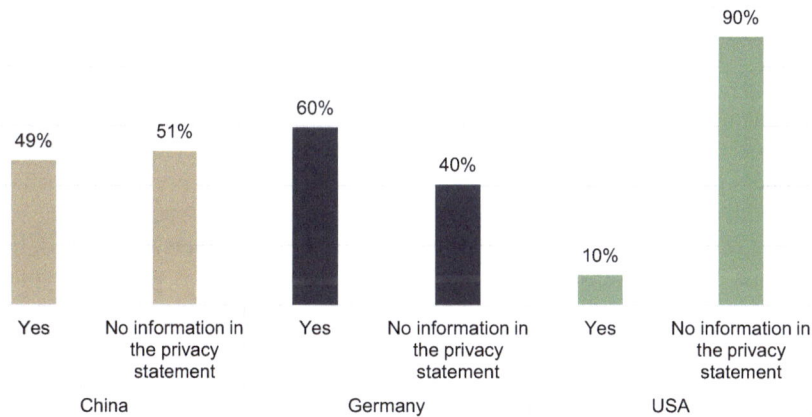

Fig. 4.21 Is it specified how long data are stored or when data are deleted? Distinction by country. Number of evaluated privacy statements $N = 416$

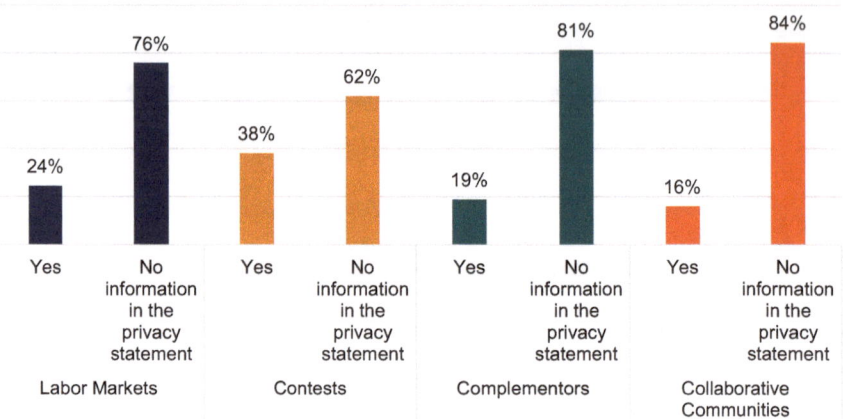

Fig. 4.22 Is it specified how long data are stored or when data are deleted? Distinction by crowdsourcing segment. Number of evaluated privacy statements $N = 416$

4.2   Processing of Data by Third Parties

This sub chapter addresses three research questions: In which form is data processed and potentially forwarded? To whom is this data forwarded? And, if applicable, which third parties provide further information to the platform companies? We again investigate each research question for China, Germany, and the U.S. We also examine differences between different types of crowdsourcing platforms. Finally, we again investigate differences in the processing of data between crowdsourcing platforms and the fintech sector in Germany.

Art. 4 (9) GDPR defines the recipient of data as a "natural or legal person, public authority, agency or another body, to which the personal data are disclosed." Recipients include "third parties" in the narrow legal sense and other possible recipients of data such as data processors that act on behalf of the platform. The business model of some crowdsourcing platforms makes it necessary to share user data with other parties. For example, the crowdworker's name and bank data must be transmitted to a payment service provider so that crowdworkers can be paid. In order to make the data transmission secure, the data not only has to be encrypted, but should also be pseudonymized or anonymized. Pseudonymization removes the immediate identification of a crowdworker while the data is processed. If, for example, a pseudonymized user name can be matched with the real name of the crowdworker later on, the data keep the reference to the crowdworker. If merging of further information does not result in a clear association between the data and a natural person, the data are anonymized. Before investigating the processing of user data by third parties and other recipients more thoroughly, we first analyzed the privacy statements of the crowdsourcing platforms regarding whether they pseudonymize or anonymize the data of their users when processing it. As

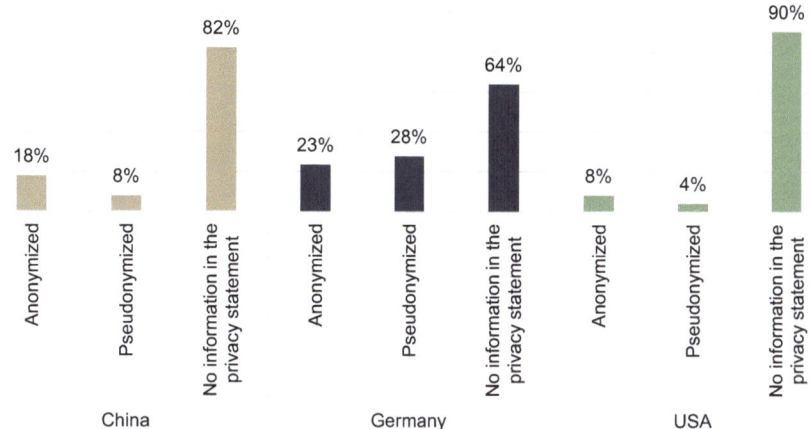

Fig. 4.23 Are data processed anonymously or pseudonymously? Distinction by country. Number of evaluated privacy statements $N = 416$

mentioned above, anonymization and pseudonymization are important tools for companies to implement privacy by design.

In general, the mentioning of pseudonymization or anonymization is rare in all three countries and all four crowdsourcing categories. As Fig. 4.23 shows, in the U.S. only 10% of the privacy statements included a respective note regarding pseudonymization and/or anonymization; in China only 18% mentioned the anonymization of user data, while *de-identification*—the Chinese equivalent for pseudonymization—was explicitly referred to in only 8% of the privacy statements. The pioneer with respect to pseudonymization or anonymization appears to be Germany, where almost every third privacy statement mentioned either of the two privacy practices or both. In comparison with the other three crowdsourcing categories, platforms operating collaborative communities make slightly greater effort to protect data privacy through pseudonymization or anonymization. Overall, 23% of these platforms mentioned either of the two privacy practices or both, as Fig. 4.24 shows.

When we compare these practices with the German fintech sector, it is noticeable that pseudonymization and anonymization are, at least in Germany, used much more frequently on crowdsourcing platforms (only 7% in the fintech sector). This is a remarkable result considering the fact that employee data are almost as sensitive as financial data.

While third parties often receive user data through contracts with the platform, some data can also be accessed on the internet, transferred, and processed without the user knowing. For example, marketing agencies or researchers might gather user data by programming a web crawler or bot that systematically browses the public part of the crowdsourcing website.

Almost half of the crowdsourcing platform companies from the U.S. mentioned that they publish personal data; in Germany that figure is 38% and in China only

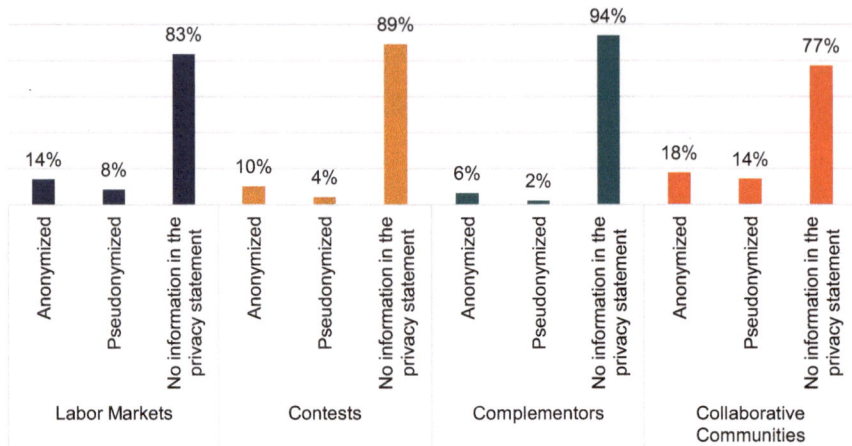

Fig. 4.24 Are data processed anonymously or pseudonymously? Distinction by crowdsourcing segment. Number of evaluated privacy statements $N = 416$

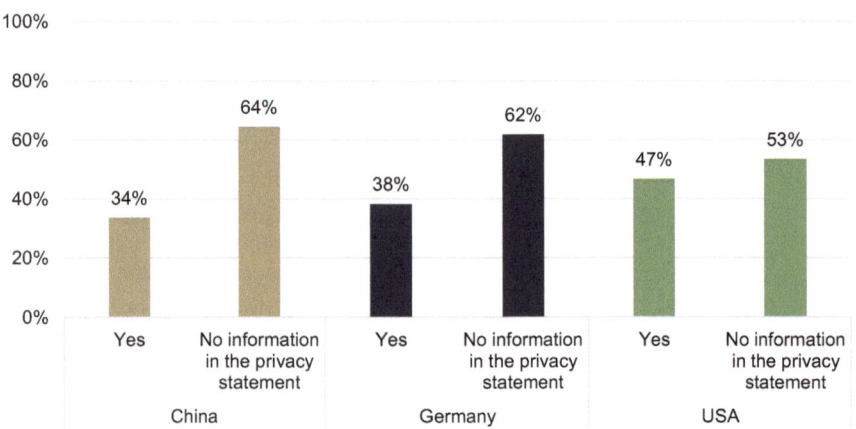

Fig. 4.25 Are personal data published? Distinction by country. Number of evaluated privacy statements $N = 416$

34%, as Fig. 4.25 shows. The majority of crowdsourcing platforms did not include relevant information in the privacy statement in all three countries. It is probably in the nature of the business that collaborative communities make more user data public; however, this is also what we observe empirically. As Fig. 4.26 shows, more than half of the collaborative community platforms publish user data, while only slightly more than one-third do so among the other three crowdsourcing platform categories. In comparison with the German fintech sector, we find that significantly more user data is published through crowdsourcing platforms. Only 18% of companies in the German fintech sector published user data, according to

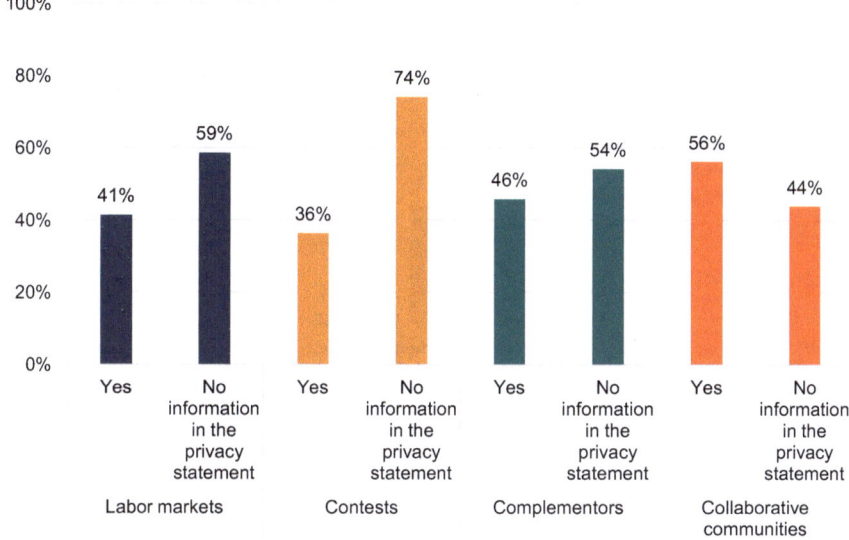

Fig. 4.26 Are personal data published? Distinction by crowdsourcing segment. Number of evaluated privacy statements $N = 416$

privacy statements (Dorfleitner & Hornuf, 2019, p. 71). This could be due to the fact that not all fintech business models have the sort of platform that makes the publication of user data necessary or useful. For example, payment data is only rarely published to the general public.[2]

In a next step, we investigate why user data are published. As Fig. 4.27 shows, especially German and U.S. privacy statements mentioned that the publication of personal data was necessary for a public or nonpublic user profile (17% and 15%, respectively) or for comments or blog functions (36% and 37%, respectively). At 35%, other reasons were most frequently mentioned in Chinese privacy statements. Among them were national security, the protection of the public interest, and mandatory requirements of the relevant government agencies. These reasons could stem from the fact that Chinese data protection law, such as the Cybersecurity Law, emphasizes the importance of national security and public interest. The processing of personal data for comments or blog functions was particularly important for online labor market platforms, as Fig. 4.28 shows. Except for China, the reasons for sharing personal data are generally very similar to the German fintech sector.

Are personal data shared with third parties with the consent of the user? As Fig. 4.29 shows, the privacy statements of Chinese and German crowdsourcing platforms very frequently mention that data is transferred to third parties (81% and 89%, respectively). Only around half of the U.S. platforms state that user data leaves the platform. Moreover, in the U.S. around 1% of the privacy statements explicitly

---

[2]For a noteworthy exception, see www.vicemo.com

Fig. 4.27 For what reason are personal data published? Distinction by country. Number of evaluated privacy statements $N = 416$

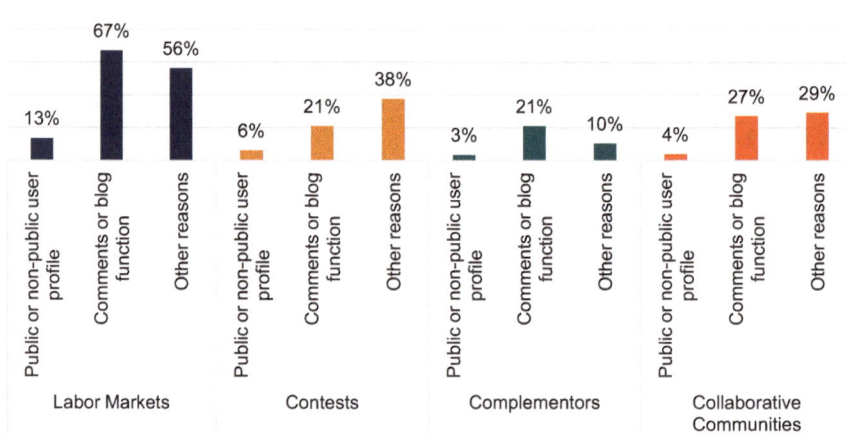

Fig. 4.28 For what reason are personal data published? Distinction by crowdsourcing segment. Number of evaluated privacy statements $N = 416$

mention that personal data is not shared with third parties. There is no such privacy practice in any other country. When investigating the four crowdsourcing categories, we find that all share such data with third parties to approximately the same extent. Crowd complementors never mention explicitly that no personal data is shared with third parties, while all other crowdsourcing categories sometimes do (Fig. 4.30). In the German fintech sector it was never mentioned explicitly that personal data is not transferred to third parties.

In a next step we explicitly test whether personal data of crowdworkers are shared with third parties with consent of the user. One reason to share personal data of

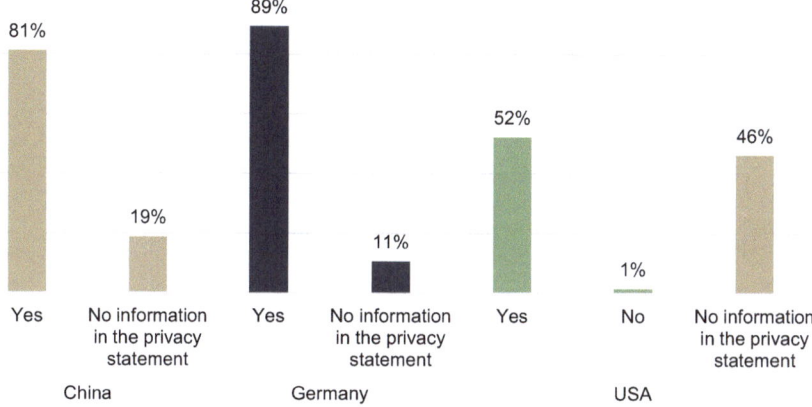

Fig. 4.29 Are personal data shared with third parties with consent? Distinction by country. Number of evaluated privacy statements $N = 416$

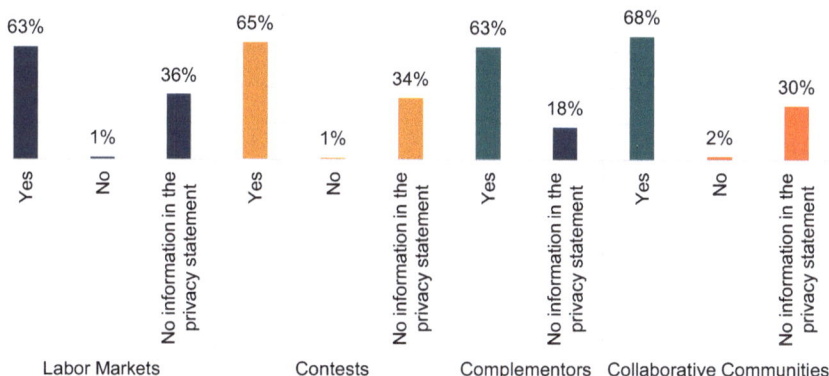

Fig. 4.30 Are personal data shared with third parties with consent? Distinction by crowdsourcing segment. Number of evaluated privacy statements $N = 416$

crowdworkers could be to create a profile of their performance, which is then shared with other platforms the crowdworkers are active on. The sharing of performance and reputation data can be to the advantage of a high-performing crowdworker, but can also be to the detriment of low-performers (Ciotti et al., 2021). As Fig. 4.31 shows, we find that especially German crowdsourcing platforms (28%) mention in their privacy statements that personal data of crowdworkers are shared with third parties, while Chinese and U.S. privacy statements mention such data transfers less frequently (6% and 17%, respectively). Few privacy statements from any of the three countries explicitly mention that they do not share personal data of crowdworkers with third parties. Figure 4.32 presents the frequency by crowdsourcing segment of whether personal data of crowdworkers are shared with crowdsourcing companies or other clients.

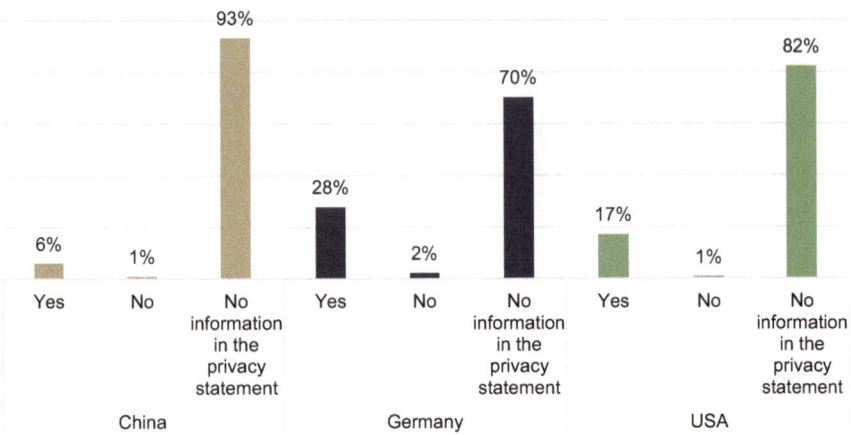

Fig. 4.31 Are personal data of crowdworkers shared with crowdsourcing companies or other clients? Distinction by country. Number of evaluated privacy statements $N = 416$

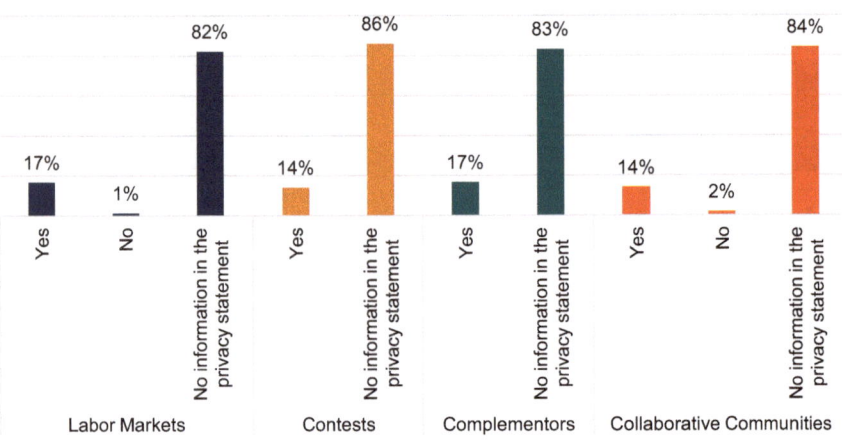

Fig. 4.32 Are personal data of crowdworkers shared with crowdsourcing companies or other clients? Distinction by crowdsourcing segment. Number of evaluated privacy statements $N = 416$

As Fig. 4.33 shows, only a few of the crowdsourcing platforms exhaustively listed in their privacy statement what types of personal data of users they share with third parties. Among Chinese crowdsourcing platforms such an exhaustive list was never provided. However, in Germany and the U.S., approximately half of the platform companies at least provide a non-exhaustive list of the types of personal data they share with third parties (55% and 38%, respectively). The least transparent platform category is crowd contests, in which only 20% provided an exhaustive or non-exhaustive list of user data they share with third parties. When we compare the German fintech segment with the German crowdsourcing segment, it becomes

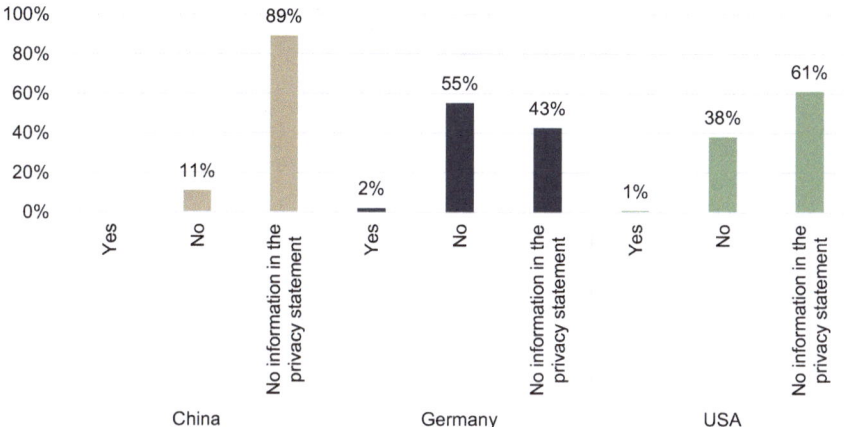

Fig. 4.33 Is there an exhaustive statement on what personal data are shared with third parties? Distinction by country. Number of evaluated privacy statements $N = 416$

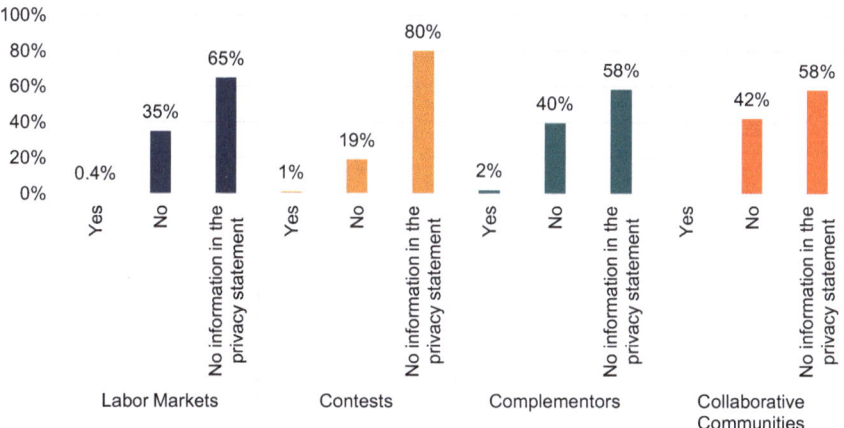

Fig. 4.34 Is there an exhaustive statement on what personal data are shared with third parties? Distinction by crowdsourcing segment. Number of evaluated privacy statements $N = 416$

evident that crowdsourcing platforms much more frequently provide a non-exhaustive list of the data shared with third parties (26% vs. 75%). Figure 4.34 presents the frequency by crowdsourcing category of whether platforms exhaustively listed in their privacy statement what types of personal data of users they share with third parties.

Most privacy statements did not exhaustively clarify what personal data are shared, even though they mentioned the sharing of data with third parties. Figure 4.35 shows what data were shared with third parties. Often, the crowdsourcing platforms shared information about the bank, account, and payment data of the users, or the

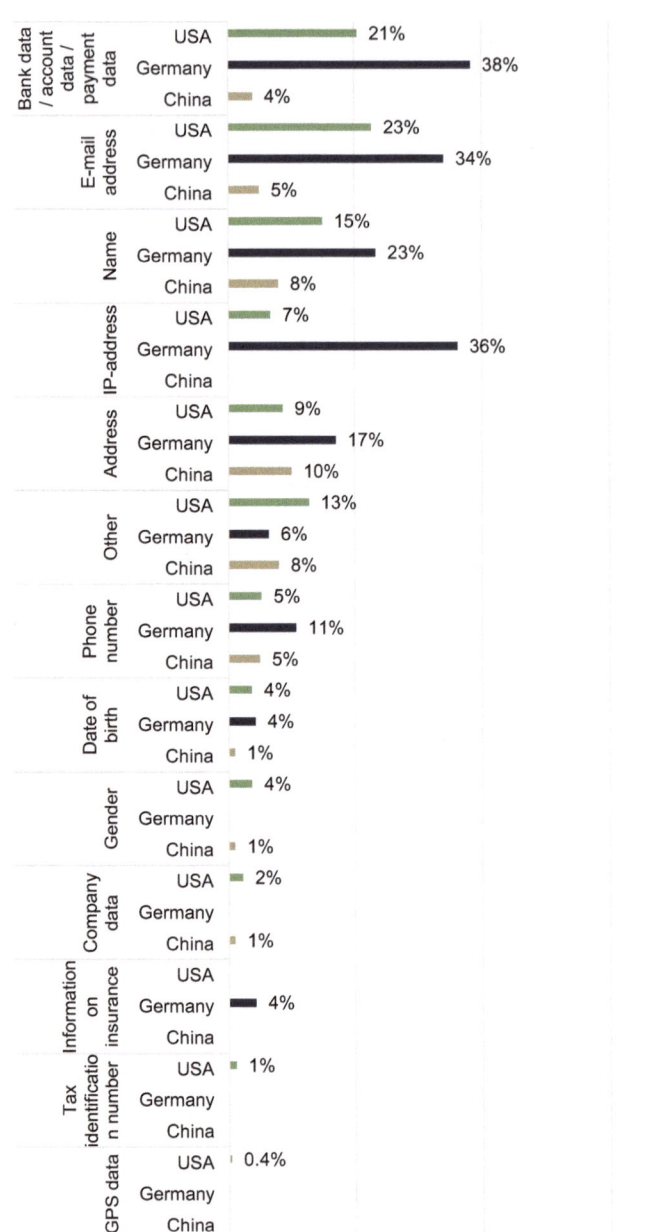

Fig. 4.35 What personal data are shared with third parties? Distinction by country. Number of evaluated privacy statements $N = 416$

e-mail address, name, IP address, and address of the user. In rare cases, U.S. platforms even shared the GPS data of the user with third parties. German platforms generally more frequently specified which data is shared with third parties, while Chinese platforms were least transparent in that respect. A look at the categories of crowdsourcing platforms shows that it depends entirely on the platform category when it comes to which data is passed on to third parties. Payment data is more frequently forwarded by collaborative communities and less often by crowd contests. For crowd complementors, yet again other data types seem to be important. Figure 4.36 presents the frequency of what personal data are shared by crowdsourcing category. If we compare the personal data that is shared with that of the German fintech industry, the list of data looks very similar, although in a different order of rank.

Figure 4.37 and 4.38 give an overview of the reasons for the disclosure of personal data mentioned in the data protection statements. According to the information provided by the crowdsourcing platforms, data was transferred primarily for the purpose of fulfilling contracts, processing orders or providing services, or due to obligations arising from the user relationship (77%), for claims processing (38%), fraud and abuse prevention and risk identification and management (37%), and advertising, marketing and the dispatch of newsletters (34%). Except for the first stated reason for the disclosure of personal data, most other reasons are of higher importance to Chinese and U.S. platforms than to German platforms. Reasons other than those explicitly mentioned for data disclosure appear to have played an important role in Chinese privacy statements. Among them were national and defense security, the protection of public security or vital public interests, and requests of the competent administrative or judicial authorities. The reasons stated most likely stem from the fact that Chinese privacy laws, such as the Cybersecurity Law, emphasize the importance of national security and public interest. Interestingly, the last most frequent reasons mentioned were changes in the corporate structure and the optimization of the business idea or further development of the product. If we compare the reasons for the disclosure of personal data mentioned in the data protection statements with those of the German fintech industry, the stated reasons appear very similar, although the ranking is slightly different.

Figure 4.39 shows that in the U.S. around three-quarters of the privacy statements provide information about whom the user data will be shared with. More rarely, this information is provided in 47% of the German privacy statements and almost never mentioned in Chinese privacy statements. Figure 4.40 shows that crowd complementors very frequently indicate to which third parties data are shared; for crowd labor market companies and collaborative community platforms it is only about half. For crowd contest platforms only 25% of the privacy statements are transparent about the destination of the data exchange. If we compare the Germany privacy statements with those of the fintech sector, it turns out that crowdsourcing platforms are on average slightly less transparent about whom the user data will be shared with. Overall, 54% of the companies in the fintech sector revealed this information (Dorfleitner & Hornuf, 2019, p. 75).

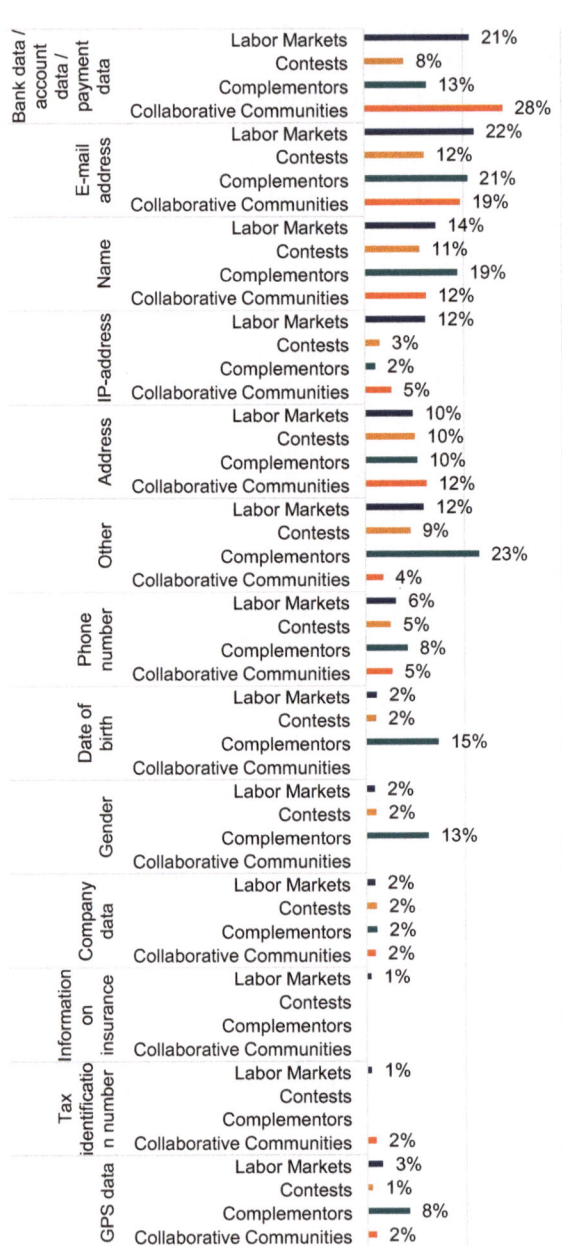

Fig. 4.36 What personal data are shared with third parties? Distinction by crowdsourcing segment. Number of evaluated privacy statements $N = 416$

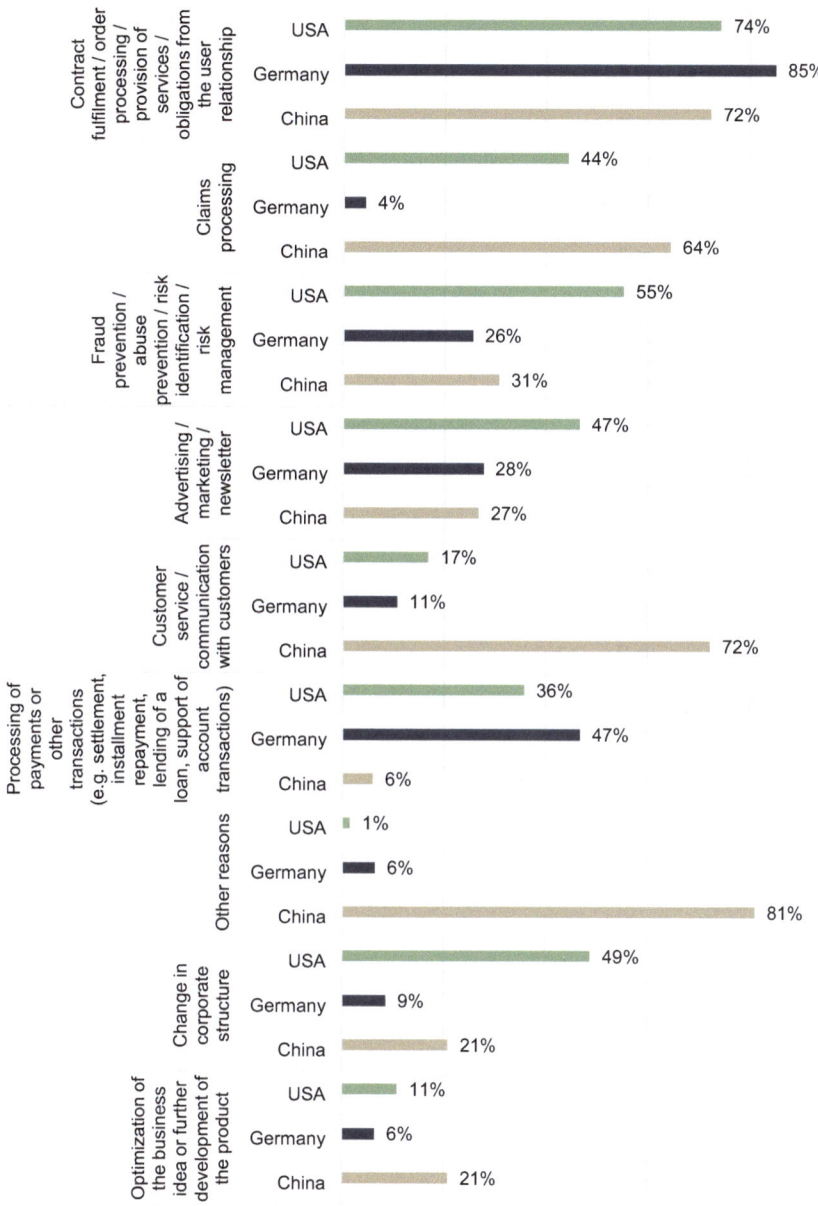

Fig. 4.37 For what purpose are personal data shared with third parties? Distinction by country. Number of evaluated privacy statements $N = 416$

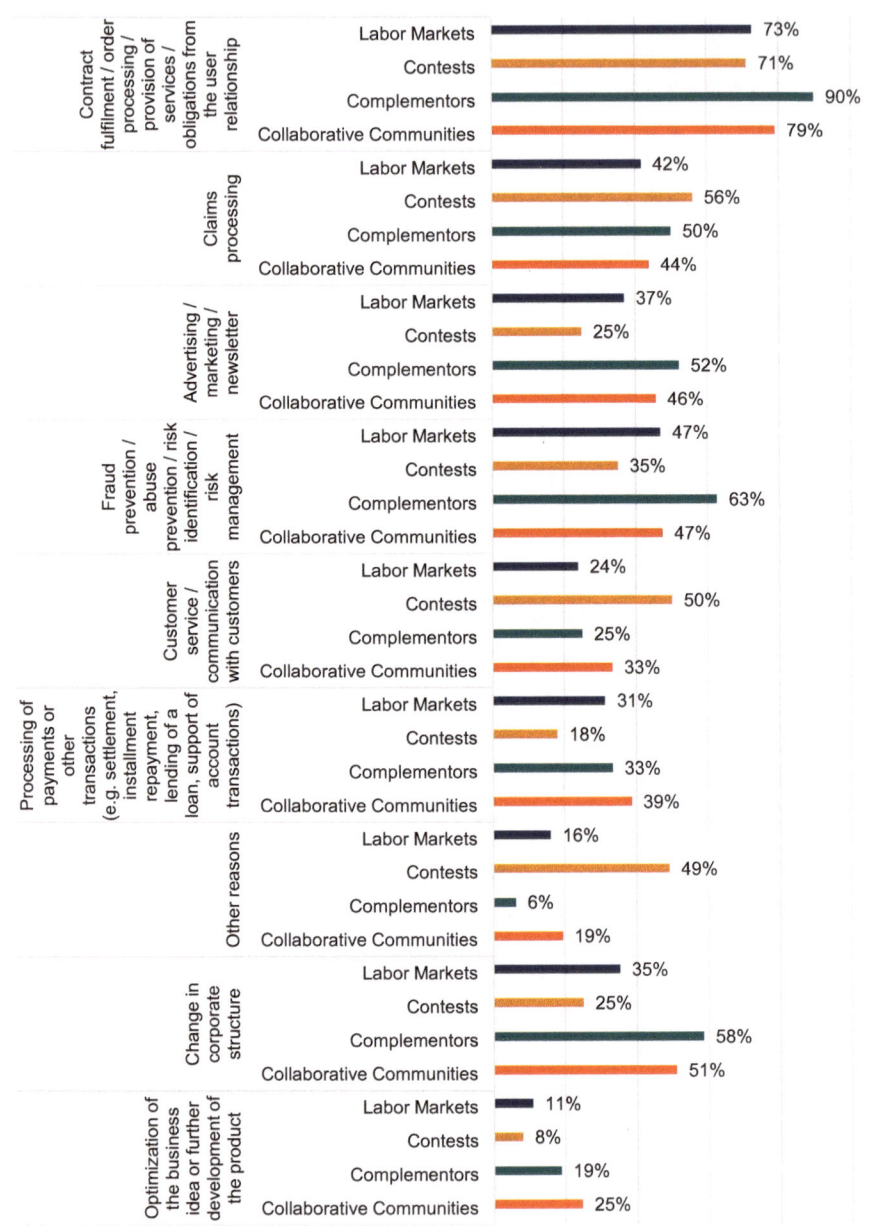

Fig. 4.38 For what purpose are personal data shared with third parties? Distinction by crowdsourcing segment. Number of evaluated privacy statements $N = 416$

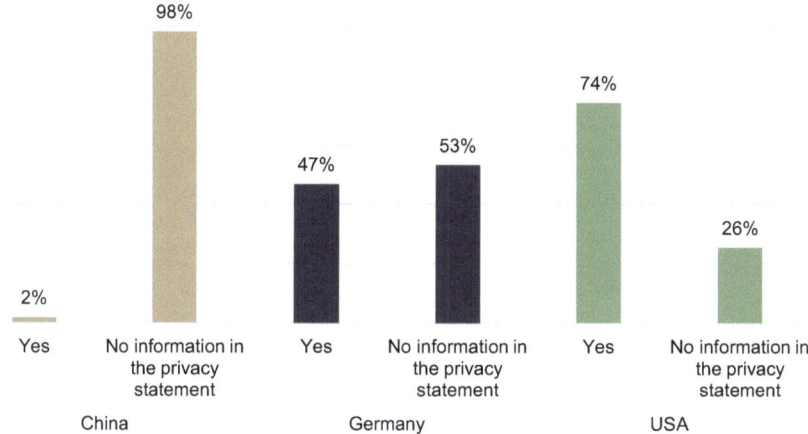

Fig. 4.39 Is it indicated to which third parties data are shared? Distinction by country. Number of evaluated privacy statements $N = 416$

While often the list of whom the user data will be shared with was not exhaustive, the crowdsourcing platforms also often stated, as Fig. 4.41 shows, that users' personal data are passed on to third parties "only in exceptional cases." This was named in around three-quarters of the Chinese and German privacy statements and somewhat less frequently in U.S. privacy statements (only 40%). Crowd contests and collaborative community platforms named this reasoning for sharing personal data with third parties slightly more often, whereas crowd complementors only used it in less than one-third of the privacy statements (Fig. 4.42).

Some privacy statements also mention that information is not only shared with third parties but also collected by the crowdsourcing platforms from third parties and linked to the data of their own users. Figure 4.43 shows that 29% of the U.S. privacy statements and 22% of the Chinese privacy statements mentioned that data from third parties is collected. The reasons mentioned for reaching out to third parties were, for example, identity and creditworthiness inquiries, and the merging and comparison with social media and marketing data of the user. It is worth mentioning that some U.S. platforms explicitly note that employers or background reporting companies are contacted to obtain information on skills and other characteristics of crowdworkers.[3] However, the third party was explicitly named in only 4% and 9%, respectively. German privacy statements only indicated in 11% that data from third

---

[3] For example, the platform Appen states in its privacy statement: "We may also collect personal data from third parties such as your employing organization, regulatory authorities, recruitment agencies [. . .]." The company Alegion emphasizes in its privacy policy: "We may collect information about you from other sources and add it to the other information we collect, directly or automatically, about you. This information may include [. . .] information about workers, such as user name and skills, from a Worker's employing entity, accreditations, qualifications, education, and other relevant information."

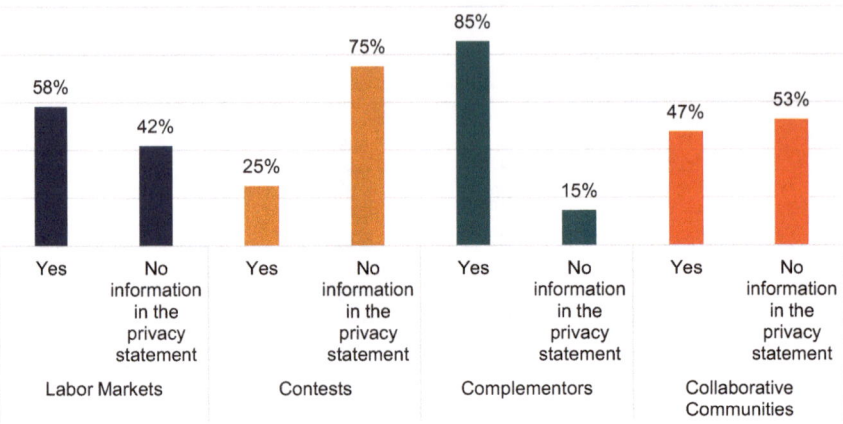

Fig. 4.40 Is it indicated to which third parties data are shared? Distinction by crowdsourcing segment. Number of evaluated privacy statements $N = 416$

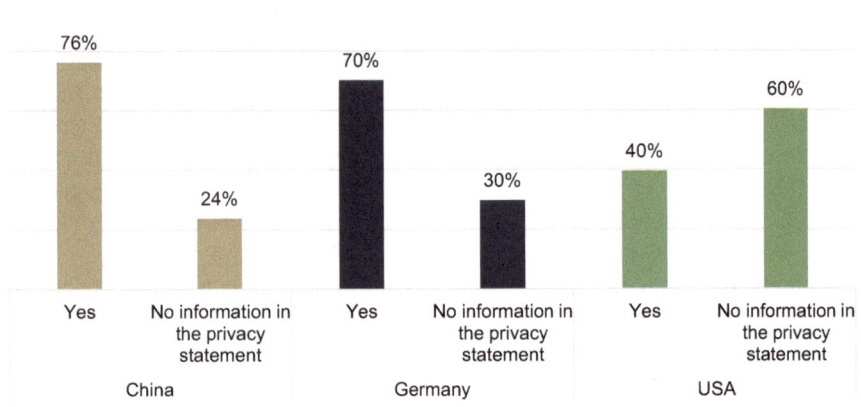

Fig. 4.41 Is it stated that personal data will only be passed on to third parties in exceptional cases? Distinction by country. Number of evaluated privacy statements $N = 416$

parties was collected, while only explicitly naming the third party in 9% of the privacy statements. As Fig. 4.44 shows, crowd complementors and collaborative communities more frequently collected data from third parties and merged them with existing user data, especially when compared to crowd contest platforms. For all platform categories, the third party was only rarely explicitly named. This picture is very much in line with the German fintech sector.

As Fig. 4.45 shows, especially in Germany the crowdsourcing platforms (72%) stated in their privacy statements that they integrated social plug-ins in their services.

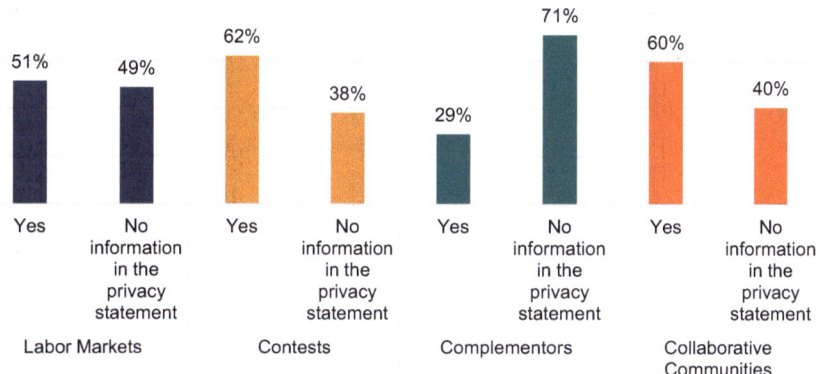

Fig. 4.42 Is it stated that personal data will only be passed on to third parties in exceptional cases? Distinction by crowdsourcing segment. Number of evaluated privacy statements $N = 416$

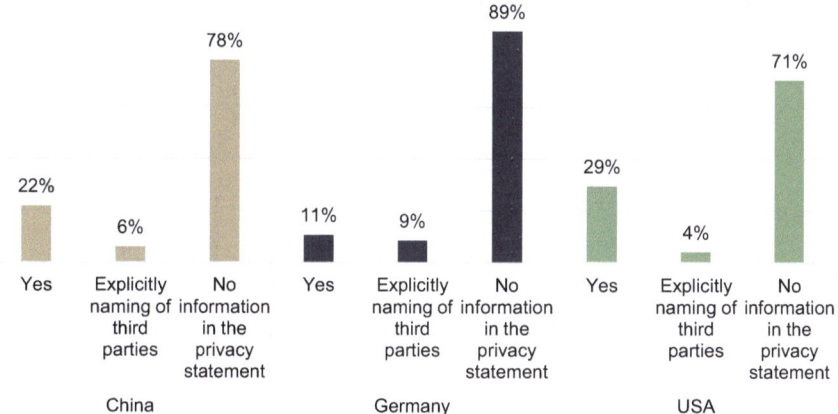

Fig. 4.43 Are personal data collected from third parties? Distinction by country. Number of evaluated privacy statements $N = 416$

Social plug-ins, which provide access to third parties, help distribute the content of the users or the crowdsourcing platform. Well known examples are Facebook's "Like" button and Twitter's "Tweet" button, which allow users to share the content from the crowdsourcing platform on the social media website. Information is transferred from the browser of the user to the respective third parties. In the U.S., privacy statements mention the use of social plug-ins less often (44%) and in China social plug-ins are even less popular, which might result from the fact that services are often based on mobile applications and Facebook and Twitter are banned in

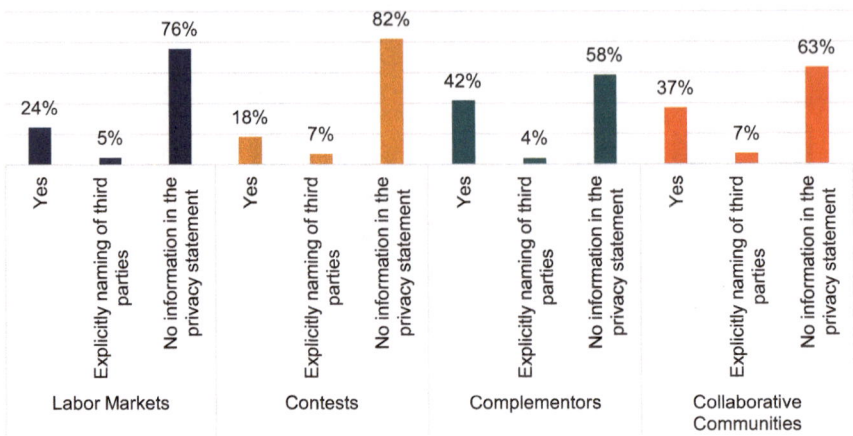

Fig. 4.44 Are personal data collected from third parties? Distinction by crowdsourcing segment. Number of evaluated privacy statements $N = 416$

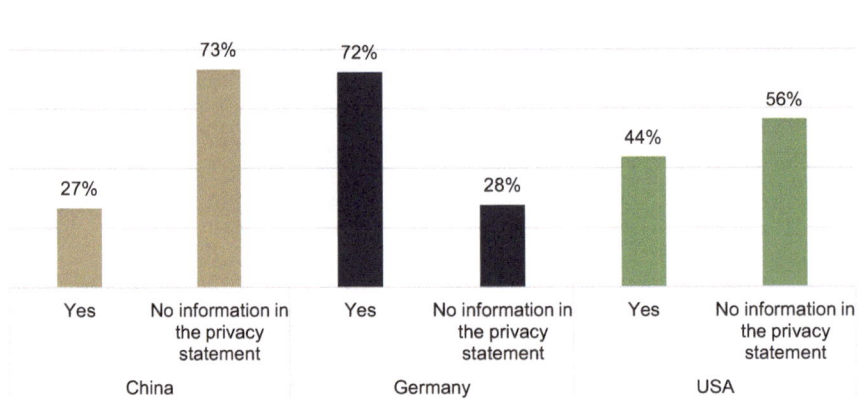

Fig. 4.45 Does the company's website use social plug-ins or are third-party services integrated? Distinction by country. Number of evaluated privacy statements $N = 416$

China. Although some Chinese platforms collect the data of WeChat or QQ accounts from platform users as a requirement to log into the websites or apps,[4] their privacy policies do not mention the use of such social plugins at all. Collaborative communities and crowd complementors use social plug-ins slightly more often than the other two crowdsourcing categories, as Fig. 4.46 shows.

---

[4]For example, the authors had to enter QQ account information when they wanted to log into the K68 platform. However, K68's privacy statement does not mention that the platform processes QQ account information.

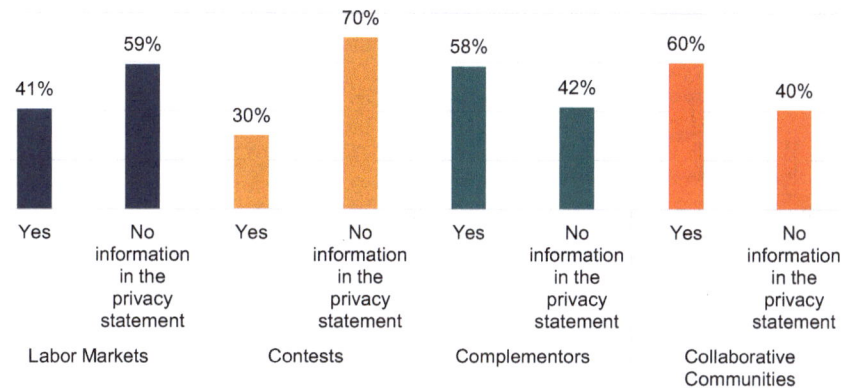

Fig. 4.46 Does the company's website use social plug-ins or are third-party services integrated? Distinction by crowdsourcing segment. Number of evaluated privacy statements $N = 416$

Figure 4.47 lists the companies whose social plug-ins were used by crowdsourcing companies. Around half of German crowdsourcing companies stated in their privacy statement that they used a social plug-in from Facebook (64%), Twitter (43%), LinkedIn (36%), and YouTube (32%). Social plug-ins from Google+, Xing, Instagram, Pinterest, Slideshare, Myspace, Shariff, Snapchat and Widgets were less frequently included (less than 50% each). Chinese platforms only rarely mentioned the use of plug-ins from companies such as WeChat, Weibo, QQ, Ding Talk, Bajie IM, and MSN (no more than 10% each).

As Fig. 4.48 shows, especially German crowdsourcing companies (94%) stated in their privacy statement that they use tracking services to collect and evaluate data on the behavior of users on their website. Web tracking enables crowdsourcing platforms to track which internet sites users visit before or at the same time, which content they call up on the website, how often and for how long they view this content, and where they subsequently migrate to (Dorfleitner & Hornuf, 2019). Four out of five U.S. privacy statements mentioned the use of tracking services; in China it was not even two-thirds. Collaborative communities and crowd complementors mentioned the use of tracking services more often than crowd labor markets and crowd contest platforms, as indicated by Fig. 4.49. Finally, and as Fig. 4.50 shows, some privacy statements mentioned the use of more than one web tracking service. The most popular service in the U.S. and Germany is Google Analytics, which is in line with usage behavior in the German fintech sector. Other services that are not reported in Fig. 4.51 (because they were only named in one privacy statement) are: UserVoice, Heatmaps, LinkedIn Analytics, NewRelic, Unbounce, HQ, Jetpack, GetSiteControl, Kissmetrics, Mandrill, Tumblr, Segmento.io, Google Optimize, and CrazyEgg for Germany; and NewRelic, Mouseflow, Inspectlet, Unbounce,

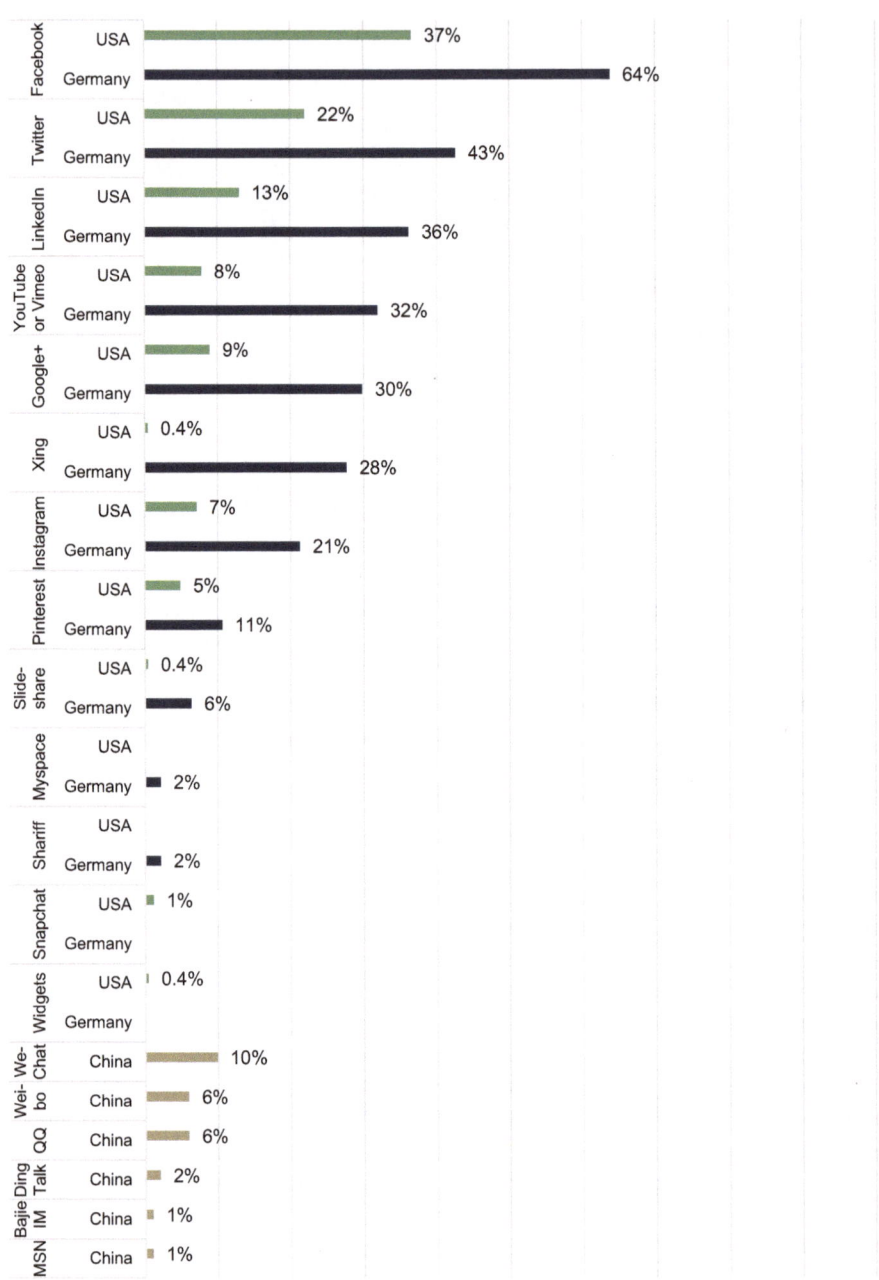

Fig. 4.47 Does the company's website use social plug-ins or are third-party services integrated? Distinction by country. Number of evaluated privacy statements $N = 416$

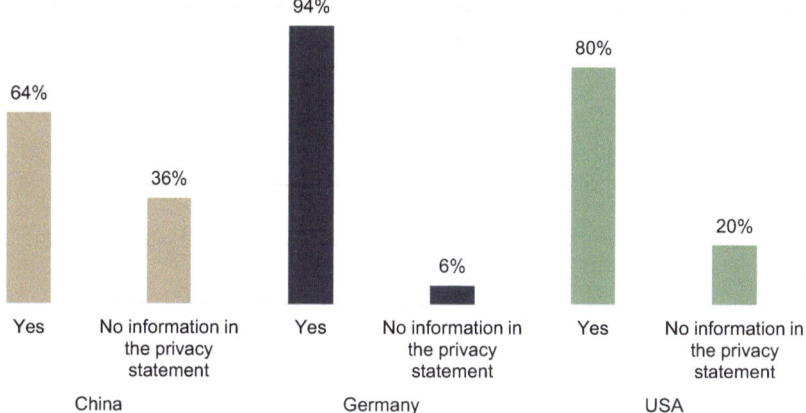

Fig. 4.48 Are behavioral, usage, or movement data processed or are tracking services used? Distinction by country. Number of evaluated privacy statements $N = 416$

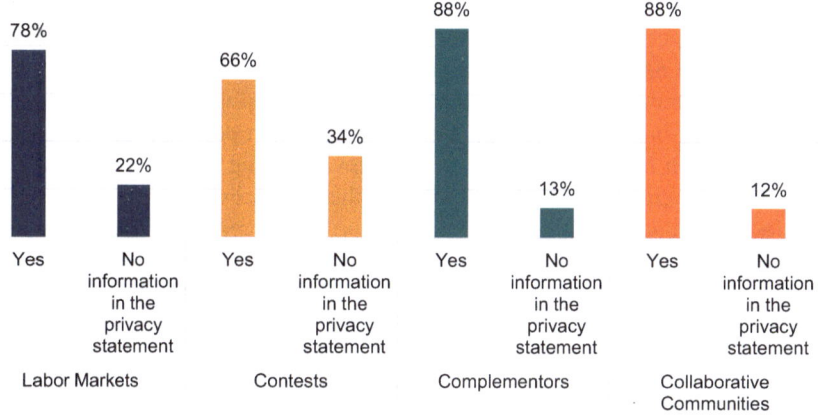

Fig. 4.49 Are behavioral, usage, or movement data processed or are tracking services used? Distinction by crowdsourcing segment. Number of evaluated privacy statements $N = 416$

Optimizely, MaxMind, GetSiteControl, Flurry, Twilio, Kissmetrics, Newrelic, Tumblr, and Criteo for the U.S.

We identified different advertising services in the privacy statements that crowdsourcing companies use to increase user activity on the platform. As Fig. 4.52 shows, some crowdsourcing platforms used up to nine different advertising services. Figure 4.53 lists the advertising services mentioned in the privacy statements. Of the services, Google, LinkedIn, Facebook, AdRoll, Bing Ads, and Twitter were frequently used in Germany and the U.S. Generally, the evidence shows that

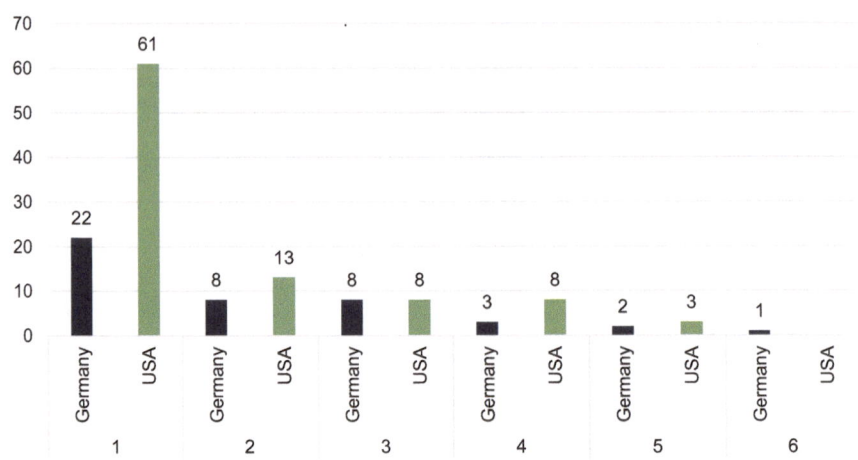

Fig. 4.50 Number of analytics services used by companies. Distinction by country. Number of evaluated privacy statements $N = 416$

crowdsourcing companies remain rather silent about the advertising services they use. The German fintech sector has been somewhat more transparent in that respect.

The purpose of cookies is, among others, to store information associated with a website locally on the computer of the user for a certain period and then to transmit this information back to the server of the crowdsourcing platform on request. The website of the crowdsourcing platform can then be individualized for the user, if cookies allow authenticating the user when he or she returns to the platform web page. As Fig. 4.54 shows, German and U.S. platforms frequently mention the use of cookies in their privacy statements (96% and 90%, respectively); Chinese platforms report the use of cookies significantly less often (27%). The remaining crowdsourcing platforms did not provide any information on the use of cookies. German and U.S. platforms also differentiate between the use of temporary and permanent cookies, while Chinese privacy statements do not make such a distinction. The evidence shows that the use of both temporary and permanent cookies is mentioned more frequently in German (49% and 40%) than in U.S. (27% and 24%) privacy statements. In the remaining privacy statements, the crowdsourcing platforms provided no information about the type of cookies used. Some companies used both temporary and permanent cookies. Figure 4.55 shows how often the use of cookies is mentioned among the different crowdsourcing platform categories. Crowd contests mention the use of cookies less frequently than the other platforms categories. Generally, the use of cookies among German crowdsourcing platforms is very similar to the use of cookies in the German fintech sector.

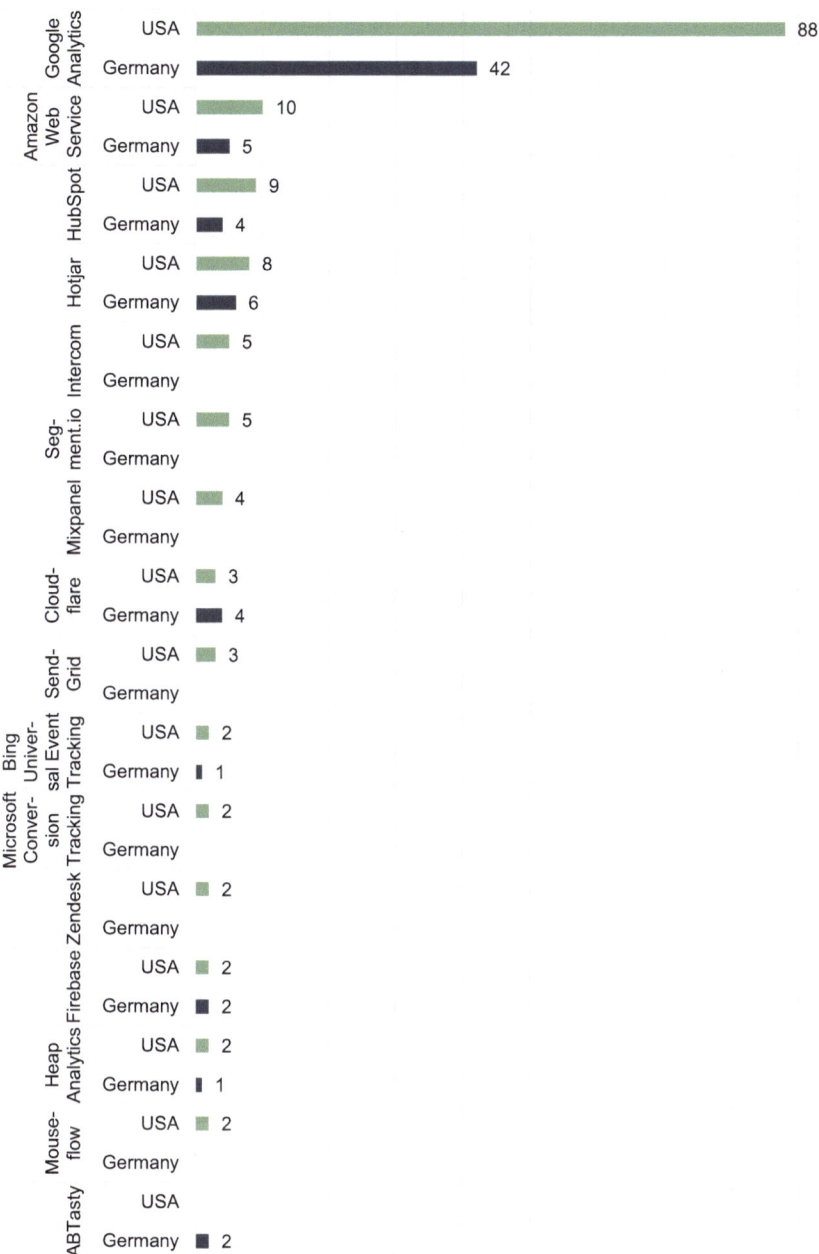

Fig. 4.51 Frequency of analytics services used by companies. Distinction by country. Number of evaluated privacy statements $N = 416$

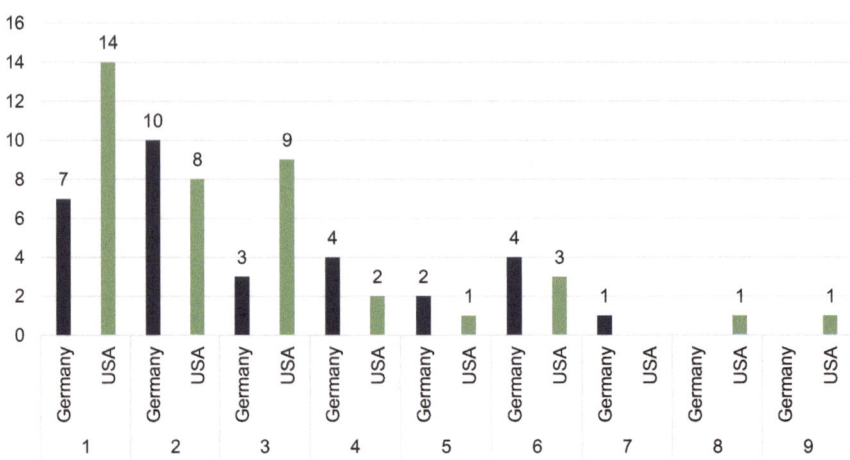

Fig. 4.52 Number of advertising services used by companies. Distinction by country. Number of evaluated privacy statements $N = 416$

Finally, data were also transmitted to the crowdsourcing platforms by the user's browser, smart phone or tablet through server log files. As Fig. 4.56 shows, in all three countries, fewer than one-fifth of the crowdsourcing platforms provided an exhaustive list of the data processed. In fact, in China an exhaustive list of the data processed was never provided. Platforms in the U.S. (78%) and Germany (79%) at least provided a non-exhaustive list of the data processed through log files, while in China only 31% of the privacy statements provided such a list. As Fig. 4.57 shows, collaborative communities and crowd complementors more frequently provide a non-exhaustive list of the data processed via log files, while crowd contests only rarely do so. Figures 4.58 and 4.59 show the data processed using log files. In general, Chinese platforms less frequently name the type of data processed through log files, while German and U.S. platforms often mention the IP address or domain name, referrer URL or referring website, and the browser type and version. The general geographic location was also frequently named in U.S. privacy statements.

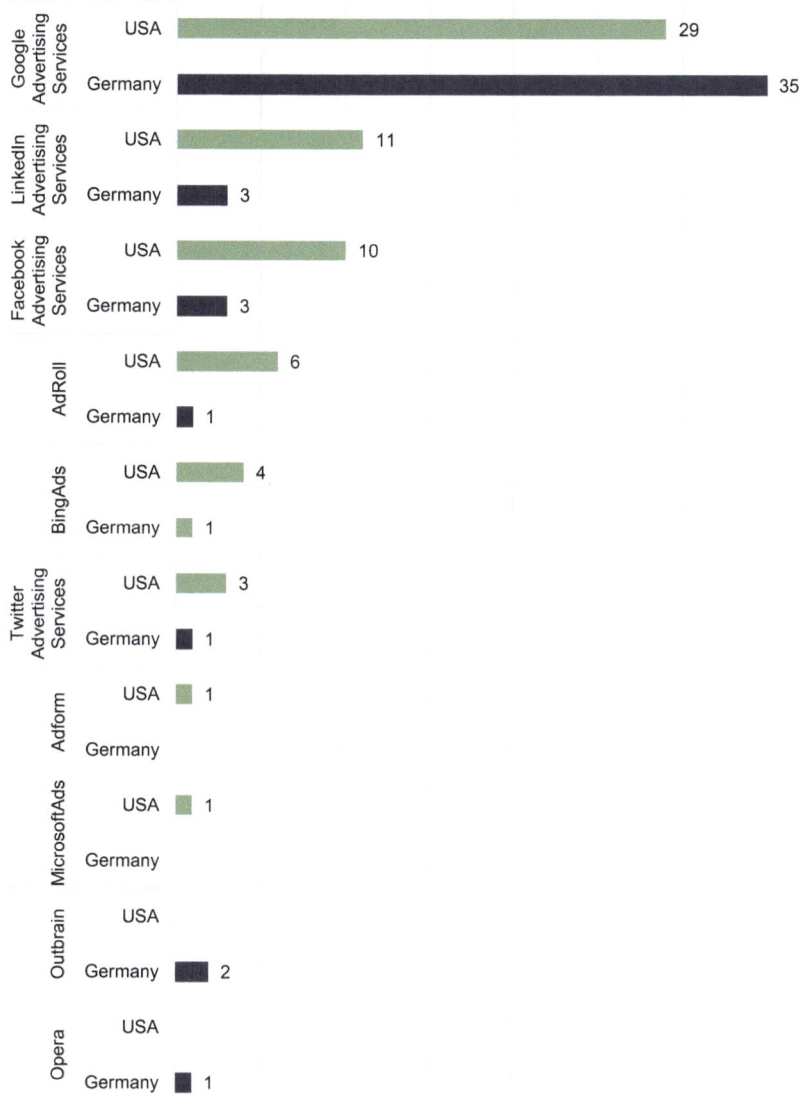

Fig. 4.53 Frequency of advertising services used by companies. Distinction by country. Number of evaluated privacy statements $N = 416$

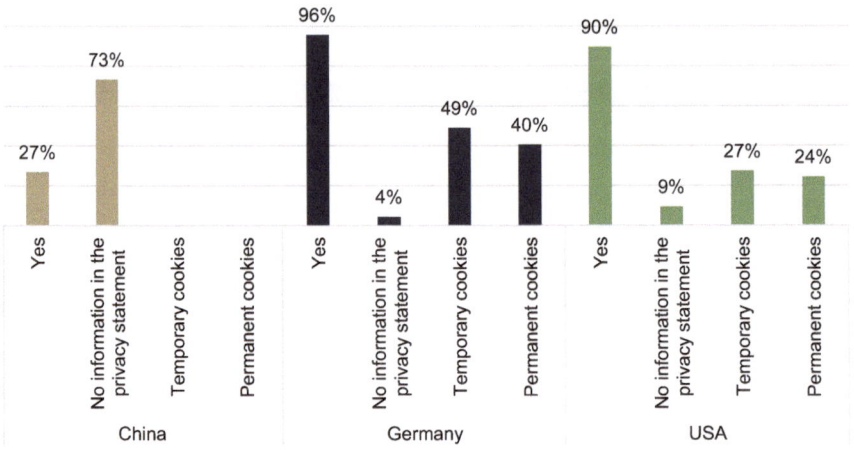

Fig. 4.54 Does the company provide information on the use of cookies? Distinction by country. Number of evaluated privacy statements $N = 416$

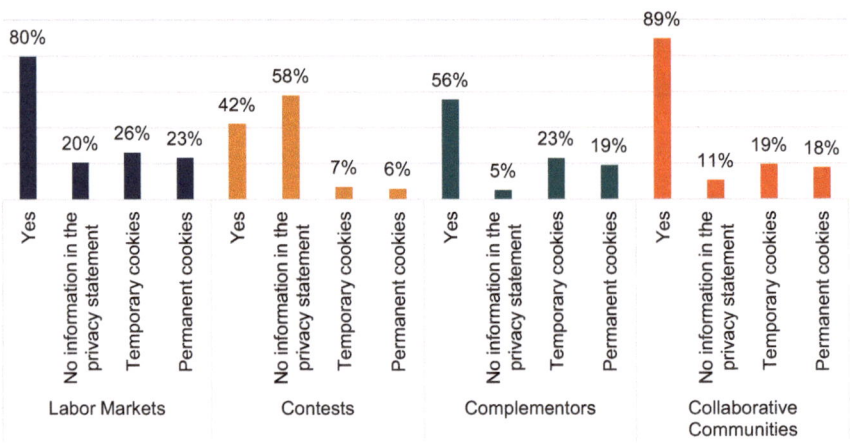

Fig. 4.55 Does the company provide information on the use of cookies? Distinction by crowdsourcing segment. Number of evaluated privacy statements $N = 416$

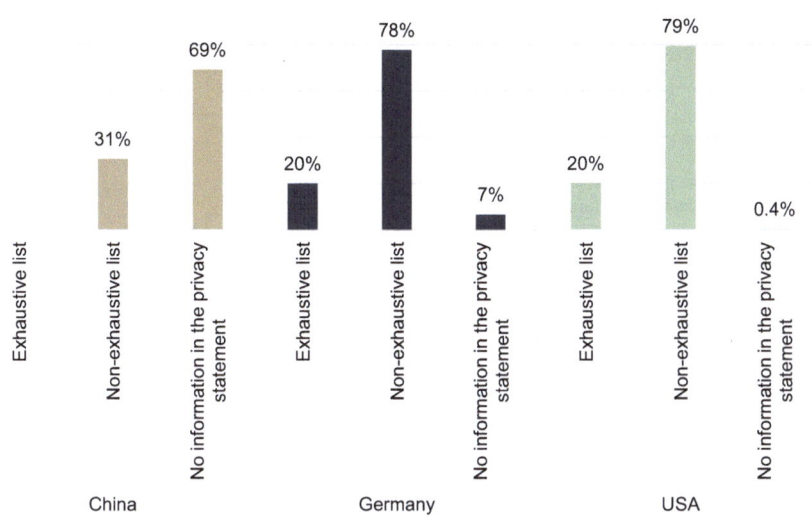

Fig. 4.56 Frequency with which the privacy statements provide an exhaustive or non-exhaustive list of what data are transmitted through server log files. Distinction by country. Number of evaluated privacy statements $N = 416$

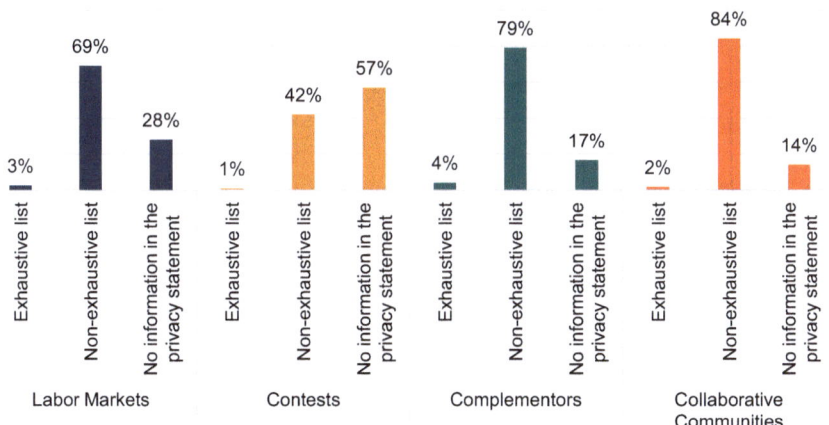

Fig. 4.57 Frequency with which the privacy statements provide an exhaustive or non-exhaustive list of what data are transmitted through server log files. Distinction by crowdsourcing segment. Number of evaluated privacy statements $N = 416$

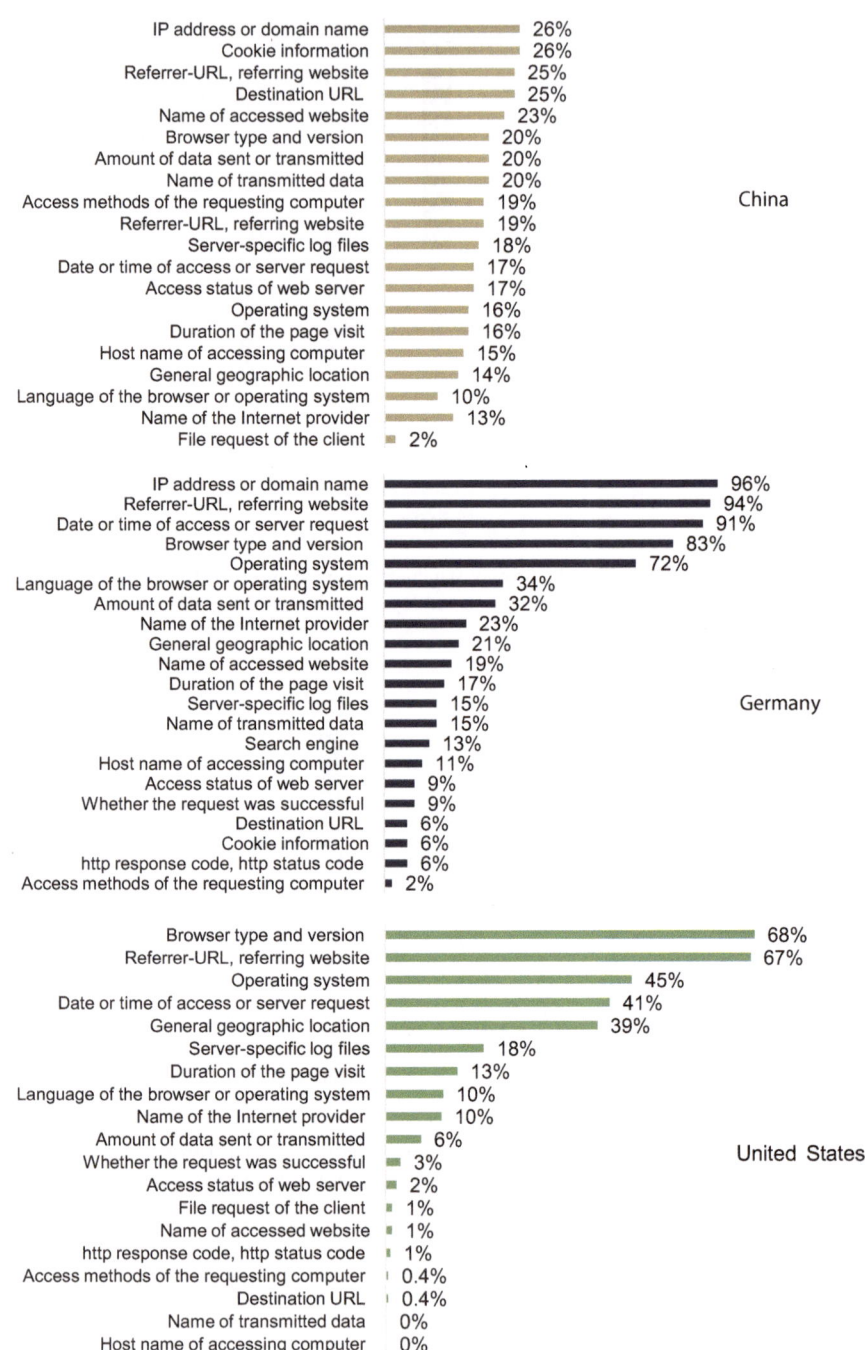

Fig. 4.58 Frequency of data processed by log files. Distinction by crowdsourcing segment. Number of evaluated privacy statements $N = 416$

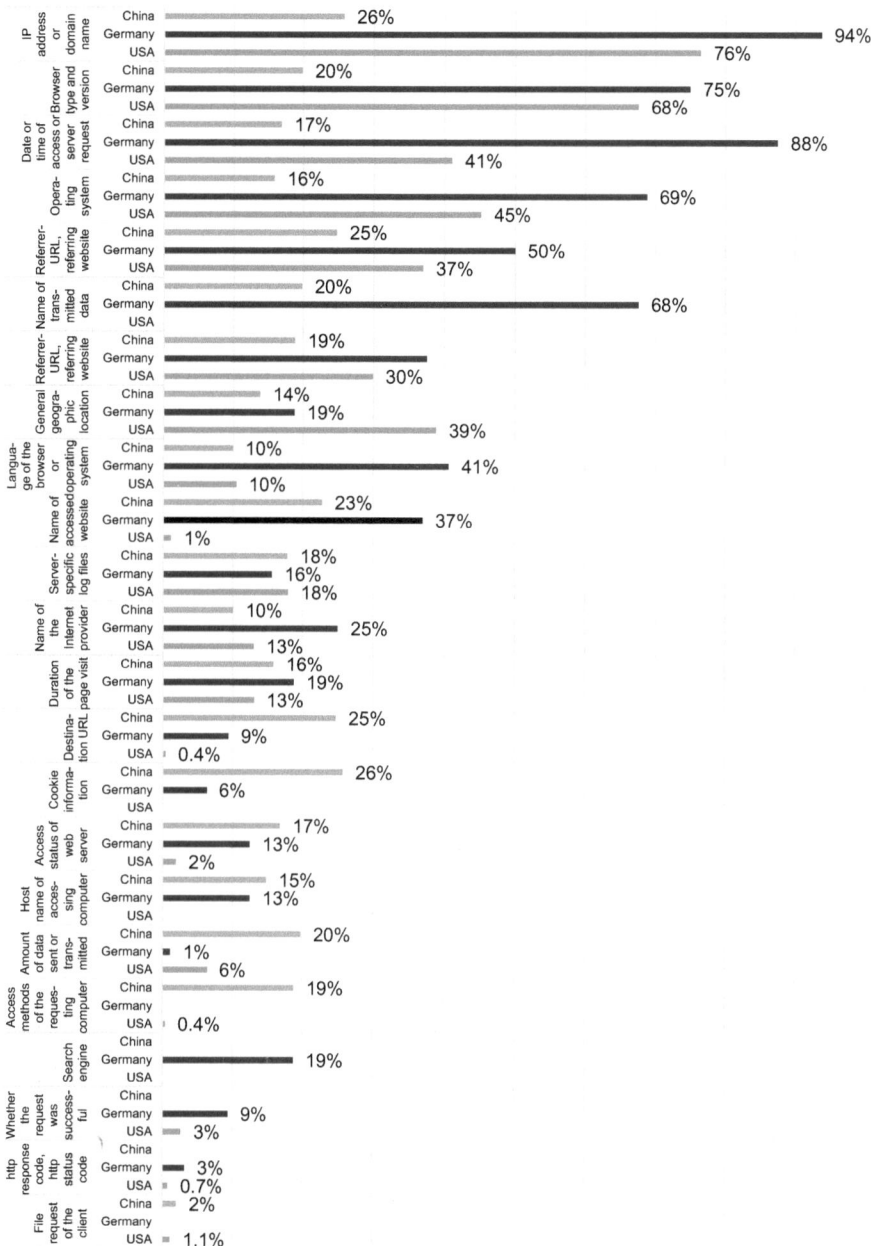

Fig. 4.59 Frequency of data processed by log files. Distinction by crowdsourcing segment. Number of evaluated privacy statements $N = 416$

References

Boudreau, K. J., & Lakhani, K. R. (2013). Using the crowd as an innovation partner. *Harvard Business Review, 91*(4), 60–69, 140. Accessed from https://europepmc.org/article/med/23593 768

Ciotti, F., Hornuf, L., & Stenzhorn, E. (2021). *Lock-in effects in online labor markets. CESifo Working Paper No. 9379.* Accessed from https://papers.ssrn.com/sol3/papers.cfm?abstract_ id=3953015

Dorfleitner, G., & Hornuf, L. (2019). FinTech and data privacy in Germany: An empirical analysis with policy recommendations. *FinTech and Data Privacy in Germany: An Empirical Analysis with Policy Recommendations, 2019*, 1–121. https://doi.org/10.1007/978-3-030-31335-7

Dorfleitner, G., Hornuf, L., & Kreppmeier, J. (2023). Promise not fulfilled: FinTech, data privacy, and the GDPR. *Electronic Markets*, forthcoming.

Geminn, C., Leon, F., & Karl-Raban, H. (2021). Die Informationspräsentation im Datenschutzrecht – Auf der Suche nach Lösungen. *ZD-Aktuell, 05335*.

Lee, J.-A., & Liu, C.-Y. (2012). Forbidden City enclosed by the great firewall: The law and power of internet filtering in China. *Minnesota Journal of Law Science & Technology, 13*(1), 125–151. Accessed from https://scholarship.law.umn.edu/mjlst/vol13/iss1/6

McDonald, A. M., & Cranor, L. F. (2009). The cost of reading privacy policies. *I/S: A Journal of Law and Policy for the Information Society, 4*(3), 543–568. Accessed from https://heinonline. org/HOL/Page?handle=hein.journals/isjlpsoc4&id=563&div=&collection=

Mrass, V., & Leimeister, J. M. (2018). Crowdworking-Plattformen als Enabler neuer Formen der Arbeitsorganisation. In H. Fortmann & B. Kolocek (Eds.), *Arbeitswelt der Zukunft: Trends – Arbeitsraum – Menschen – Kompetenzen* (pp. 139–151). Springer Fachmedien. https://doi.org/ 10.1007/978-3-658-20969-8_10

Chapter 5
Summary and Conclusion

5.1 Increasing Regulation and Regulatory Competition

To date, there is no specific regulation for data protection on crowdsourcing plat-forms in China, Germany and the U.S. In all three countries, however, there has been an increase in legislative activities addressing the handling of data on such platforms in recent years. In Germany, the EU GDPR provides a comparatively strict data protection framework for the digital market. The GDPR has led public lawmakers in other countries, including China and the U.S., to enact similar legislation. This points to a regulatory "race to the top" in privacy regulation. On the other hand, the spillover effects of the GDPR have been limited in the privacy statements of Chinese and U.S. platforms. Only a minority of the U.S. platforms and none of the Chinese platforms identified in the present volume refer to the GDPR. This confirms existing studies (Frankenreiter, 2022), according to which the impact of EU data protection law on U.S. online firms is lower than has been assumed.

5.2 Processing of User Data

5.2.1 Privacy Statements as Main Source of Information

Almost all crowdsourcing platforms in China, Germany and the U.S. process per-sonal data on their users. All German and most U.S. companies provide this information in a separate privacy statement. In China, on the other hand, most platforms do not publish a privacy statement, but integrate privacy information into the general terms and conditions. Similar to the German fintech sector, platforms in the three countries and different crowdsourcing segments seldom state

---

This chapter was written by Sonja Mangold.

conclusively what personal data are processed. The privacy statements of the platforms are quite long. The average reading time for users ranges from 16 minutes to almost half an hour. This indicates that many users do not read the privacy statements at all or at least not in their entirety. Standardization or alternative ways of presenting information, such as icons, could be a user-friendly solution (Dorfleitner & Hornuf, 2019; Geminn et al., 2021).

5.2.2   Processing of Crowdworkers' Data

Crowdsourcing platforms provide a framework for matching clients to workers, primarily freelancers. Personal data of crowdworkers is usually collected and processed throughout the entire business process. The majority of German platforms and a significant number of U.S. platforms distinguish in their privacy statements which data from crowdworkers and other users they process. Only a few Chinese platforms make such a distinction. Crowdsourcing platforms should seek to be even clearer and more transparent in their privacy statements regarding the processing of crowdworker data. In this way, customer trust could be strengthened and fears of excessive surveillance among crowdworkers dispelled. Moreover, early information and transparency would make it easier for crowdworkers to effectively exercise their data protection rights.

5.2.3   Collection of Sensitive Data

According to Art. 9 GDPR, the processing of sensitive data, such as data relating to racial or ethnic origin, health status, or biometric data is only permitted in exceptional cases. Nevertheless, a large number of crowdsourcing platforms in China, Germany and the U.S. process such sensitive data. U.S. platforms in particular collect a wide range of sensitive information, including data on religious affiliation, political opinion, sexual orientation and trade union membership. Chinese platforms stand out for their collection of data on nationality and citizenship. Some U.S. platforms are explicit in stating which personal and sensitive data is not processed. By specifying what data is not collected, platforms can increase user trust and positively differentiate themselves from other competitors. In this respect, the information practices of U.S. crowdsourcing portals could serve as a role model.

5.3   Processing of Data by Third Parties

5.3.1   Data Sharing

The majority of Chinese and German platforms share personal data with third parties. Significantly fewer U.S. platforms state that user data leaves the platform. Similar to German fintech companies, many crowdsourcing platforms are unclear about what data is shared with third parties and to whom the data is transferred. Under European data protection law, platforms must inform their users about data disclosures and the recipients of the data. China's Personal Information Privacy Law establishes similar obligations. In this respect, the crowdsourcing platforms fail to meet legal requirements. Companies should be more transparent about transfers of personal data. Standardization could be helpful in the presentation of information about data disclosures (Dorfleitner & Hornuf, 2019).

5.3.2   Use of Social Plugins and Web Analytics

Many crowdsourcing platforms use social plugins such as Facebook's "Like" button. Especially German platforms state that they integrate social plugins on their websites. Chinese platforms mention the use of social plugins less frequently, referring to national services such as WeChat. Social plugins allow users to share content from the crowdsourcing platforms' website on the social media website. Social plugins can be problematic from a data protection point of view because users' personal data, such as their IP address, is transferred to the social network (Spittka & Mantz, 2019). Something that may be helpful for platforms in practice would be the "double click" solution, whereby a text field informing the user about the data protection concern is displayed automatically when the user hovers the mouse over the button. If the user activates the button with the first click, a server connection is established with the social network. A further click triggers the actual function of the button (e.g., "liking" the platform's content on the social media website). The majority of crowdsourcing platforms in China, Germany and the U.S. use web tracking services to collect and analyze data on user behavior on their websites. German crowdsourcing platforms mention most frequently that they use tracking services. The most popular service in the U.S. and Germany is Google Analytics. This result is in line with the German fintech sector. Many platforms also mention advertising services that allow them to display advertising outside their own websites. Compared to the German fintech sector, crowdsourcing platforms are less transparent about which advertising services they use.

5.3.3   Use of Cookies

Most German and U.S. platforms state that they use cookies. Chinese platforms mention cookies less frequently in their privacy statements. In a comparison of the different platform categories, relatively few crowd contest platforms say that they use cookies. Cookies are small text files which platforms place on users' computers. Cookies are used to make websites more user-friendly, but also to send targeted personalized advertising. A distinction must be made between temporary cookies, which are deleted when the user leaves the website, and permanent cookies, which are stored even after the browser is closed. Permanent cookies are also used for marketing purposes. Numerous German and somewhat fewer U.S. platforms mention the use of permanent cookies in their privacy statements. A significant proportion of crowdsourcing platforms do not provide information about the type of cookies used.

5.3.4   Data Protection Efforts by Platforms and Outlook

Anonymization and Pseudonymization of data are important tools to protect users' privacy. A considerable number of crowdsourcing platforms declare in their privacy statements that they anonymize or pseudonymize personal information. German platforms mention anonymization and pseudonymization most frequently and even distinguish themselves positively from German fintech companies. In a comparison of the crowdsourcing segments, collaborative communities are particularly privacy-friendly in this respect. Furthermore, a number of U.S. and German crowdsourcing portals advertise on their websites that they go through data protection certification procedures or use data protection seals and audits. For example, U.S. platforms mention that they are TRUSTe certified.

In contrast to public regulation, protection measures initiated by platforms are based on the knowledge and self-interest of the actors involved. Other self-regulatory initiatives, such as the Code of Conduct of German crowdsourcing providers, also integrate data protection measures for users and crowdworkers. Self-initiative efforts made by platforms on data protection and fair business practices should be strengthened by legal policymakers and legislators in the future (Mangold, 2022).

In addition to (voluntary) self-initiatives by platform businesses, pressure is needed from civil society, consumer organizations and labor unions. This book can provide important information for policymakers, the platforms themselves and other actors involved about which data protection problems actually exist in the global crowdsourcing market and need to be tackled in the future.

References

Dorfleitner, G., & Hornuf, L. (2019). *FinTech and data privacy: An empirical analysis with policy recommendations*. Springer.

Frankenreiter, J. (2022). The missing "California effect" in data privacy law. *Yale Journal on Regulation, 1068*(2022). Accessed June 9, 2023, from https://papers.ssrn.com/sol3/papers.cfm?abstract_id=3883728

Geminn, C., Francis, L., & Herder, K.-R. (2021). Die Informationspräsentation im Datenschutzrecht – Auf der Suche nach Lösungen. *ZD-Aktuell, 2021*, 05335.

Mangold, S. (2022). Crowdwork. Aktuelle rechtliche Entwicklungen und Bedeutung wirtschaftsethischer Selbstinitiativen. *Recht Digital (RDi), 2022*, 478–483.

Spittka, J., & Mantz, R. (2019). Datenschutzrechtliche Anforderungen an den Einsatz von Social Plugins. *Neue Juristische Wochenschrift (NJW), 2019*, 2742–2745.

Appendices

A. Chinese Crowdsourcing Platforms

A.1 Platforms with a Privacy Statement

1. 猪八戒网 https://www.zbj.com/
2. 一品威客网 http://www.epwk.com/
3. 时间财富网 (原威客中国) https://m.680.com/
4. K68 http://www.k68.cn/
5. 创意猫 http://www.chuangyimao.com/
6. 阿里云众包 https://zhongbao.aliyun.com/
7. 淘宝客威客 https://weike.taobao.com/
8. 无忧案例网https://www.51case.com/
9. 软件项目交易网 https://www.sxsoft.com/
10. 三打哈网http://www.sandaha.cc/
11. 微差事 http://www.weichaishi.com/
12. 微推推 http://www.weituitui.com/
13. 丑皮匠网 http://www.cpjwk.com/
14. 多人维网 http://www.duorenwei.com/
15. 万创中国 https://www.innochina.com/
16. 中移在线众包平台http://zhongbao.10085.cn/index.html
17. 集贤网https://www.xianjichina.com/
18. 大圣创意 http://www.dsook.com/
19. 特创意 http://www.techuangyi.com/
20. 花瓣美思 https://muse.huaban.com/
21. 牛社网 http://www.niushe.com/
22. 思维网 http://www.siweiw.com/
23. 小鱼儿网 https://www.xiaoyuer.com/
24. 21ic中国电子网 http://www.21ic.com/
25. 软件外包平台 http://www.waibaoba.com/

L. Hornuf et al., *Data Privacy and Crowdsourcing*, Advanced Studies in Diginomics and Digitalization, https://doi.org/10.1007/978-3-031-32064-4

26. 牛人众包 only App
27. 码客帮 https://www.make8.com/index
28. 极客众包 http://taskzb.com/
29. 解放号 https://www.jfh.com/
30. 码易https://www.mayigeek.com/
31. 任务中国 http://www.taskcn.wang/
32. 庖丁技术http://www.paoding.cc/
33. 开发宝 https://www.rdplat.com/
34. 实现网 https://shixian.com/
35. 开源中国 https://www.oschina.net/
36. 众包就要事了了 http://www.thingok.com/
37. YesPMP http://www.yespmp.com/
38. 大学士网 https://www.dxueshi.com/
39. 通力互联 http://b2b.tonelink.com/
40. BIM众包网 https://www.bimzb.com/
41. 快码 https://www.kuai.ma/
42. 码市 https://codemart.com/
43. 程序员客栈 https://www.proginn.com/
44. 电+ https://www.365power.cn/
45. 人人开发 http://rrkf.com/
46. 芽叶云 https://www.yayeyun.com/
47. 米鼠网 https://www.misuland.com/
48. 软件商务网http://www.bizsofts.com/
49. 我要外包网 http://www.51waibao.net/
50. 云沃客 https://www.clouderwork.com/
51. 互帮网http://www.bangcn.com/
52. A5任务 http://task.a5.cn/
53. 汇图网 http://www.huitu.com/
54. 汇新云https://www.huixinyun.com/
55. 玩码http://www.playcode.com.cn/
56. 一牛网http://zb.16rd.com/
57. 聚能力网http://www.junengli.com/
58. Sobug漏洞悬赏平台https://www.sobug.com/
59. 班墨云(人人测) http://www.yunceshi.com/index.html
60. 知安人工测试平台https://www.knowsafe.com/
61. 知道创宇https://www.seebug.org/
62. 众测平台http://alltesting.cn/index.html
63. 攒粒 https://www.zanli.com/
64. 敲宝网https://www.qiaobaoba.com/
65. 做到!https://www.zuodao.com/guest/index.html
66. 译言网http://g.yeeyan.org/
67. 数据堂任务平台 only App
68. 米画师https://www.mihuashi.com/
69. 特赞https://www.tezign.com/
70. zb1 98.com 时与中众包网http://www.zb198.com/

71. 蚂蚁微客 (only App)
72. 巨子令工程任务众包网http://www.jzl365.com/
73. 百度众测https://test.baidu.com/
74. 话梅糖工程任务众包网 https://www.huameitang.com/
75. 先迈网https://www.xianmai88.com/article/210
76. 博彦集智https://www.byjizhi.com/crowdsourcing
77. 有道众包http://zb.youdao.com/
78. 蚂蚁众包 www.antzb.com
79. 智汇+众包平台 www.ggdzhj.com
80. 魔叮 www.emoding.com
81. trycan http://c.trycan.com/
82. 金领英才 www.linkin.net
83. 二一教育众包网 www.zb.21cnjy.com
84. 科易网 www.rdc.1633.com
85. 三维家众包平台https://wk.3vjia.com/
86. 云赚 http://user.yunzhuan.com
87. 点我98 http://www.dianwo98.com/?sj16121261
88. 测客网 http://www.iceke.com
89. 推客网 http://twker.com/
90. 芝麻菜会计作业众包平台 www.zhimacaipt.com
91. 我爱方案网http://www.52solution.com/
92. 衍鹤众包汇https://www.yanhe51.com/
93. 图虫网 https://tuchong.com/
94. 500px https://500px.com.cn/
95. 昵图网 http://www.nipic.com/
96. 千库网 https://588ku.com/
97. 千图网 https://www.58pic.com/
98. 我图网 https://www.ooopic.com/
99. 素材公社 https://www.tooopen.com/
100. 必然美享 https://www.biransign.com/
101. VJshi https://www.vjshi.com/

A.2 Platforms Without a Privacy Statement

1. 智城网https://www.taskcity.com/
2. 译心译意翻译网 http://www.1x1y.com.cn/
3. 中国赏金写手 http://weike.rrrwm.com/
4. ALIDUTY众包 http://www.aliduty.com/
5. 天下威客网 http://www.wkgogo.com/
6. 猿急送网 https://www.yuanjisong.com/
7. 我要赚钱网 http://iwtmm.com/
8. 小白广告语 http://hislogan.com/index.html
9. 爱品名 http://ipming.com/index.html

10. 我要久久发 http://www.woyao998.com/?sj16121261
11. 技聊-技能社交平台 https://www.upjiliao.com/homepage
12. 补天众测 https://zhongce.butian.net/Zhongce.html
13. 杰客网 http://www.geekoo.cn/
14. 点点赚 http://www.ddzhuan.cn/
15. 东莞科技在线众包平台 www.dkzx.org/kjzb/Default.aspx
16. 沐风工业云平台https://www.mfcad.com
17. 周八时间 http://www.zhoubatime.com/
18. 机自网- 机械自动化众包平台www.jiiizi.com
19. http://zb.mfcad.com/
20. Logo天下 https://www.logotianxia.com/
21. 人气窝 http://www.renqiwo.com/
22. 红动中国 https://www.redocn.com/

A.3 Platforms with No Website

1. PP外包网
2. 软推网
3. 拍拍赚
4. RFsister
5. 呼叫云
6. 800威客网(跨境电商营销配套服务)
7. 猩猩威客
8. 空心科技
9. 全球设计网
10. 赏金网
11. 自由意
12. 微力公社
13. V5威客网
14. 多推推
15. 钱打钱
16. 猎金网
17. 九推客
18. 创梦小豆
19. 58任务网
20. 欢乐赚
21. 别叉掉
22. toidea创易网

B. German Crowdsourcing Platforms

B.1 Platforms with Privacy Statements

1. 99designs GmbH https://99designs.de
2. ACCOM http://www.accomm.de/datenschutz.html
3. Across Systems GmbH https://www.across.net/impressum/datenschutz
4. Aestium GmbH/empfohlen de https://www.empfohlen.de/datenschutz/
5. Alternate GmbH https://techrush.de/impressum/datenschutz/
6. appjobber https://www.appjobber.de/info/datenschutz
7. Applause GmbH https://www.applause.com/de/datenschutzerklaerung
8. Brandnooz Media Gmbh https://www.brandnooz.de/datenschutzerklaerung
9. BrandsYouLove https://www.brandsyoulove.de/article/datenschutz/show.html
10. Clickworker GmbH https://www.clickworker.de/agb-datenschutz/
11. Connected GmbH https://www.konsumgoettinnen.de/datenschutzhinweise.html
12. Codingpeople GmbH https://codingpeople.com/de/datenschutzerklaerung
13. Content.de AG https://www.content.de/datenschutz
14. Crowd Guru GmbH https://www.crowdguru.de/datenschutz/
15. Crowdsite B.V. https://www.crowdsite.com/privacy-policy/
16. expert.cloud http://www.expertcloud.de/datenschutzerklaerung/
17. Focus Online Group GmbH https://www.netmoms.de/unternehmen/datenschutz/
18. freelance.de https://www.freelance.de/datapolicy.html
19. greatcontent AG https://www.greatcontent.com/de/datenschutzerklaerung/
20. Gruner Jahr GmbH https://www.markenjury.com/de/informationen/datenschutz
21. HYVE AG https://www.hyve.net/de/privacy/
22. iAdvize GmbH (ibbü) https://kurzelinks.de/u60w
23. Innovationskraftwerk https://www.innovationskraftwerk.de/Plattform/Information/Datenschutz
24. innosabiGmbH https://innosabi.com/datenschutz/
25. Insiders Deutschland GmbH https://www.theinsidersnet.com/de-de/info/privacy/
26. Jovoto GmbH https://www.jovoto.com/legal/privacy/
27. Junior Medien GmbH https://www.mama-reporter.de/home/datenschutz
28. Kjero GmbH https://www.kjero.com/datenschutzbestimmungen/
29. LocalMotorsBerlin https://localmotors.com
30. machdudas https://www.machdudas.de/securitypolicy
31. Media Factor GmbH https://testnow.de/datenschutzerklaerung/
32. miBaby GmbH https://www.mibaby.de/Datenschutz
33. MilaAG https://static.mila.com/legal/Privacy_Policies/CH-EN_PrivacyPolicy_current.pdf
34. Mylittlejob GmbH https://www.workgenius.com/de/datenschutz
35. Passbrains AG https://www.passbrains.com/top/privacy.html

36. Phantomminds https://www.phantominds.com/datenschutz/
37. POSPulse https://www.pospulse.com/en/privacy-policy
38. rapidusertest https://rapidusertests.com/crowd-test/datenschutz
39. Sparheld International https://www.sparheld.de/agb#datenschutzbedingungen
40. Streetspotr GmbH https://www.app.streetspotr.com/de/privacy
41. Strör Media Brands GmbH https://www.stroeermediabrands.de/datenschutz.html
42. twago https://www.twago.de/static/data-protection-privacy/
43. Testbirds GmbH https://www.testbirds.de/datenschutz-und-cookies/
44. testCloud.de https://test.io/de/data-privacy/
45. Testtaylor Gmbh https://www.testbee.com/datenschutzerklaerung/
46. Textbroker https://www.textbroker.de/datenschutz
47. Vorwärts GmbH https://reviewjoy.com/privacy-policy/

C. U.S. Crowdsourcing Platforms

C.1 Platforms with Privacy Statements

1. 10xManagement LLC www.10xManagement.com
2. 110Designs LLC www.110designs.com
3. 20/20Panel www.join.2020panel.com
4. 99designs Inc. www.99designs.com
5. Ad Tournament/ResidentLocal www.adtournament.com
6. Adobe Stock www.stock.adobe.com
7. Alegion www.alegion.com
8. Allegis Transcription Inc. www.allegistranscription.com
9. AllFreelanceWriting www.allfreelancewriting.com
10. Amara.org www.amara.org
11. AmazonMechanicalTurk www.mturk.com
12. Analysia www.analysia.com
13. Angellist www.angel.co
14. Appen Limited www.appen.com
15. Aquent LLC www.aquent.com
16. ArticleOnePartners/RWS Group LLC www.rws.com
17. artwanted/ Slam www.artwanted.com
18. AssembleTV www.assemble.tv
19. AssistantMatch www.assistantmatch.com
20. AudioTranscriptionCenter www.audiotranscriptioncenter.com
21. Autodesk Inc./ Instructables www.instructables.com
22. Behance www.behance.net
23. Belay Inc. www.belaysolutions.com
24. Bigstockphoto/Shutterstock www.bigstockphoto.com
25. BKAContent www.bkacontent.com

26. BloggingPro www.blogging.pro.com
27. BrandedSurveys www.surveys.gobranded.com
28. Bugcrowd Inc. www.bugcrowd.com
29. Bunny Inc. www.weare.bunnystudio.com
30. Cambly Inc. www.cambly.com
31. Carbonmade www.carbonmade.com
32. CastingWords www.castingwords.com
33. Catalant www.gocatalant.com
34. CDBaby www.cdbaby.com
35. Challenge Gov. www.challengegov.com
36. Chegg Inc. www.chegg.com
37. ClearVoice Inc. www.clearvoice.com
38. ClickNwork www.clicknwork.com
39. Clickworker www.clickworker.com
40. CloudFactory www.cloudfactory.com
41. CloudPeeps Inc. www.cloudpeeps.com
42. CMNTY www.cmnty.com
43. Cobalt Labs Inc. www.cobalt.io
44. CoContest/GoPillar www.gopillar.com
45. Codementor/Perideea Inc. www.codementor.iu
46. CodePen www.codepen.io
47. CodersClan LLtd. www.codersclan.com
48. Codersera www.codersera.com
49. Compose.ly/LLC www.compose.ly.com
50. Concentrix/Solv www.solvnow.com
51. Constant Content www.constant-content.com
52. Contena/Heroic LLC www.contena.co
53. Contently www.contently.net
54. ContentRunner www.contentrunner.com
55. Coroflot/Core 77 inc. www.coroflot.com
56. Coupons.com/Quotient Technology Inc. www.coupons.com
57. CourseHero www.coursehero.com
58. CreateMyTattoo LLC www.mcreatetemytattoo.com
59. CreativeMarket Labs Inc. www.creativemarket.com
60. Crowd Surf www.crowdsurfwork.com
61. Crowded/Valilly Inc. www.crowded.com
62. Crowdmade www.crowdmade.com
63. Crowdsource Solutions Inc. www.crowdsource.com
64. CrowdSpring www.crowdspring.com
65. DailyTranscription www.dailytranscription.com
66. Damongo www.damongo.com
67. Degreed Inc. www.degreed.com
68. Designboom Competitions www.designboom.com
69. DesignContest LLC www.designcontest.com
70. DesignCrowd LLC www.designcrowd.com

71. Designfier www.designfier.com
72. Designhill www.designhill.com
73. Designquote www.designquote.net
74. Dice/DHI Group Inc. www.dice.com
75. DoJobsOnline www.dojobsonline.com
76. Dribbble LLtd. www.dribbble.com
77. dscout LLtd. www.dscout.com
78. Dynata LLC/Opinion Outpost www.opinionoutpost.com
79. Easyshift/Quiry Inc. www.easyshift.app.com
80. Ebates/Rakuten Inc. www.rakuten.com
81. Ebyline/IZEA Inc. www.app.ebyline.com
82. eScribers LLC www.escribers.net
83. EzineArticles www.ezinearticles.com
84. FancyHands Inc. www.fancyhands.com
85. Field Agent/Delaware www.fieldagent.net
86. FieldNation LLC www.fieldnation.com
87. Figure Eight/Appen www.figure-eight.com
88. Findeavor www.findeavor.com
89. Fiverr US Inc. www.fiverr.com
90. FiverUp www.fiverup.com
91. Fixya www.fixya.com
92. Flickr/SmugMug Inc. www.flickr.com
93. Folyo LLC. www.folyo.me.com
94. Freedom With Writing www.freedomwithwriting.com
95. Freeeup/Next Media LLC www.freeeup.com
96. Freelanced www.freelanced.com
97. FreelanceMyWay www.freelancemyway.com
98. FreelanceWriting LLC www.freelancewriting.com
99. FreelanceWritingGigs/ Splashpress Media www.frelancewritinggigs.com
100. Fusioncash Inc www.fusioncash.com
101. Gengo Inc. www.gengo.com
102. GeoHive/Maxar www.geohive.com
103. GettyImages Inc. www.gettyimages.com
104. Gigbucks www.gigbucks.com
105. Gigster Inc. www.gigster.com
106. Gigwalk www.gigwalk.com
107. GMR Transcription Services inc. www.gmrtranscription.com
108. GoLance Inc www.golance.com
109. Grab Points www.grabpoints.com
110. Gun.io www.gun.io.com
111. Hatchwise/Geekface LLC www.hatchwise.com
112. Helium Inc. www.helium.com
113. HireCoder www.hirecoder.com
114. HireOwl www.hireowl.com
115. HireWriters www.hirewriters.com

116. Hive Work www.hivemicro.com
117. Hubpages/Maven Inc. Delaware www.hubpages.com
118. Hubstaff Talent www.talent.hubstaff.com
119. IdeaScale www.ideascale.com
120. IDEO LLC www.iodeocolab.com
121. ilovecreatives www.ilovecreatives.com
122. InnoCentive Inc. www.innocentive.com
123. InnovationExchange www.innovationexchange.com
124. InstaGC www.instagc.com
125. iPoll www.ipoll.com
126. Job Boy www.jobboy.com
127. Jobspotter Indeed www.jobspotter.indeed.com
128. JoomLancers www.joomlancers.com
129. JustAnswer/PearlCom www.justanswer.com
130. KellyServices Inc. www.kellyservices.com
131. Krop www.krop.com
132. Language Line Solutions www.languageline.com
133. LifePoints www.lifepointspanel.com
134. LiveOps Inc. www.liveops.com
135. Logo Contest www.logocontest.com
136. Logo Design Guru Inc. www.logodesignguru.com
137. Logo Lounge LLC www.logolounge.com
138. LogoMoose www.logomoose.com
139. Logomyway www.logomyway.com
140. Lorem www.asklorem.com
141. MediaBistro www.mediabistro.com
142. Microburst/Zillion www.zilliondesigns.com
143. microWorkers www.microworkers.com
144. MindsPay www.mindspay.com
145. MiniFreelance www.minifreelance.com
146. Minijobz www.minijobz.com
147. Minted LLC www.minted.com
148. MobileWorks/Leadgenius Inc. www.leadgenius.com
149. MojoMarketplace www.mojomarketplace.com
150. Moonlighting App.com Inc. www.moonlighting.com
151. Moonlightwork Inc. www.moonlightwork.com
152. MorningCoffeeNewsletter www.freelancewriting.com
153. My Starbucks Idea www.mystarbucksidea.com
154. MyCrowdQA www.mycrowdqa.com
155. MyFonts/Delaware Corp. Inc. www.myfonts.com
156. MyPoints/Prodege LLC www.mypoints.com
157. NamingForce/Degree LLC www.namingforce.com
158. NasaClickworkers www.nasaclickworkers.com
159. NexRep www.nextrep.com
160. NineSigma/Nine Sights www.ninesights.ninesigma.com

161. ninja VA www.ninja-va.com
162. Olaxr www.olaxr.com
163. OnlineMicrojobs/Digital Paper Products Inc. www.onlinemicrojobs.com
164. OnlineVerdict www.onlineverdict.com
165. Outsource.com www.outsource.com
166. PaidViewPoint/Umongous Inc. www.paidviewpoint.com
167. Panda Research www.pandaresearch.com
168. PayU2Blog www.payu2blob.com
169. Picoworkers Inc. www.picoworkers.com
170. Pinecone.reasearch/Nielsen LLC www.pineconeresearch.com
171. PoeWar www.poewar.com
172. Points2Shop LLC www.points2shop.com
173. PowerToFly www.powertofly.com
174. PrizeRebel/iAngelic Inc. www.prizerebel.com
175. ProductionHUB www.productionhub.com
176. Programmermeetdesigner www.programmermeetdesigner.com
177. Project4Hire www.project4hire.co
178. Proz.com www.proz.com
179. PubLoft/GigLoft Inc. www.publoft.com
180. Q A Mentor Inc. www.qamentor.com
181. Qualitrix www.qualitrix.com
182. QuickRewards www.quickrewards.net
183. Quicktate www.quicktate.com
184. Quirky www.quirky.com
185. Quiry www.quiry.com
186. RainForestQA www.rainforestqa.com
187. Ranker Inc. www.ranker.com
188. RapidWorkers/Uniscript Inc. www.rapidworkers.com
189. Reddit Inc. www.reddit.com
190. Remotasks/Ecosystem Inc. www.remotasks.com
191. Respondent Inc. www.respondent.io
192. RetailMeNot Inc. www.retailmenot.com
193. Rev. Inc. www.rev.com
194. RocketGenius Inc. www.rocketgenius.com
195. Samasource Inc. www.samasource.com
196. Scalable Path www.scalablepath.com
197. Scribie www.scribie.com
198. SEOClerks www.seoclerks.com
199. ServiceScape www.servicescape.com
200. ShopAtHome www.shopathome.com
201. ShopKick Inc. www.shopkicks.com
202. Shutterstock Inc. www.shutterstock.com
203. Skyword Inc. www.skyword.com
204. SliceThePie Ltd. www.slicethepie.com
205. Slidejoy www.getslidejoy.com

206. SmartCrowd/Lionbridge www.thesmartcrowd.com
207. Snagajob www.snagajob.com
208. Sortfolio www.sortfolio.com
209. Sound Better Inc. www.soundbetter.com
210. Spare5, Mighty LLC www.spare5.com
211. SpeakWrite www.speakwrite.com
212. Speechpad www.speechpad.com
213. Speedlancer Inc. www.speedlancer.com
214. Spoonflower www.spoonflower.com
215. Spreadshirt Inc. www.spreadshirt.com
216. SpringboardAmerica www.springboardamerica.com
217. Squadhelp Inc. www.squadhelp.com
218. Stack Overflow Inc. www.stackoverflow.com
219. Stage32Job LLC www.stage32.com
220. Steem.it www.steemit.com
221. StudentFreelance.com/Talei LLC www.studentfreelance.com
222. SuperPoints/Rakuten US www.rakuten.com
223. SurveyJunkie www.surveyjunkie.com
224. Swagbucks/Prodege LLC/Ysense www.swagbucks.com
225. Teespring Inc. www.teespring.com
226. Textbroker www.textbroker.com
227. The Game Crafter, LLC www.thegamecrafter.com
228. TheCreativeGroup/Robert Half Inc. www.roberthalf.com
229. TheCreativeLoft www.thecreativeloft.com
230. TheMomProject www.themomproject.com
231. Thesecondshift LLC www.thesecondshift.com
232. Theshelf Inc. www.theshelf.com
233. Threadless www.threadless.com
234. Timeetc USA Ltd. www.web.timeetc.com
235. Toluna Ltd. www.toluna-group.com
236. Tongal www.tongal.com
237. TopCashbackb Inc. www.topcashback.com
238. Topcoder LLC www.topcoder.com
239. Toptal www.toptal.com
240. TranscribeMe Inc. www.transcribeme.com
241. Translatorsbase www.translatorsbase.com
242. TryMyui www.trymyui.com
243. Twine/Clowdy Ltd. www.twine.fm
244. Ubertesters www.ubertesters.com
245. Unbabel Inc. www.unbabel.com
246. Univox Community/Market Cube LLC www.univoxcommunity.com
247. Upwork Global Inc. www.upwork.com
248. UserTesting www.usertesting.com
249. uTest/Applause Inc. www.applause.com
250. Verblio Inc. www.verblio.com

251. Vindale Research/Dynata LLC www.vindale.com
252. WeLokalize www.welocalize.com
253. Witmart www.witmart.com
254. Workana LLC www.workana.com
255. WorkingNotWorking www.workingnotworking.com
256. WorkingSolutions LLC www.workingsolutions.com
257. Worldwide101/Boldly www.boldly.com
258. Wow!Women on writing www.wow-womenonwriting.com
259. Writeraccess www.writeraccess.com
260. Writers Write Inc. www.writejobs.com
261. Xprize Foundation Inc. www.xprize.org
262. YouGov www.yougov.com
263. YourEncoreHub Inc. www.yourencore.com
264. Yubster LLC www.yubster.com
265. Zazzle Inc. www.zazzle.com
266. Zeerk www.zeerk.com
267. Zerys www.zerys.com
268. Zooppa Com Inc. www.zooppa.com

C.2 Platforms Without a Privacy Statement

1. CallCenter QA www.callcenterqa.org
2. CrowdSurf www.crowdsurfwork.com
3. DoMyWork www.domywork.net
4. EZgig www.ezgig.work
5. Fair Play Alliance www.fairplayalliance.org
6. Gig Me 5 www.gigme5.wordpress.com
7. Hello Rache www.hellorache.com
8. 48HOURSLOGO www.48hourslogo.com
9. Humanatic www.humanatic.com
10. Ibotta www.home.ibotta.com
11. InboxDollars www.inboxdollars.com
12. MicroMappers www.micromappers.qcri.org
13. Paid to Blog www.paidtoblog.co
14. Photography Jobs Online www.photography-jobs.net
15. Solid Gigs/Millo.co www.solidgigs.com
16. Support Driven www.supportdriven.com
17. The Source www.thesourceagents.com
18. UpCounsel Technologies Inc www.upcounsel.com
19. VickyVirtual www.vickyvirtual.com
20. Zirtual www.zirtual.com

C.3 Platforms with No Website

1. AirPair
2. Greatlance
3. Imgigz
4. Livework Studios LLC
5. Photography Jobs Finder